A HISTORY OF EAST TENNESSEE AUTO RACING

The Thrill of the Mountains

David McGee

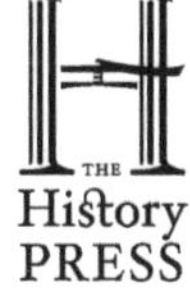

THE History PRESS

Published by The History Press
Charleston, SC 29403
www.historypress.net

Front cover, top: Volunteer Speedway. *Courtesy Joey Millard*; *middle left*: Joe Lee Johnson's trophy. *Photo by author*; *middle right*: Smoky Mountain Raceway. *Courtesy Ray Taylor*; *bottom*: L.D. Ottinger (2) and John A. Utsman (26). *Courtesy John A. Utsman.*
Back cover, top: Courtesy Jimmie Warden; *inset*: Courtesy Carl Moore Collection; tickets courtesy Melvin Corum.

First published 2014

Manufactured in the United States

ISBN 978.1.62619.137.2

Library of Congress CIP data applied for.

Notice: The information in this book is true and complete to the best of our knowledge. It is offered without guarantee on the part of the author or The History Press. The author and The History Press disclaim all liability in connection with the use of this book.

Dedicated to Melvin Corum, Paul Lewis, Tony Morton and everyone else who preserves and promotes racing history.

Contents

Acknowledgements

Thank you to commissioning editor Banks Smither, project editor Julia Turner and the dedicated staff of The History Press for your support, belief in this project and efforts to make it successful.

A book of this scope would be utterly impossible without trusted sources of information, and Melvin Corum, Tony Morton and Robert Walden have been invaluable in that regard. I leaned heavily on their decades' worth of knowledge, uncanny ability to recall the tiniest details and reliable advice. Each also shared a number of photographs.

It was truly an honor to spend time with the drivers and their families who sat for hours, patiently answering questions and sharing priceless stories.

This project also relied on access to the extensive newspaper microfilm holdings of East Tennessee State University's Sherrod Library, the Hamblen County Public Library in Morristown and the *Bristol Herald Courier*. Much data also came from my collection of more than five-decades' worth of NASCAR media guides and reference publications.

Some information would have remained forever buried without super sleuth Danette Welch and her co-workers at the McClung Collection of the Knoxville Public Library. Thanks for your interest and support.

Thank you to Herb Adcox, David Allio, Larry Baker, Jeff Birchfield, Steve Blevins, Bonnie Carter, Mike Cline, Ernie Collins, Eddie Gannaway, Floyd Garrett, Don Good, Rick Harris, Robbie Henry, Harmon Jolley, A.D. Jones, Cindy Lane, Bob Lawrence, Michael Moats, Carl Moore, Randall Perry, Gary and Mike Potter, John Potts, Bob Richey, Rick Sheek, Kevin

Triplett, Tim Weiss, Steve Willinger and Lori Worley among many others, who shared recollections and encouragement or helped locate people. If only there had been time to interview everyone.

Thanks also to Brian Katen and his remarkable Virginia speedways project, fellow author Perry Allen Wood, Mike Bell and the folks at GeorgiaAutoRacingHistory.com, Bill Holder and the National Dirt Late Model Hall of Fame, ARCA historian Brian Norton, Jeff Gilder at RacersReunion.com and the AAA Dirt Car Research Project for preserving and promoting the heritage.

Some of these interviews occurred years ago and, if not for some meaningful encouragement, might have continued to languish. Thank you to good friend and fellow author Joe Tennis for supplying a much-needed shove.

A very special thank-you to Debbie Helton for your willingness to accompany and assist on countless research trips and for advice, support, patience and sacrificing our time so I could focus on this work. You are my true champion.

This book showcases the wonderful black-and-white photographs of Ray Taylor, generously shared by Robbie Henry and Becki Johnston. In addition, photographers John Beach, Chris Haverly, Joey Millard, Michael Moats and the late Mike O'Dell were great resources.

Others who generously allowed access to their photos include the *Bristol Herald Courier*, Bristol Motor Speedway, Mike Cline, Ernie Collins, Brownie King, Paul Lewis, Carl Moore, Mike Potter, John A. Utsman and Jimmie Warden.

Please peruse the bibliography because I highly recommend each book listed, especially Allan Brown's *The History of America's Speedways, Past & Present* and everything written by Greg Fielden.

Introduction

Just like moonshine or biscuits and gravy, oval-track racing has been an integral part of East Tennessee's culture for a century, so thoroughly documenting all of this region's racing history would require a book three or four times this size.

Tennessee's eastern time zone stretches from Bristol westward along the mountainous underbelly of Virginia and Kentucky to the Big South Fork and then juts southward west of Knoxville to Chattanooga and the Georgia border. Dozens of racetracks operated within those twelve thousand square miles, frequently serving as social and entertainment centers for communities large and small.

Ovals of red clay, weathered asphalt and brushed concrete still dot the landscape across this corner of Appalachia, attracting gladiators by the score and fans by the thousands. On warm summer nights or crisp fall afternoons, they dab on high-octane cologne and bask in the raw, unmuffled ambience. For many, the experience is more vital than breathing.

Yet for each surviving track, many more have fallen silent, swept away by progress or simply abandoned. Each driver who buckles on a helmet today follows a well-traveled path of men who risked life, limb and often their last dime for tin trophies, meaningless kisses and paltry paydays.

A warning: some details conflict with published and online accounts but represent the best information available. Auto racing received scant news coverage in bygone days, and many successful drivers failed to keep up with their own accomplishments. Accurate record keeping was also often an afterthought for tracks, which sometimes changed promoters like socks—especially those dastardly few who skipped out with the money while races were going on.

This book's overarching aim is to take readers to some unique places and introduce them to some truly remarkable people whose undying passion for their chosen path entertained and enriched us all.

1
Diverse Beginnings

Autumn was in the air as an excited crowd filed into the grandstands to witness Louis Chevrolet and Barney Oldfield—two of the most recognizable figures in early American motorsports—compete for victory. The mechanized drama was not on the bricks of Indianapolis, the steeply banked boards of Brooklyn or Chicago or even the exotic seaside site of the Vanderbilt Cup but on the flat, half-mile dirt oval of Chattanooga's Warner Park fairgrounds.

Billed as the "world track championship," the October 17, 1917 contest was actually a three-heat match race between two of racing's greatest early stars and a momentary diversion for a city still sending its sons to war.

Their Monday afternoon duel was the grand finale of the Chattanooga district fair and included heats of ten, fifteen and thirty laps. The Swiss-born Chevrolet won the first and third, driving a green French-made Delage owned by Oldfield. It seems Chevrolet's own Frontenac—a Ford-powered speedster designed by the driver and brother Gaston—never arrived by rail.

Chevrolet led all ten laps of the first heat, outrunning Oldfield's enclosed cockpit "Golden Submarine" by about four car lengths. His average speed was a course record 48.6 miles per hour, muted by the tight confines since both cars were capable of going twice that fast.

Oldfield got a better start in the twenty-lap contest and also led all the way, posting an average speed of nearly forty-eight miles per hour. He won by half a car length in his four cylinder–powered car constructed in California by Fred Offenhauser and Harry Miller.

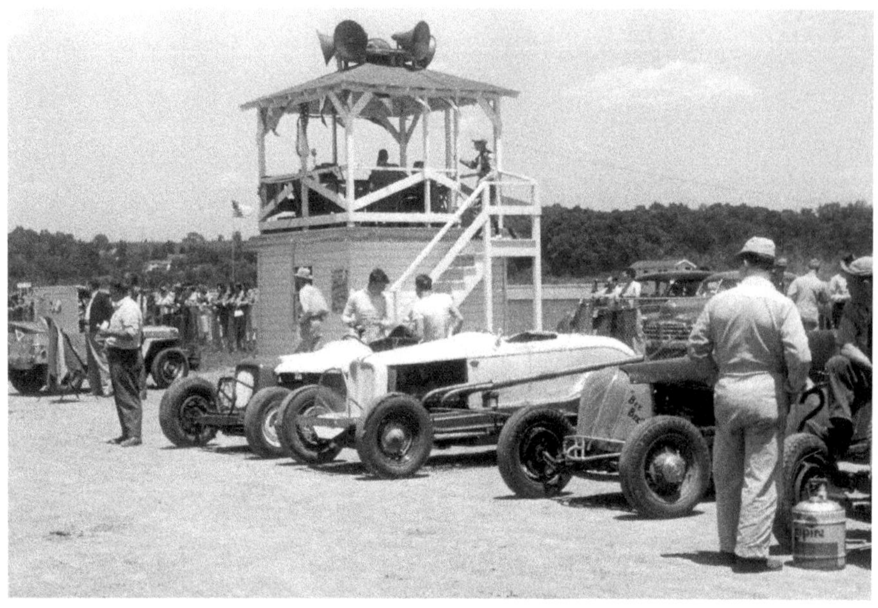

Racers line up prior to competing. *Courtesy Jimmie Warden.*

In the rubber match, Oldfield gained an early advantage and led the first ten circuits before his machine drifted wide entering the first turn. The daring Chevrolet shot the gap for the lead and never looked back. With his ever-present cigar clenched in his teeth, Oldfield charged up to his rival's rear bumper on the final lap, but he couldn't complete the pass. The traffic jam afterward didn't clear for hours.

While their matchup wasn't the first time automobiles raced in East Tennessee, it was certainly the most celebrated to that point.

Out to Pasture

Horseless carriage racing first captured the nation's fancy in the late 1890s, but only the wealthy could afford the noisy contraptions. Competition soon seeped into America's heartland on fairgrounds tracks designed for horses. Tennessee's once-notable Thoroughbred racing industry was dealt a fatal blow in 1906 when the general assembly banned betting, but that decision opened equine tracks, including Warner Park and the Morristown Fairgrounds, to contests between automobiles.

Another once-successful horse track near Knoxville's Chilhowee Park switched over to auto racing around 1916, but its first season was marred by the death of racer W.E. Lockett, whose car went out of control and crashed. Lockett's ride-along mechanic Harmon Kreis was spared, and the track closed by the 1920s, though its outline remains today.

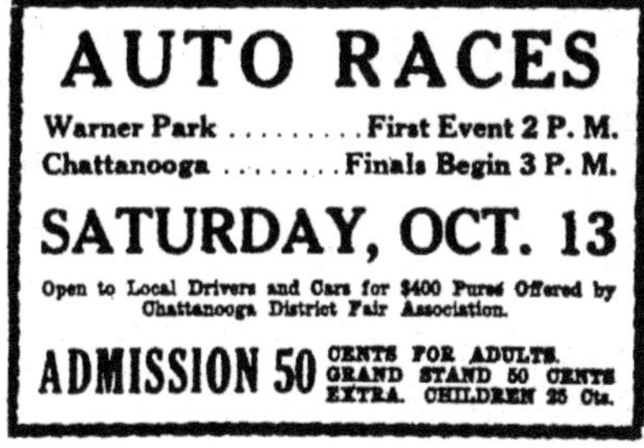

A 1917 advertisement promotes auto racing at Warner Park in Chattanooga. *Author's collection.*

Tragedy Strikes

Harmon Kreis's younger brother, A.J. "Pete" Kreis, started competing on the region's dirt tracks when he was just fifteen, after their father, John, purchased his first race car. The Knoxville native quickly graduated to faster machines and more treacherous environments, driving a Duesenberg on steeply banked wooden board tracks from California to Maryland. He qualified eighth and finished ninth in his first Indianapolis 500 in 1925, the same year he first raced in the Italian Grand Prix.

Kreis returned to the brickyard in 1926 with a new supercharged eight-cylinder Miller racer but was ill and unable to drive. Rookie Frank Lockhart convinced Kreis to let him qualify the car. Lockhart broke the track record on his first lap but slowed during the subsequent three laps and started twentieth. On race day, Lockhart drove to the front and won the first rain-shortened Indianapolis 500 in the Kreis-owned car.

That same year, Kreis and co-driver Earl Cooper stood on the podium at Monza, Italy, after a third-place finish in the Italian Grand Prix.

During the Great Depression, Kreis spent more time working at his father's business but remained a regular at Indianapolis. He made five more starts on the original brick course between 1927 and 1933, but mechanical woes limited his success.

He returned to Indianapolis in 1934 driving for 1932 race winner Fred Frame. During practice on May 30, a car spun in front of Kreis, who steered to avoid it but lost control. His car climbed onto the wall in the south end of the speedway at ninety miles per hour and rode the wall briefly before flying out of the track and striking a tree, splitting the machine in half and killing Kreis instantly. Ride-along mechanic Bob Hahn also died at the scene.

A tombstone in Knoxville's Asbury Cemetery features a detailed engraving of the track and a single race car on the outside wall. The inscription reads, "A.J. Pete Kreis, The Last Lap, Indianapolis Speedway."

Homegrown Stars

A pair of East Tennessee brothers was among the nation's most accomplished racers during the 1920s and 1930s.

Phillip Bird "Phil" Cline and younger brother, Frontis Graydon "Major" Cline, grew up just east of Knoxville in Jefferson City but gained fame far from home with their exploits behind the wheel. They combined to win more than one hundred feature races, primarily on midwestern tracks at the Illinois State Fair in DuQuoin, the Ozark State Fair in Missouri and a Kansas track where Major won despite suffering eleven flat tires caused by leftover horseshoe nails.

Their cars were sleek for that era—fenderless, single-seat roadsters with tall, thin tires and wire-spoke wheels. Major raced a Frontenac, the short-lived brand produced by the Chevrolet brothers but based on the Ford Model T and powered by a four-cylinder Ford engine. Phil Cline raced a Laurel Special.

Major once broke his back in Kansas, but even that didn't keep him from racing. Doctors put him in a full body cast, and after Major healed some, the brothers suspended a hammock between the two race cars for Major to lie in while being driven down highways. Once he was lifted into the race car, he drove while wearing the body cast.

The brothers supplemented racing income by repairing cars and farm machinery during their travels. As the Great Depression wore on, however, many tracks reduced or eliminated cash prizes. Unable to subsist on trophies, they returned home and opened Cline Brothers Garage on Mechanic Street in Jefferson City, where their motto was "We fix anything."

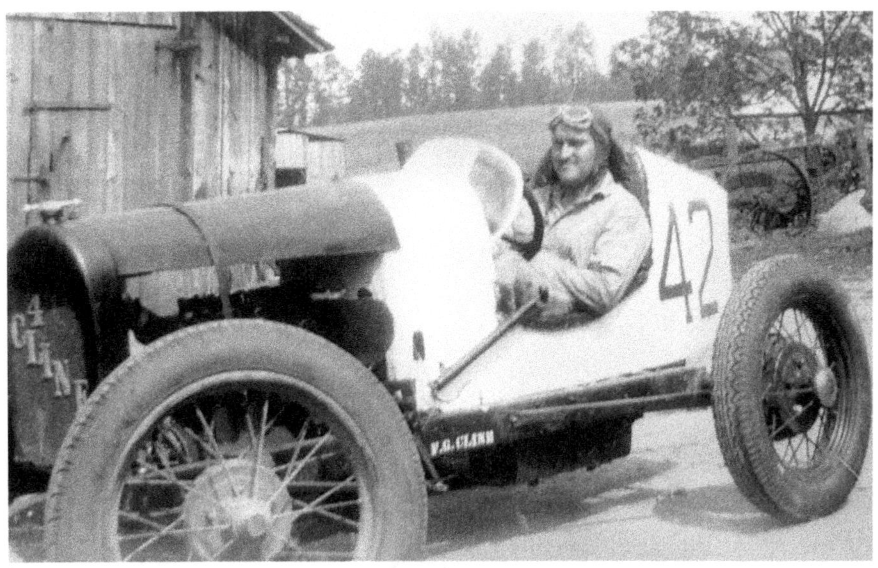

Brothers Major (above) and Phil Cline (below) left Strawberry Plains in the 1920s to race all over the nation. They won more than one hundred races. *Courtesy Mike Cline.*

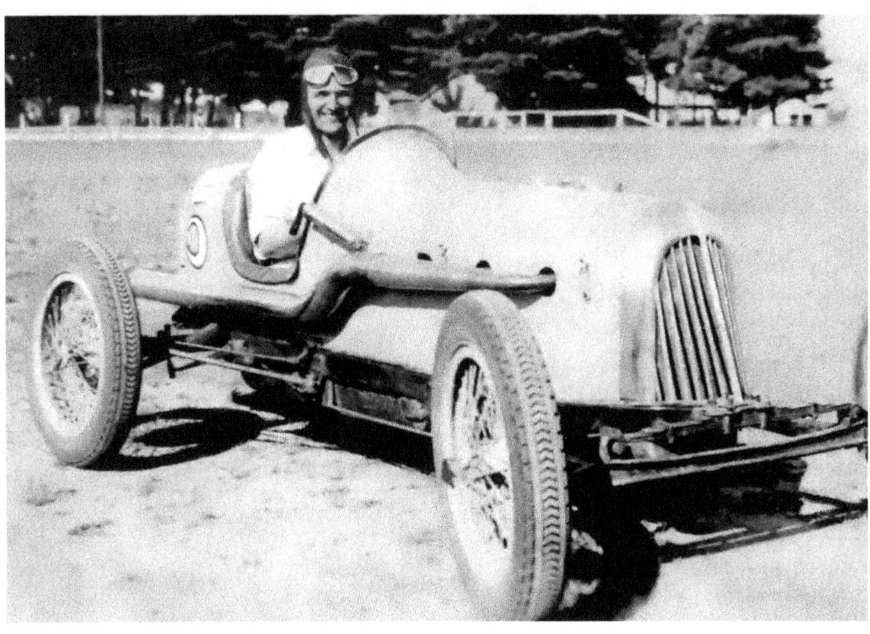

Hill Climb Hysteria

Hill climbs—organized, timed speed contests on public roads—were wildly popular in Europe in the early 1900s and soon popped up around the United States. The Pikes Peak hill climb in Colorado remains the nation's most enduring event, but it didn't begin until 1916.

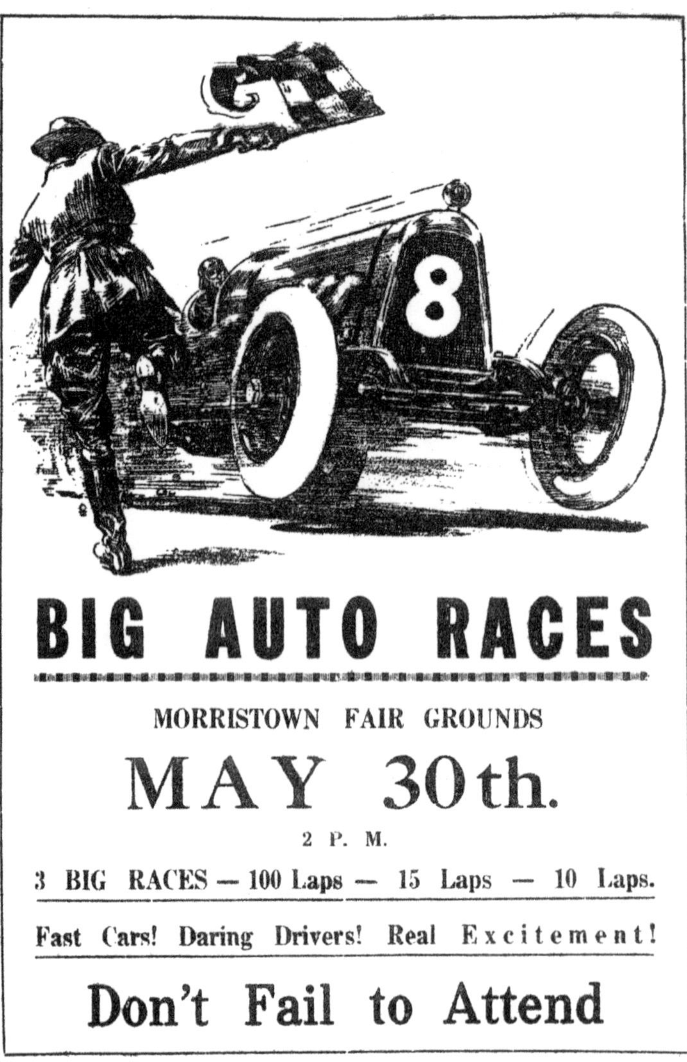

Auto racing was popular in East Tennessee in the 1920s when the Morristown Fairgrounds regularly hosted racing events. *Author's collection.*

In April 1909, Louis Chevrolet drove a Buick up a 4.9-mile course on Chattanooga's Lookout Mountain in six minutes and thirty seconds. The record-setting run garnered national headlines and is believed to be among the first speed contests held in East Tennessee.

Motorsports pioneer David Abbott "Ab" Jenkins embarked on a nationwide trek to shatter every existing hill climb record in 1931, an effort promoted by automaker Studebaker and sanctioned by the American Automobile Association.

On April 2, 1931, Jenkins needed just 12.75 seconds to drive his eight-cylinder Studebaker President roadster to the top of Paterson Road hill in Knoxville. The Thursday afternoon climb covered just 671 feet, or roughly one-eighth of a mile. The competition shifted to Chattanooga, where Jenkins swept all three events. He raced 4.4 miles up Signal Mountain in four minutes, 37.1 seconds and needed seventeen minutes, 26.2 seconds to conquer the 7.4-mile sprint to the top of Lookout Mountain on Easter Sunday.

A Utah native and former homebuilder, Jenkins captured an amazing thirty-eight consecutive hill climb records that year in forty events from New England to California. He went on to establish one hundred land-speed records on the barren salt flats of Bonneville, Utah, in a career documented by both book and film.

The Knoxville hill climb was never repeated, but Chattanooga hosted four climbs in March 1933. Indy 500 regular Al Miller won each in a Hudson Essex.

Hot Rod Roadsters

Auto racing returned from sabbatical after World War II as ex-GIs drove stripped down, fenderless racers known as "hot rods" on dirt ovals from coast to coast. Numerous tracks across East Tennessee regularly featured these daredevils and briefly spawned the South East Racing Association in Bristol and the Hard Top Racing Association in Knoxville. The South East group was organized by driver Bill Warden of Bluff City, who offered guaranteed payouts at races in East Tennessee, Virginia, Kentucky, North Carolina, Ohio and his native West Virginia.

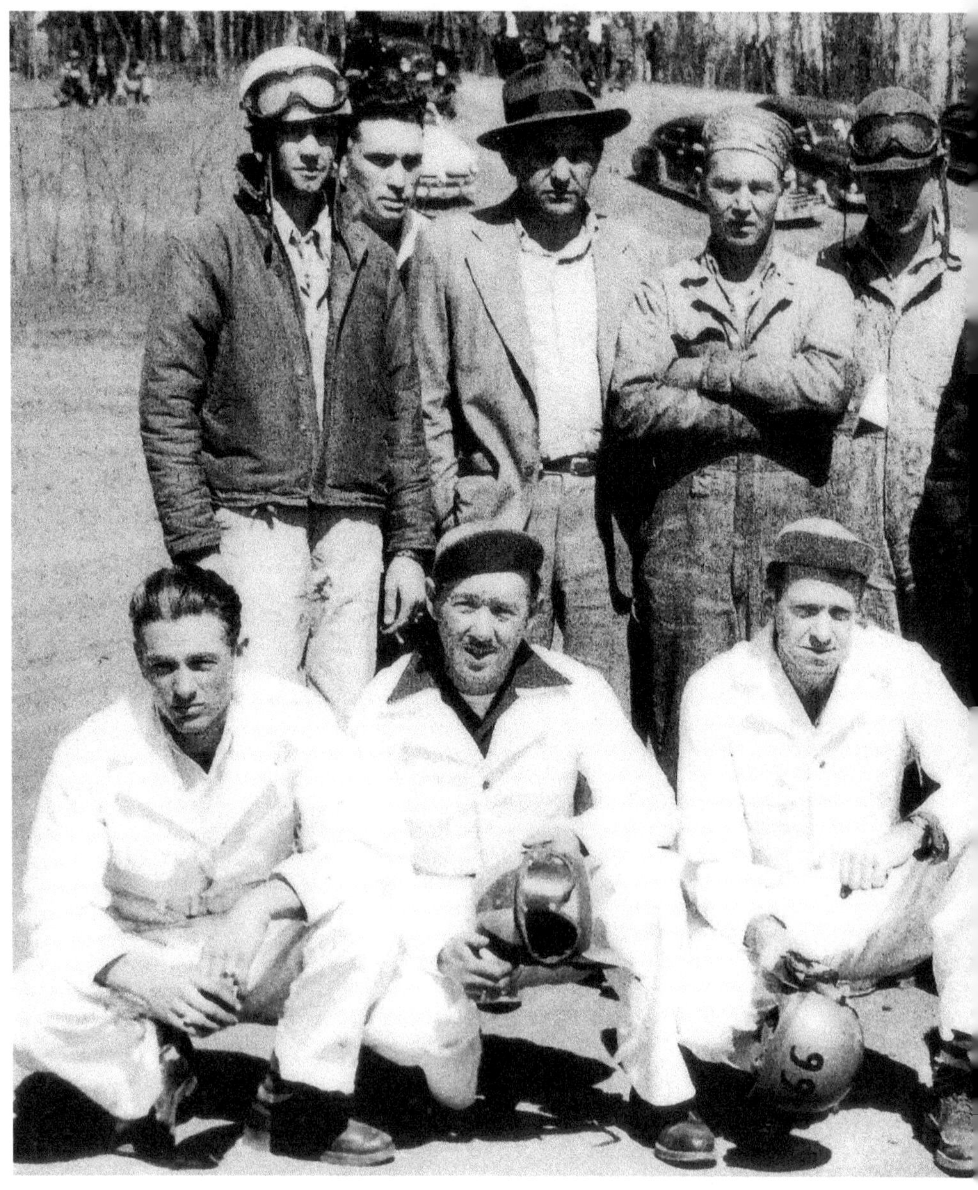

Pictured left to right, back row: Tyler Cabaugh, Harry Morris, B. Hughes, John Utsman, K. Hicks, R. Hicks, Sammy Diggs, Sherman Utsman, Bo Diggs, B. Hicks and Casey Jones; *front row:* Dub Utsman, Willard Gott, Bill Warden, Jimmie Warden and Albert Greenway. Picture from 1949. *Courtesy John A. Utsman.*

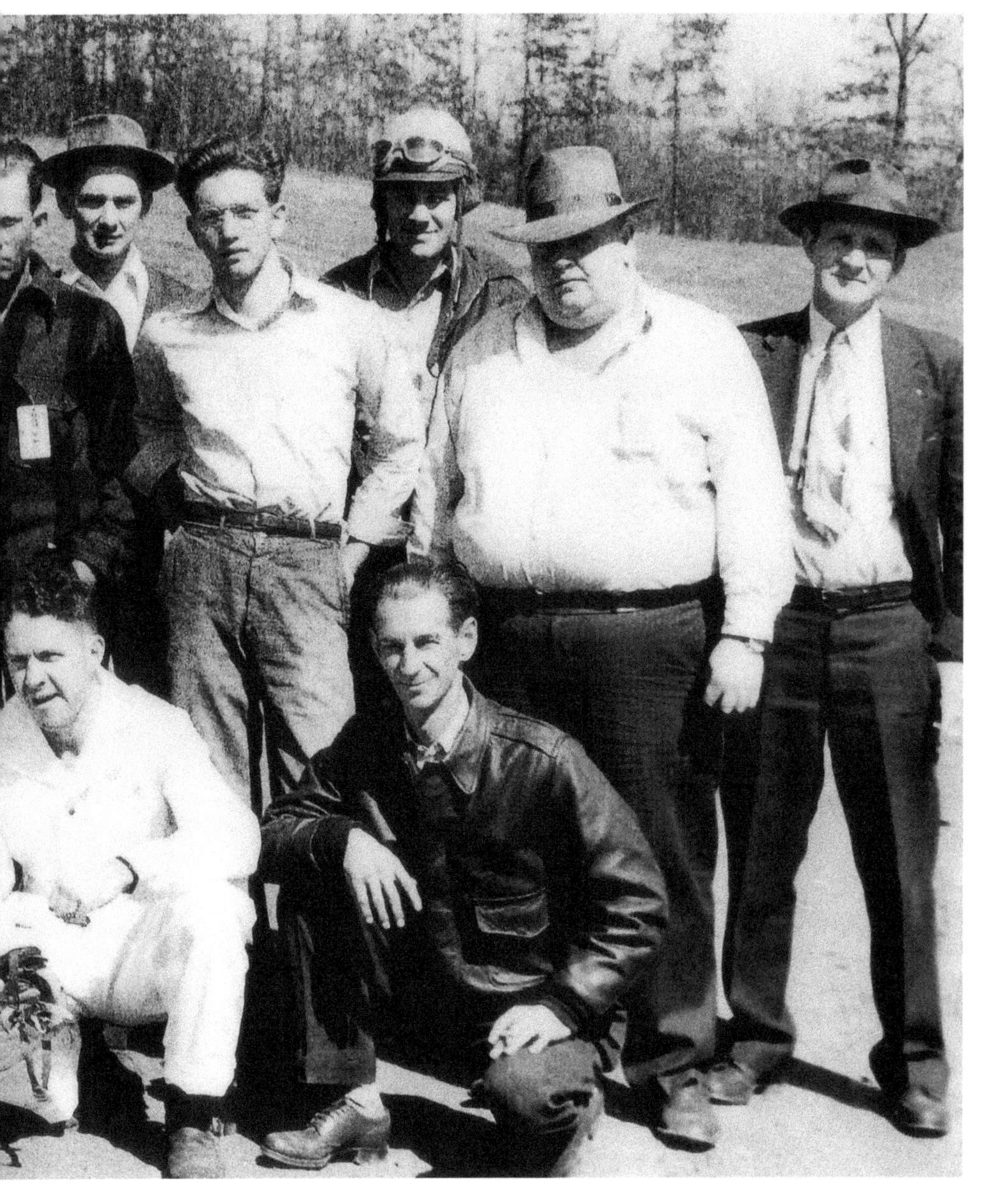

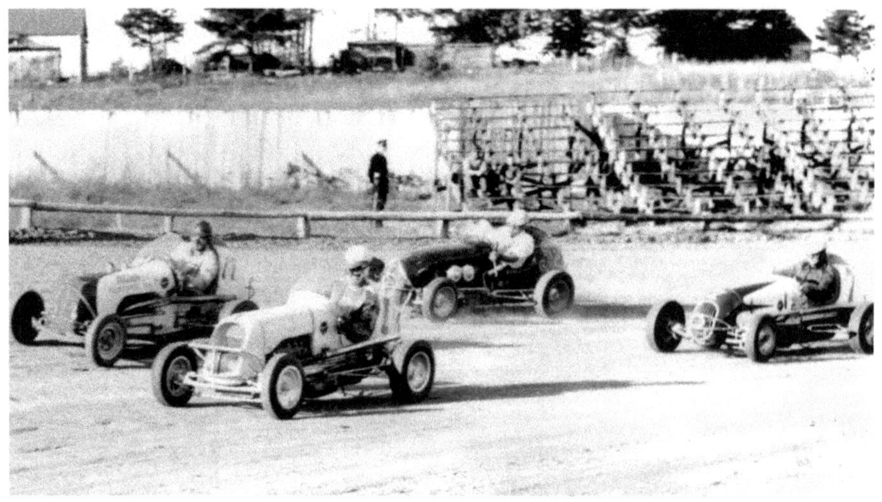

Midget cars race around the Broadway Speedway near Knoxville in the late 1940s. *Courtesy Melvin Corum.*

Mighty Midgets

As early as 1948, flyers and newspaper advertisements proclaimed "Midget Auto Racing Back at Tri-City Speedway" or "Midget Auto Races Every Saturday Night" in Johnson City. Fans flocked to watch the nimble open-wheel cars compete at startling speeds.

Memorial Stadium was the pride of Johnson City, and Midget cars raced there in the 1940s. They also competed on nearby Tri-City Speedway and were once the featured class at Broadway Speedway, starting in 1948. Broadway attracted many of auto racing's biggest names to compete in national touring Midget races sanctioned by the American Automobile Association.

Rex Easton of Springfield, Illinois; Johnnie Tolan of Denver, Colorado; Jimmy Bryan of Phoenix, Arizona; and George Tichenor of Logansport, Indiana, were among the Broadway winners. Bryan went on to claim seven United States Auto Club champ car wins and race in Formula One. Tolan won the 1952 AAA National Midget Championship, and "Squeaky" Easton won the 1954 AAA Midwest Midget Championship. Chuck Weyant won Broadway's final AAA Midget race in May 1956.

Bristol's NASCAR-sanctioned half mile provided an even greater stage for Midget cars when it hosted the Midget 200 on August 19, 1962. It was one of the last events sanctioned by NASCAR's Midget division, but racers from other sanctioning groups, including the United States Auto Club, competed for a $5,000 payday.

Buddy Martin of Cleveland, Ohio, was never seriously challenged during the event, wheeling his red-and-white No. 22 Buick-powered machine to the win. Martin's only hiccup occurred during his lone pit stop, when a mechanic couldn't remove one of the lug nuts retaining the right rear tire. Martin jumped out to survey the problem and then climbed back into his machine to finish the race on the old tire.

Martin also posted the fastest qualifying time, circling the Bristol oval in 21.89 seconds, or 82.94 miles per hour, faster than the Grand National track record of 22.12 seconds (81.37 miles per hour) held by Fireball Roberts.

Black and White

With its alternating black-and-white squares, the waving checkered flag remains an indelible racing symbol, but in the segregated South, those colors took on an entirely different meaning. The few dedicated black race car drivers of that era weren't allowed to compete on the same tracks as white drivers. In the late 1940s and early 1950s, an organization called the Atlanta Stock Car Club provided a platform for black drivers to race on southeastern dirt tracks, including those in Tennessee.

Promoter Edward Gannaway worked with Otis Ealy to bring the group to his Chattanooga Speedway.

"My dad didn't have a racist bone in his body. We ran several races in the time of total segregation, and it went over really well. That was very unusual for the time," Gannaway's son Eddie recalled. Gannaway helped put up posters promoting races featuring "All Colored Drivers."

The series helped launch the career of Charlie Scott, who later raced in NASCAR, and apparently attracted a special visitor:

"When Martin Luther King Jr. was on TV—when the civil rights movement was going on—my dad kept saying he looked familiar. He remembered that, as a younger man, King came to our track. He said he always wore a suit and he was always with a number of other young men."

Fayte Irwin, the promoter of Knoxville's Broadway Speedway, also staged an all-black racing event.

Sprint Cars

Sprint cars, larger and more powerful versions of the open-wheel Midgets, christened a new half-mile dirt oval at Newport's Tennessee-Carolina Fairgrounds on June 23, 1956. Texas native Jud Larson won a furious battle with Bobby Grim of Coal City, Indiana; 1953 national champion Bud Randall; and Ray Knepper. The race was sanctioned by the International Motor Contest Association.

Larson later became a United States Auto Club regular, scoring five victories, racing in the Indianapolis 500, competing in Formula One and posthumously being inducted into Midget Auto Racing Hall of Fame. The IMCA sprint cars returned to action in Newport on May 12, 1957, with Buzz Barton of Chickasha, Oklahoma, nabbing one of sixteen wins in his illustrious career.

Modifieds and Sportsman

East Tennessee's racing landscape continued evolving during the 1960s as Modifieds—cut down older coupe- and sedan-bodied cars with liberally modified engines—and Sportsman cars, usually mid-1950s Chevrolets and Fords, gained favor. Both divisions were regular fare on dirt ovals and the region's three primary paved tracks: Bristol, Chattanooga and Oak Ridge.

A week after the gleaming new Bristol International Speedway established a regional record of eighteen thousand fans for its 1961 Volunteer 500, promoters Larry Carrier and Carl Moore hosted the initial program of Modifieds and Sportsman. During the next couple seasons, a mixture of Tri-Cities drivers raced against invaders primarily from Virginia and the Carolinas on Saturday nights. The two classes usually raced simultaneously, with points awarded in each division.

Bill Morton won back-to-back Modified titles in 1961 and 1962, while Earl Hatcher and Brownie King won the Sportsman championships.

Nashville native Red Farmer won a four-hundred-lap NASCAR Modified championship race at Bristol in October 1961, held in conjunction with the Southeastern 500. The next year it was split into two two-hundred-lap races, as Joe Bill Adams won the Modified-Sportsman portion and Malcolm Brady of Columbia, Tennessee, won the Modified-Special race.

Newly paved and NASCAR-sanctioned in 1962, Boyd's Speedway near Chattanooga became another hotbed for Modified racing. The field

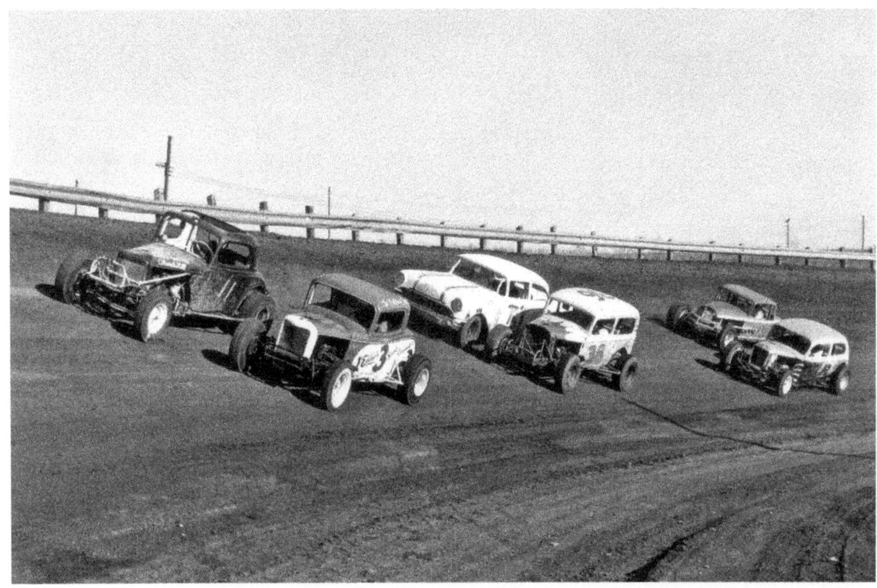

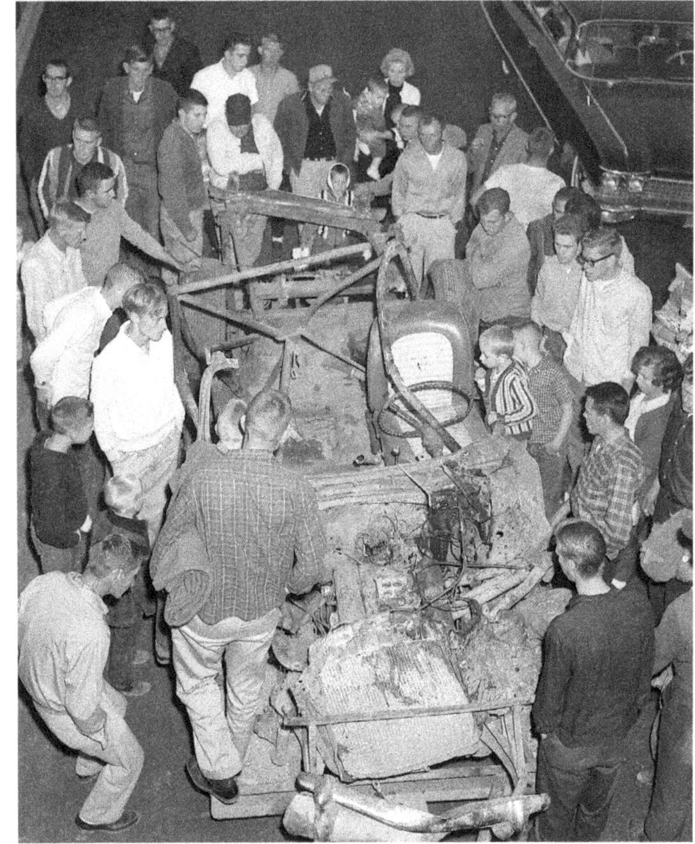

Above: Modifieds circle the original dirt oval at Smoky Mountain Raceway in Maryville in 1964 and include Claude Lay (3), Gene Glover (11), John A. Utsman (36) and Jim Hunter (51). *Ray Taylor photo.*

Right: A crowd encircles what remained of a Chevrolet driven by Pete Clouse, who died in a crash at Smoky Mountain Raceway in 1964. *Ray Taylor photo.*

typically included Tri-Cities drivers battling Freddy and Harold Fryar of Chattanooga, Tootle Estes of Knoxville and Georgia aces Charlie Mincey and Leon Sells, along with Kentuckian Wayne McGuire.

Modifieds were also the feature class on dirt when Smoky Mountain Raceway opened in 1964 and Kingsport Speedway opened in 1965, but they soon gave way to the Sportsman cars.

2

Tracks Through Time

Race drivers and the tracks they compete on are nothing without the other. Ranging from dusty fairgrounds with temporary seating for a couple hundred to Bristol Motor Speedway—one of the world's largest, most opulent sports stadiums—oval tracks have long operated in every corner of East Tennessee. Here are brief accounts of the most widely known.

Northeast

Appalachian Speedway

Promoted as the Southeast's finest dirt track when it opened in April 1969, Appalachian Speedway was a banked half-mile oval with sixty-foot-wide straightaways and seventy-five-foot-wide corners encircled by triple-strand guardrail. Built on forty acres near Kingsport's bustling Stone Drive, the track had seating for 7,500 but operated just two miles from the NASCAR-sanctioned Kingsport Speedway, and the two tracks frequently ran on the same night.

After closing in 1973, it reopened in 1974 with ex–motorcycle racer Robert Smawley serving as promoter. Late Models were the feature class, and the track also hosted a United States Auto Club Midget race. Appalachian closed after the 1975 season, and Brookside Industrial Park now operates there.

Austin Springs Park

The half-mile dirt oval off Austin Springs Road brought auto racing to Johnson City in the 1930s. The track featured Ford Model As and Model Ts and was sometimes so muddy the cars would get stuck and have to be pulled out.

Avoca Speedway

More than a decade before Bristol Motor Speedway was conceived, Bristol daredevils briefly raced on a quarter-mile dirt oval known as the Avoca

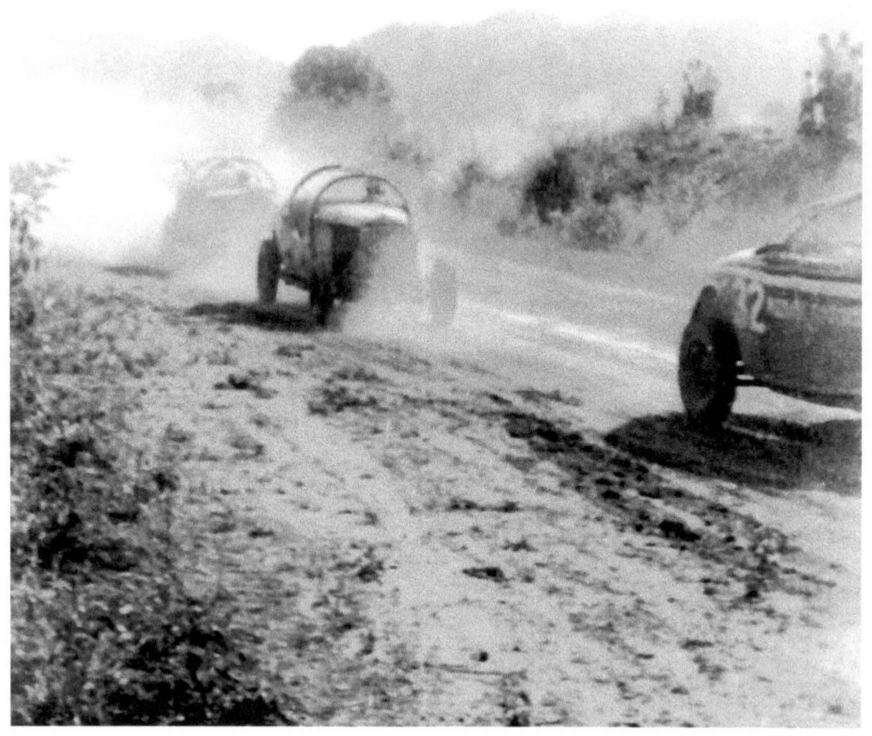

Jalopies known as hot rods race through the dust at the old Avoca Speedway in Bristol. *Courtesy Jimmie Warden.*

Speedway. Jimmie Warden, brother Bill and John "Pappy" Utsman claimed many of the wins there in 1948, the only year the track operated.

It was situated near the present Friendship import auto dealership now overlooking the Volunteer Parkway.

Black Bottom

A quarter-mile dirt oval was located a stone's throw from the Watauga River in Elizabethton, near the present Twins baseball complex.

Elizabethton was once a prominent mill town, and two nearby rayon plants employed 6,100 workers after World War II. The companies built inexpensive housing for their workers, and the nearby racetrack provided entertainment, hosting Midget cars and Modifieds during the 1950s. The track closed after a female spectator was fatally injured.

Bristol Motor Speedway

Bristol Motor Speedway towers over the rolling East Tennessee countryside on the site of a former dairy farm. Businessmen Larry Carrier, Carl Moore and R.G. Pope envisioned one of the nation's finest and fastest short tracks when they built the original iteration in 1961. More than five decades later, the massive complex historically ranks as fans' favorite NASCAR track.

Purchased by Speedway Motorsports in 1996, Bristol grew to its present 160,000-seat capacity. Originally asphalt, the track was converted to concrete in 1992 and resurfaced in 2007.

Bristol has annually hosted two races in the present Sprint Cup series, plus the Nationwide, Truck, virtually all of NASCAR's touring series and a number of other groups. It was twice covered with dirt to showcase winged Sprint Cars and Late Models.

Chinquapin Raceway

Chinquapin Raceway was a third-mile dirt oval built south of Bluff City. Tales abound of the famous drivers who competed there, but documentation is scarce. The track opened in 1959, primarily featured Modifieds and operated through 1962. Its final program included three feature races, with Layman Utsman winning two and Tiny Lund the other.

Davy Crocket Speedway

Also once known as Rogersville Speedway, this three-tenths-mile dirt oval was adjacent to the present Cherokee Dragway off Race Track Road. At one time, it operated in conjunction with Sportsman Speedway in Johnson City and Appalachian Speedway in Kingsport.

It featured Late Model stock cars with Walter Ball and Gary Myers among its most frequent winners. Surrounded by other tracks on all sides, Davy Crockett closed after the 1976 season.

Greeneville Fairgrounds

A quarter-mile dirt oval operated briefly during the 1950s at the Greeneville–Greene County fairgrounds.

I-81 Speedway

Originally designed as a motocross course known as the Dallas Ricker Complex, this three-eighths-mile dirt oval briefly hosted Late Model stock cars during the 1990s. It was also known as Northeast Tennessee Raceway. The four-hundred-acre facility near Interstate 81's exit 44 now operates as part of an off-road racing complex catering to motocross and all-terrain vehicle enthusiasts.

Island Park Speedway

After World War II, businessman Bill Warden convinced the owners of Island Park—a tiny jut in the Holston River in Bluff City—to let him carve out a primitive quarter-mile oval and conduct jalopy races. Island Park operated in the late 1940s, attracting Warden's brother, Jimmie, and John, Dub and Sherman Utsman—all of whom later raced in NASCAR's Grand National division. The island is privately owned.

Kingsport Speedway

Few who raced during Kingsport Speedway's inaugural 1965 season could imagine the significant roles it would play in racing history. Originally a quarter-mile, the track was expanded to three-eighths of a mile and secured NASCAR sanction in 1968. Kingsport hosted NASCAR's Grand National stockers for three years, plus an array of NASCAR support divisions and the Late Model Sportsman class.

Former NASCAR team owner J.D. Stacy took over in 1984 and converted it back to dirt. Kingsport hosted the mercurial National Dirt Racing Association and remained dirt until 1996, when new owner Joe Loven poured a concrete surface and regained NASCAR sanction. It closed in 2002, sitting idle for years before former NASCAR driver-turned-promoter Robert Pressley reopened it in 2011.

Memorial Stadium

In 1948, a year before North Carolina's venerable Bowman-Gray Stadium staged auto races, Midget cars raced around Johnson City's Memorial Stadium.

Built by the Works Project Administration in 1935 as part of the New Deal, Memorial Stadium was the football home of Science Hill and Langston high schools and hosted an annual college game known as the Burley Bowl. An oval running track surrounding the field proved ideal for auto racing. The opening race was held on Memorial Day weekend in 1948 in which, promoters advertised, "expert drivers from Indianapolis" would compete. Go-karts later raced there.

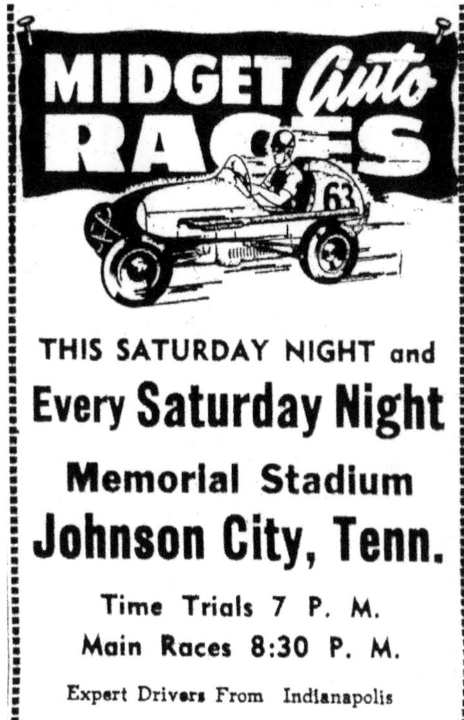

Johnson City's Memorial Stadium hosted Midget cars and other forms of racing starting in 1948. *Author's collection.*

The stadium was listed on the National Register of Historic Places in 2012 but was razed to make way for a community center and park.

Powder Branch Speedway

Located southeast of Happy Valley High School near Elizabethton, the Powder Branch Speedway featured Midgets and go-karts on its flat, clay quarter-mile surface. The track operated in the 1950s and 1960s.

Sportsman Speedway

Iconic Sportsman Speedway ran seventeen seasons on Johnson City's west side and boasts a rich, colorful history. The three-eighths-mile dirt track opened in 1958 and served as a training ground for local drivers Paul Lewis, Connie Saylor, Brad Teague and John A. Utsman, among others who went on to find success in NASCAR. It closed in 1974.

Tri-Cities Speedway

Built on land now occupied by an airport runway, the Tri-Cities Speedway near Blountville was one of the region's most successful early racetracks.

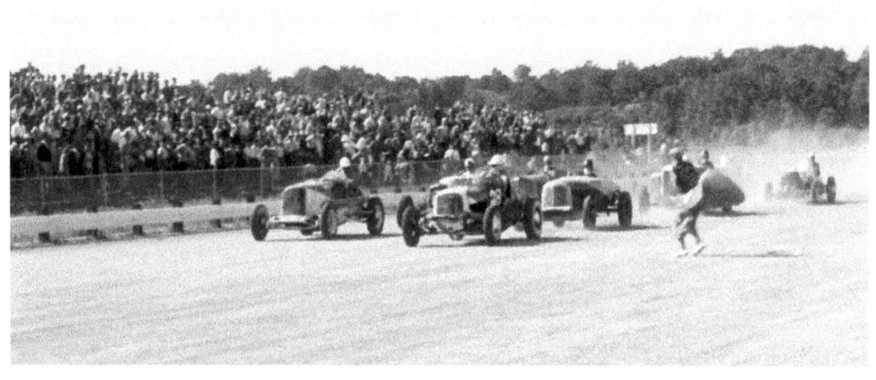

A large crowd looks on as the field takes the green flag during a race in the 1950s. *Courtesy Jimmie Warden.*

The third-mile dirt oval opened in 1948, hosting regular contests for Midget cars, roadsters, hot rods and machines that evolved into Modifieds.

Also known as Tri-City Speedway, the flagman's stand was between the banked turns, which is also where grandstands were located, offering fans a great, elevated vantage point. Progress and the growth of the adjacent Tri-Cities Regional Airport eventually claimed the track after the 1957 season.

Volunteer Speedway

Located on a bluff overlooking Interstate 81's exit 23 in Bulls Gap, the lights from Volunteer Speedway have illuminated the pathway for race fans since 1974. Built by Hugh and Louise Goan, the high-banked four-tenths-mile clay oval is among the nation's fastest, most challenging circuits.

Wendell Wallace holds the Late Model track record at 120 miles per hour, and NASCAR regular Kasey Kahne set the Sprint Car track record at more than 140 miles per hour.

The list of winners reads like a who's who of dirt-track racing. From Tennessee legends Herman Collins, Red Ledford and Walter Ball to Herman Goddard, Scott Bloomquist and Freddy Smith, all tasted victory at Volunteer. Vic Hill won five track championships, and H.E. Vineyard has four.

Central

Ashway Speedway

Speedway Circle turns off U.S. Route 25 into a Strawberry Plains subdivision, but tucked neatly away at the top of the hill is the fan entrance to Ashway Speedway. The red clay facility still hosts go-kart racing but is also a time capsule with its cracked concrete grandstands and decaying wooden buildings.

Buddy Hilliard took two years to build the original half-mile track on land that was once the family cornfield, finally opening in 1957. The track's distance was long ago shortened to a quarter-mile, but the view into the nearly flat third and fourth turns looks much like it did when Tootle Estes won the first race. He was a regular along with Herman Goddard, H.E. Vineyard, Bill McMahan and the Corums.

The track closed after the 1980 season but reopened as a go-kart facility in 1982. Often called "the pasture," the track was also labeled Asheway, referring to the nearby Asheville Highway.

Atomic Speedway

Long regarded as one of the nation's premier clay ovals, Atomic Speedway was synonymous with top-tier Late Model racing from its opening in 1970 until it closed in 2006.

Constructed just west of Knoxville off Interstate 40's Melton Hill Dam exit, Atomic showcased the best dirt racers in the region and the United States. The banked one-third of a mile was fast and entertaining, hosting major independent races along with national and regional touring series events.

Johnny Gibson won the track's first Late Model championship in 1970. Atomic was also home of the East Tennessee Racing Hall of Fame, but it closed after the 2006 season when the property was sold to make way for a truck terminal.

Big South Fork Raceway

Nestled in the hills near Huntsville in Scott County, the Big South Fork Raceway was a three-eighths-mile clay oval with long straightaways and tight, steeply-banked turns. It was named for the Big South Fork national recreation area operating nearby. The track opened in the 1990s and closed in 2002.

Broadway Speedway

Constructed north of Knoxville in heavily populated Fountain City, Broadway Speedway provided the region's first significant stage for national-caliber competition and helped shine the initial spotlight on Tootle Estes, Ed Harvey, Eddie Metler and other standouts.

The track first opened in 1948 as a quarter-mile oval featuring the wild and wooly open-wheel Midget cars. Broadway later included a half-mile oval and drag strip.

It quickly gained a national reputation, attracting many of the biggest stars of American racing to compete in national championship events sanctioned by the American Automobile Association and other organizations. It closed in 1958, and the Halls livestock auction now operates there.

Clinton Speedway

A half-mile dirt oval operated at the Anderson County Fairgrounds in Clinton in the 1920s, giving early drivers a chance to hone their skills.

411 Motor Speedway

Located a few miles south of Knoxville in Seymour, 411 Motor Speedway first opened on Easter Sunday 1960. The three-eighths-mile banked clay oval has undergone numerous changes over the years, including a stint as a paved track from 1993 to 2006, and was briefly sanctioned by NASCAR.

It also hosted an Automobile Racing Club of America race on Labor Day Weekend 1973. ARCA regular and part-time NASCAR Grand National East driver Wayne Watercutter scored the only pole and win of his ARCA career. He held off N.D. Copley, East Tennessee's "Little" Bill Corum, A. Arnold and Dave Dayton in the one-hundred-lap feature. In 1993, Scott Sutherland won a two-hundred-lap NASCAR All-Pro Series race there. The track continues to offer weekly dirt racing.

Greenback Speedway

Located some ten miles west of Maryville off Morganton Road, Greenback Speedway presented Sportsman and jalopy racing every Friday night in the 1960s on a quarter-mile dirt surface.

Melvin Corum won the track's first race in 1963. He, brother "Big Bill" Corum and cousin "Little Bill" Corum were regulars, along with Charlie Rogers and Claude Donovan.

Johnson's Race Track

Former slave turned successful businessman Cal Johnson operated a half-mile oval track near present Chilhowee Park, staging horse races there until about 1906. In 1910, Johnson drew a crowd to see the city's first airplane landing and, later, a race between a Wright brothers' biplane, a dirigible airship and a car driven by Herbert Graf. The biplane won.

Around 1916, the dirt oval known as "Johnson's Race Track" featured mechanical horsepower. Racing ended by the early 1920s, and the property was gradually developed into a residential area. The city retained the track's oval shape as a city street, and today, more than fifty modest homes and a church have a Speedway Circle address.

Knoxville Motor Speedway

The Knoxville Motor Speedway was a dirt oval that operated during the Great Depression in Knox County's Inskip community. Managed by local businessman J.B. Cate, the track was located near the present Merchant's Drive intersection with Tillery Road. It hosted roadsters similar to the Indianapolis cars of that era and early Midgets.

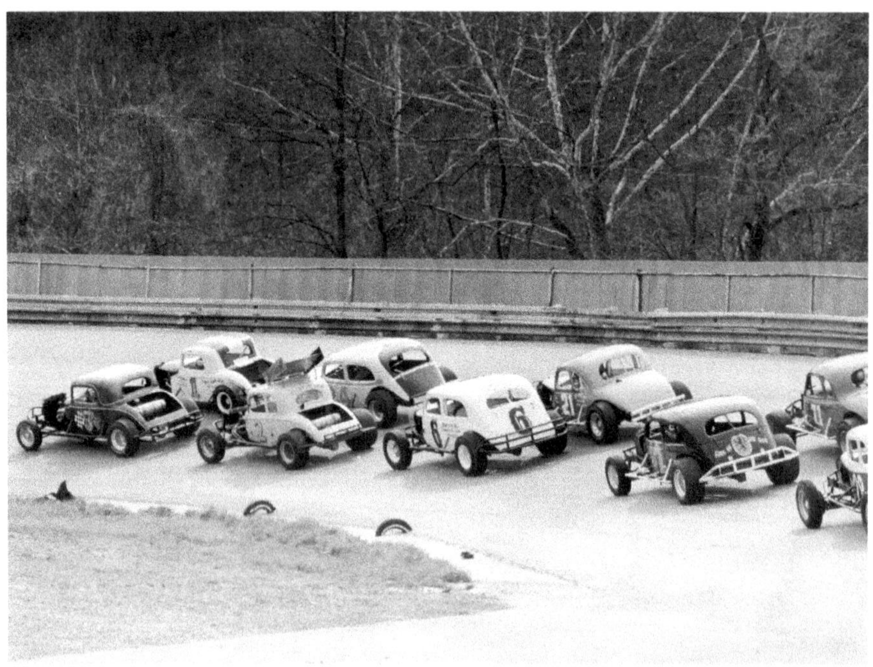

Modifieds race on the asphalt of the old Knoxville Raceway near Maynardville. *Courtesy Melvin Corum.*

Knoxville Raceway

Auto parts magnate Ed Harvey was bitten by the racing bug while driving Midgets and Modified cars. In 1965, Harvey sold land to the State of Tennessee for an interstate highway and used that money to construct Knoxville Raceway, a four-tenths-mile paved oval off the Maynardville Highway.

The track ran Modified and figure-eight races and hosted an Automobile Racing Club of America series race in May 1968. Midwest veteran Les Snow qualified on the pole and won the one-hundred-lap race, one of his eight victories in a season where he narrowly lost the championship to Benny Parsons.

It was converted to a dirt surface in 1974 and reopened in 1975 with regular Friday night shows. Despite running in conjunction with high-profile Atomic Speedway, Knoxville operated just a couple more seasons and was later reconfigured into a drag strip that opened in 1978.

Morristown Fairgrounds

Some of East Tennessee's earliest regular racing happened on the dirt half-mile oval at the Morristown fairgrounds. Starting sometime after 1910 and continuing for at least two decades, the track attracted the best drivers from East Tennessee and surrounding states.

Local plumbing contractor Will Roddy promoted many of the events on Memorial, Independence and Labor Day holidays, while a group called the Knoxville Speedway Corporation also promoted races there. Advertisements promised "plenty of cars, daring drivers and excitement," and news accounts of that era reported several thousand fans attended.

Al Roman of Louisville, Kentucky, was the big winner of a fifty-mile, one-hundred-lap race at Morristown on Labor Day 1928. The field of twenty included many drivers from East Tennessee and from as far away as Florida.

The track experienced at least two fatalities. Driver Fred Radino died from injuries sustained in a racing accident in 1914, and George Robb died in May 1928 after crashing through a fence.

Morristown Speedway

The Morristown Speedway operated for about six seasons, from 1948 to 1953, near the former Sunset Drive-In. The quarter-mile dirt oval offered the popular hot rod roadsters and Midget cars. Hometown racer Paul Gose was among its most frequent winners.

Sherman Utsman won the track championship in 1952, the same year well-known driver Paul Hilbert of Weber City, Virginia, died as the result of a crash there. The track ultimately closed after the 1953 season and was replaced by a tobacco warehouse and, later, a Bojangles restaurant.

Newport Speedway

Unlike the wrecked metal derelicts surrounding it, Newport Speedway is one of the region's survivors. The banked four-tenths-mile paved oval continues to host racing on a hill off Industrial Road, in the midst of an auto junkyard.

The track first opened with a dirt surface in 1977, featuring many of the region's best Late Model stock cars. Newport hosted the first race for what would become Robert Smawley's National Dirt Racing Association in 1978. With a wealth of dirt ovals operating in the area, the Newport track was paved in 1988 and now operates under the sanction of the American Speed Association.

Roane County Speedway

Also known as Harriman Speedway, this quarter-mile dirt oval operated from 1951 to 1968 on a site near U.S. Route 27 and Caney Creek in Harriman.

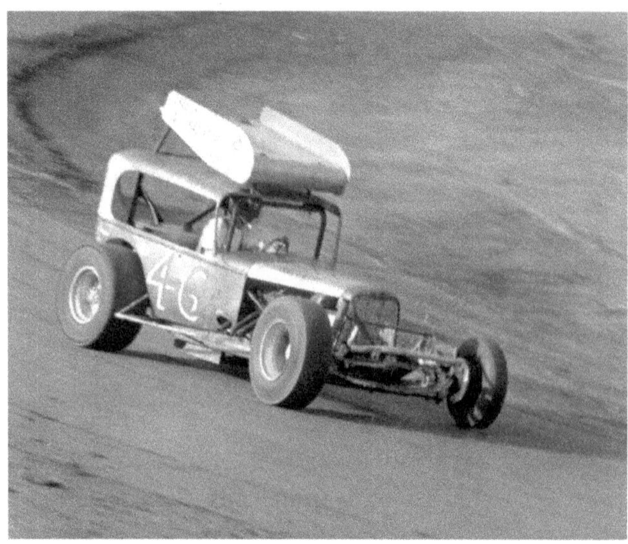

A winged "Skeeter" Modified flies around the former Sportsman Speedway in Johnson City. *Courtesy Ernie Collins.*

The track was northeast of the present Roane State Community College. Roane County's track hosted jalopies, Modifieds and Late Models.

Oak Ridge Speedway

Also known as Edgemoor Speedway and the Oak Ridge Sportsdrome, the quarter-mile oval opened as a dirt track in 1951. After about four years, promoters created what was billed as the "South's first paved oval" and hosted races until 1962. The track's Modified show regularly attracted Freddy and Harold Fryar, Friday Hassler and Bob Burcham from the Chattanooga area. Eddie Metler was also a big winner there, and it was the site of L.D. Ottinger's first victory.

While some accounts claim the American Automobile Association conducted national championship Midget races there in the 1950s, those events actually occurred at Broadway Speedway. Midgets did compete there, along with stock cars.

Scenic Raceway

The high-banked, nearly half-mile dirt oval near the Tennessee-Kentucky border regularly attracted racers from both states for weekly events from 2000 to 2006. It was located north of Oneida, just west of U.S. 27.

Scenic hosted the UDTRA national dirt Late Model tour in 2002 as Georgia's Dale McDowell led all fifty laps and held off Steve Francis and Rick Eckert for the victory. The track was scheduled to host Tennessee's first USAC Sprint Car race in forty-six years in 2006, but the event was cancelled.

Smoky Mountain Raceway

Smoky Mountain Raceway remains one of the region's most venerable facilities after five decades of operation. Located southwest of Maryville off Brick Mill Road, the track has continually evolved. It opened as a half-mile dirt oval hosting Modifieds in 1964. The following year brought a NASCAR sanction and its first Grand National race. NASCAR's biggest names ran three races on dirt and nine on asphalt between 1965 and 1971. Richard

Petty scored six victories, and Smoky Mountain produced the lone series win for Johnson City driver Paul Lewis.

When NASCAR's Late Model Sportsman division rose in popularity, Smoky Mountain hosted regular weekly shows and some touring races. The track surface was shortened to four-tenths of a mile and converted to dirt in the 1980s, and it has hosted most of the major touring series.

Tennessee-Carolina Speedway

The banked half-mile dirt oval at the Tennessee-Carolina Fairgrounds was originally called Newport Speedway but renamed to reflect where it operated. The historic track featured a large hillside grandstand and ample parking.

It opened in 1956 and hosted Tennessee's first NASCAR Grand National race that October. The Tennessee-Carolina Speedway also provided regular weekly shows featuring Tootle Estes, Paul Gose and young hometown racer Lloyd Dane (L.D.) Ottinger, who went on to win two NASCAR national championships. It closed in 1967 after the promoter and fairgrounds failed to come to terms.

Tazewell Speedway

Nicknamed the "Bad Fast Taz" for its blazing speeds, Tazewell Speedway claims the title of world's fastest one-third-mile dirt oval. Its steeply banked corners and short straightaways provide a clay-covered mixing bowl for Late Model drivers to run dizzying lap times.

Brothers Blaine and Bill Frazier built a relatively flat racetrack on their father's Claiborne County farm in 1964. They revised the track in 1982, adding steep banking in the corners that produce its now trademark action. Scott Bloomquist set the Late Model track record at 10.82 seconds in 2012.

Located north of town, just off U.S. 25E near Cumberland Gap National Park, the track operated from 1965 until 1987. It reopened in 1993 and continues to run regular weekly programs plus host regional and national touring series races.

Wartburg Speedway

The banked one-third-mile dirt oval first opened in 1958 and has operated during most of the years since, through a variety of promoters. Wartburg has run Late Models and a variety of support divisions and hosted the Southern Regional Racing Series. Fans can watch the races from the grandstands or its trademark terraced-hillside parking area.

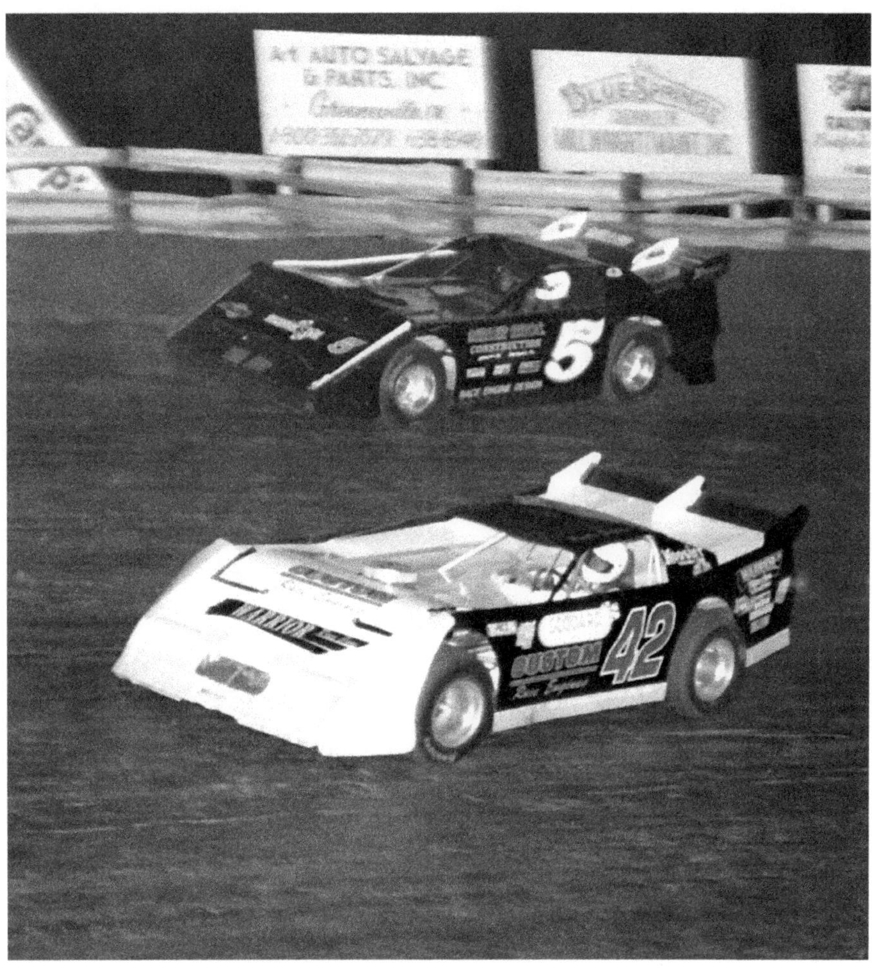

Late Model stock cars of Rusty Goddard (42) and Ronnie Johnson (5) battle on the high-banked Volunteer Speedway in the 1990s. *Joey Millard photo.*

Southeast

Boyd's Speedway

Through a string of promoters and at least six different name changes, people refer to the one-third-mile oval at the Tennessee-Georgia line as Boyd's Speedway. Namesake E.A. Boyd built and operated the original clay track in 1952, running Midgets and, later, Modifieds.

It was paved in 1962, sanctioned by NASCAR and hosted its first Grand National race on August 3. Joe Weatherly took advantage of Richard Petty's mechanical problems to post his eighth win of that season in the Confederate 200. The track was rebranded Chattanooga International Raceway in 1964, and David Pearson won its final three-hundred-lap Grand National race.

In its NASCAR days, Boyd's Modified races attracted the likes of Bobby and Donnie Allison and Red Farmer to battle with local heroes the Fryar brothers, Bob Burcham, a large Tri-Cities contingent and Kentuckian Wayne McGuire. It was converted back to dirt prior to the 1977 season and operates today.

While technically in Georgia, turns one and two are about one hundred feet south of the Tennessee border, which bisects the property.

Chattanooga Speedway

Chattanooga Speedway opened as a nearly half-mile dirt oval in 1947, but promoter Edward Gannaway shortened the track to about a quarter mile and operated it that way until its closing after the 1951 season.

Also referred to as Alton Park, the track featured stock car racing on Sunday afternoons with future NASCAR Grand National drivers Charley Griffith and Walter Hartman competing. Another regular visitor was speed shop entrepreneur and hot rod pioneer "Honest Charley" Card, who began selling high-performance parts in 1948.

There were two fatalities at the track. A racer died as a result of injuries suffered in a crash, and a fan was killed when struck by a race car's tire-wheel assembly. The track was located off Hooker Road in the flood plain of Chattanooga Creek north of the Georgia state line. An auto salvage business now operates there.

Cleveland Speedway

The one-third-mile clay oval continues operating every Saturday night, like it has for much of the past six decades. The track opened in 1954, closed briefly after the 1958 season but then reopened in 1961. For years, it was promoted by former NASCAR Convertible national champion Joe Lee Johnson, who purchased the track in 1980 and sold it in 2004.

Cleveland has been a regular stop for the Southern All Star Series, hosting more events than any other track, plus a number of large independent races and the Lucas Oil Late Models.

Johnson and his wife, Jean, were inducted into the National Dirt Late Model Hall of Fame for their promotional efforts.

Midway Speedway

Midway Speedway—so named because it was midway between the Athens and Etowah communities—was a quarter-mile dirt oval that operated just a few years in the 1950s.

Moccasin Bend Speedway

Besides owning a chain of grocery stores, Chattanooga businessman Herbert Kirk was a race fan. In the 1950s, he built a track on part of eighty acres he owned on the Moccasin Bend peninsula despite opposition from neighbors concerned about dust and noise.

The quarter-mile dirt oval was billed as the South's highest banked dirt track when it opened on August 1, 1954, and promotional flyers trumpeted races as "Chattanooga's greatest sports event[s]." The track operated primarily on Sunday afternoons. Finishes were often exciting because a freshwater spring flowed beneath the exit of turn four, making the track wet and reaching the start-finish line a challenge. It closed after the 1956 season.

Spring City Raceway

Formerly known as Rhea County Speedway, the tight quarter-mile clay oval continues offering weekly racing in a variety of classes each Saturday night from March through October. It began operating in the 1980s, closed for a few years and resumed racing in 1997. The track, nicknamed "the Bullring," is just off Rhea County Highway.

Warner Park

Originally built as the Olympia Park horse track in 1895, the City of Chattanooga purchased the forty-three acres in 1912 and renamed it to honor a local politician. The site has included an amusement park, bowling alley, petting zoo and, for many years, an auto racetrack.

The flat half-mile dirt oval first hosted car racing around 1916 and continued to do so until the 1950s. One of the track's most distinguishing features was a large oak tree with very little bark near turn three. Many a driver's day ended after hitting that tree.

Hall of Fame driver Bill Holland of Philadelphia, Pennsylvania, won a AAA Sprint Car race there in May 1948, a few days before he finished second in the Indianapolis 500.

Warner Park is now home to the Chattanooga Zoo and a city-owned sports complex.

3

Don't Mess with Jim

Former army paratrooper Jimmie Warden drove race cars like he lives life: flat out. Warden and his brother, Bill, began racing in their native West Virginia, but their careers blossomed when they moved to Bluff City in East Tennessee after World War II.

Jimmie regularly captured checkered flags at long-lost dirt ovals Island Park, Avoca, Tri-Cities and Morristown, while his brother found greater success in promoting races. For all his speed behind the wheel, Warden earned a reputation as someone who also took care of equipment. That combination prompted an unexpected telephone call in August 1951.

S.M. Cain and Les Bowman, a pair of businessmen from nearby Johnson City, liked stock car racing enough to make Warden an offer. Would he be interested in driving in the NASCAR Southern 500 if they provided a car? Despite having never raced on asphalt nor wheeled anything as bulky as a Grand National stocker, Warden immediately said yes.

"I didn't really know them, but they knew me from racing around here," Warden said. "Hudson was the fastest car back then, so they called all over the country and found a four-door that was the only one with the heavy-duty engine. That took two or three days. They got the car and drove here, and we went to Darlington, South Carolina."

NASCAR's premier event of that era established its starting field during ten days of time trials instead of one qualifying session. In a system patterned after the Indianapolis 500, drivers posting the five fastest times on the first day earned the top five starting positions. The fastest five from day two

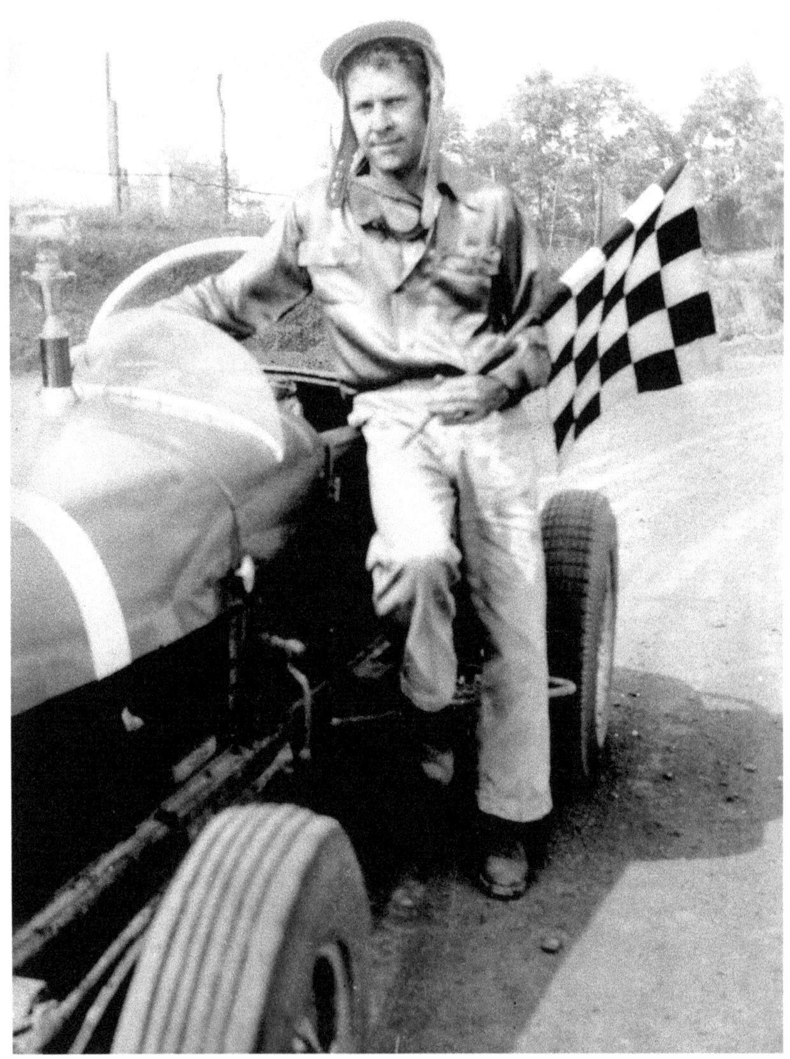

Jimmie Warden captured many checkered flags in races all over the Appalachian region. *Courtesy Jimmie Warden.*

would start in positions six through ten until the massive field was filled. The Tennesseans arrived with only two days remaining before "the world's greatest stock car race."

For a young man from Appalachia who'd never seen anything larger than a half-mile dirt oval, Darlington Raceway's sprawling original 1.25-mile layout with its 1,566-foot-long, 85-foot-wide straightaways and sweeping, banked corners might have seemed imposing.

"It should have scared the hell out of me. But we were so busy trying to get lined up and get our gasoline and get our pit, I didn't have time to do a whole lot of thinking," Warden recalled.

After driving the Hudson to South Carolina, he and his new team taped over the headlights, removed the windshield wipers and hubcaps and got in line to qualify. In those days, the flagman stood on the race track at the start-finish line, and as Warden's turn approached, he asked the official for some help.

"I've never been here before," Warden said. "Could I get a couple laps of practice first?"

"No," the man responded curtly. "You go right now, or you don't go at all."

Warden climbed in without a word, started the Hudson's factory-stock six-cylinder engine, pulled onto the track and picked up speed as the green flag waved. Warden aimed toward the top groove, barreled into the fourteen-degree banking of turn one, cut the wheel left and promptly spun out, ending his chances for that day.

With one last opportunity to qualify, Warden heeded the advice of others and never let off the throttle through Darlington's tricky corners. Despite no

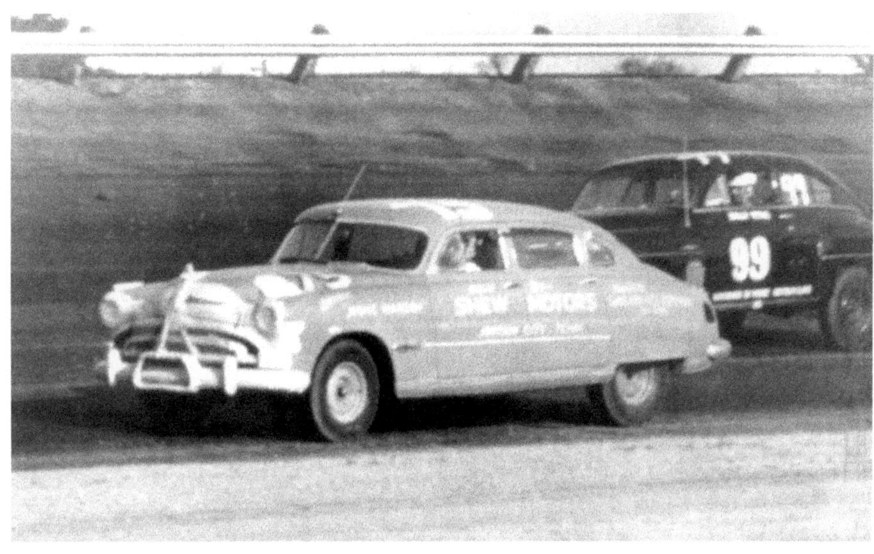

Jimmie Warden (75) races alongside Billy Myers (99) in the 1951 Southern 500 in Darlington, South Carolina. *Courtesy Jimmie Warden.*

practice, he recorded one of the week's fastest laps at 83.90 miles per hour, compared to Frank Mundy's pole-winning lap of 84.65 mph.

Cars were lined up three wide to start the race, but getting into the program on the final day meant Warden would start sixty-ninth of eighty-two cars, the largest field in NASCAR history. When all were positioned, cars filled the entire frontstretch and turn four.

"I was in the middle of three lanes of traffic going around there. I couldn't go forward, couldn't go backward and somebody would bump you occasionally," Warden recalled. "You'd be going down the straightaway, and there would be cars all around you—and you'd hear 'pop' when one of those tires would blow. You wouldn't believe it to have that many flat tires and not wreck everybody on the track."

Six hours and thirty minutes after it began, Herb Thomas was first beneath the checkered flag aboard his Marshall Teague–owned, factory-sponsored Hudson Hornet. He received $8,800, while Warden got $50 for fiftieth place, an improbably good showing given the circumstances. Even more so if one considers legendary racers Buck Baker, Curtis Turner, defending race winner Johnny Mantz and polesitter Frank Mundy all finished behind him.

"I didn't wreck, and a whole lot of them did," Warden said with a laugh. It remains a bittersweet memory for someone used to winning because Warden never returned to NASCAR.

"Money was pretty hard to come by back then. I was lucky to find somebody who would sponsor me one time because I didn't have money," Warden said. What he did accomplish was dominating the East Tennessee scene for a time.

Competing primarily in brother Bill's Tennessee-based South East Racing Association, Warden raced in "junkyard derby" events with Modified cars called hot rods. Constructed for a few hundred dollars, the cars featured cut-down bodies, scrapyard-survivor engines and no power steering (which hadn't been invented yet). A driver's only protection was a seatbelt, a small helmet similar to what jockeys wore and goggles. Some cars sported roll bars, but many were merely single, shoulder-high hoops behind the driver. The idea, Warden said, was to duck down in the car if a rollover appeared imminent.

Those primitive, stripped-down cars evolved into roadsters featuring a lower center of gravity, the driver in the center and modified engines. Warden's greatest success came behind the wheel of a sleek DeSoto-powered roadster owned and prepared by Harry Morris. Racetracks progressed, too, from short-lived, primitive quarter-mile tracks at Island Park in Bluff

City and Avoca Speedway near Bristol to Tri-Cities Speedway, Northeast Tennessee's first significant track.

"They rented the [Bluff City] island and went in there and scraped out a race track. We only raced there a year or so. Avoca wasn't much. We only raced there a few times," Warden said. "A lot of tracks were just nothing. There was one track where we ran with tire chains on because it was a mud hole. If you ran regular tires, you'd just spin."

Bill Warden constructed a track on land adjacent to Tri-Cities Airport, and racing began there in 1948. Primitive by modern standards, the track featured banked corners, grandstand seating, a control tower and one truly distinctive feature: the wooden flagman's stand located between turns one and two.

Warden finished second in the Tri-Cities track points in 1950 and then dominated the 1951 season. Warden won sixteen times in twenty-three races at Tennessee tracks including Morristown and Chattanooga.

"We raced in Greeneville one time, and it was so dusty you couldn't see. Bill and I were both racing. We were just guessing, but we lapped those other

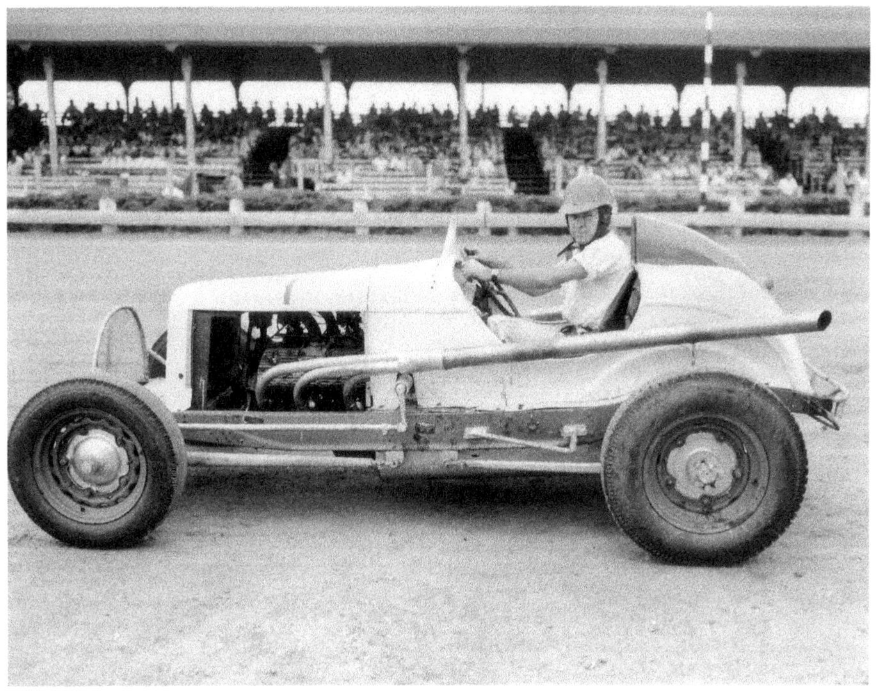

Jimmie Warden gets ready to go on track at the national Sprint Car race at Williams Grove, Pennsylvania. *Frank Smith photo, courtesy Jimmie Warden.*

cars every two laps. I couldn't pass him because I couldn't see. He won, and I ran second," Warden said. "One time over next to Kingsport, I was out front by half a lap. I had them covered, and a rainstorm came up. They didn't wave the red flag, and I went down in the turn and spun and went from first to last in one lap. That old clay dirt is slick as glass when it gets wet."

He also competed at the 1950 national championship roadster races in Williams Grove, Pennsylvania.

"I qualified real good and was running right behind the world champion. I felt like I could pass him, but he went down in the turn and spun. I saw a rock come up off his tire, and it knocked the top off all four of my spark plugs," Warden said.

Warden retired in 1952 while still in his prime. Car owner Morris hired former rival Paul Hilbert, but Hilbert was killed in a racing crash a few weeks later in Morristown.

"They weren't paying much prize money, so I quit. I'd gotten married and had a little girl, so I didn't want to get hurt or killed," Warden said.

He went on to operate a successful business and became friends with entrepreneurs Larry Carrier and Carl Moore, who established Bristol International Speedway in 1961.

4

Broadway Lights

From the biggest names of open-wheel racing and the Indianapolis 500 to many of stock car racing's greatest early stars, Broadway Speedway attracted them all during a notable ten-year run from 1948 to 1957.

Broadway built its reputation by hosting national championship Midget car races sanctioned by the American Automobile Association. Indianapolis 500 winners Jimmy Bryan, Johnnie Parsons and Bill Vukovich and midwestern stars Woodie Campbell, Johnny Chaplin, Gene Force, Dick Frazier, Joe James, Bob Reuther and George Tichenor regularly competed at Broadway along with Oklahoma hotshots Buddy Cagle, Bud Grace and Angelo "Angie" Howerton.

With little more protection than a leather helmet, goggles and a basic seat belt, fan favorites muscled the open-cockpit cars around the track at more than fifty miles per hour. How wild was it? In an advance news story about a Labor Day AAA National Championship Midget race, the track's race director said the "100-lap event would not be stopped regardless of accidents and stalled cars would not be moved" because rules forbid stopping the race!

Promoter Sterling Lafayette "Fayte" Irwin cultivated local fans and drivers with a steady diet of Midgets, Modifieds and later stock cars competing within the racetrack's wooden guardrails.

Hometown fans cheered for Ed Harvey, Kenny Milligan, Eddie McPhettridge, Kenny Sharp, Eddie Metler, Clay Buckner and a young Herbert "Tootle" Estes—locals who became legends.

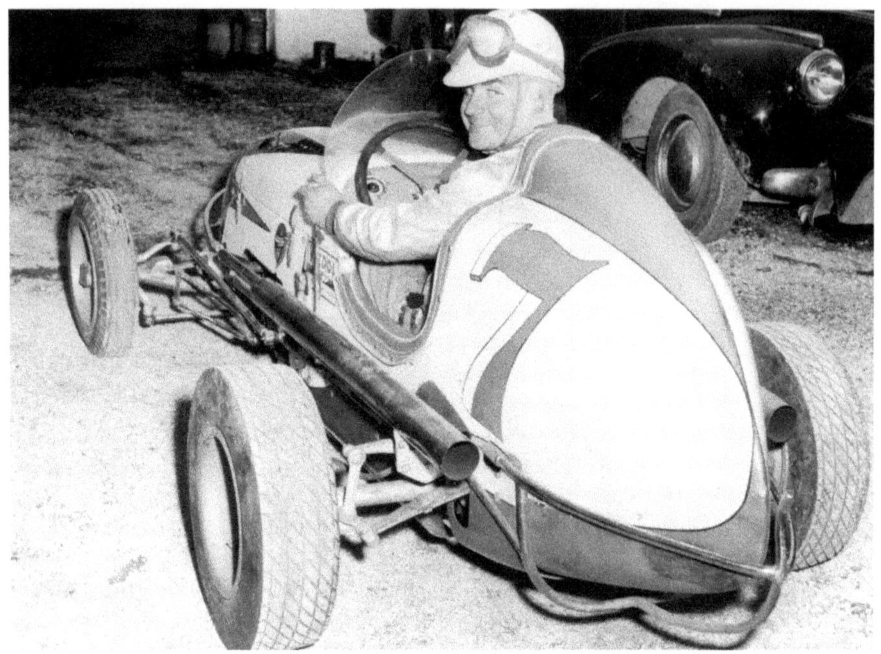

Ed Harvey of Knoxville sits behind the wheel of his No. 7 Midget at Broadway Speedway. *Melvin Corum collection.*

The final major Midget race at Broadway saw Chuck Weyant capture the checkered flag over pole-sitter Hank Nykaza in April 1956.

Stock car racing's popularity rose in the 1950s, and Broadway became the state's first track to attract that era's major touring series.

The American Automobile Association held four races there in 1954 and 1955. Its successor, the United States Auto Club, held four stock car races there in 1956 and 1957. John Marcum's Midwest Auto Racing Club, which later became the Automobile Racing Club of America, made multiple stops at Broadway in 1956 and 1957. Some of the era's biggest names—Nelson Stacy, Marshall Teague, Les Snow and Frank "Rebel" Mundy—all claimed victories.

Mundy, an Atlanta native who served as a personal driver for U.S. general George S. Patton during World War II, dominated early AAA races at Broadway. His first win came in May 1954, wheeling a Hudson Hornet past future Indy 500 winner Jim Rathmann in the one-hundred-lap affair.

Mundy captured the 1955 AAA national championship in dominant fashion driving a Chrysler 300 owned by NASCAR pioneer Carl Kiekhaefer.

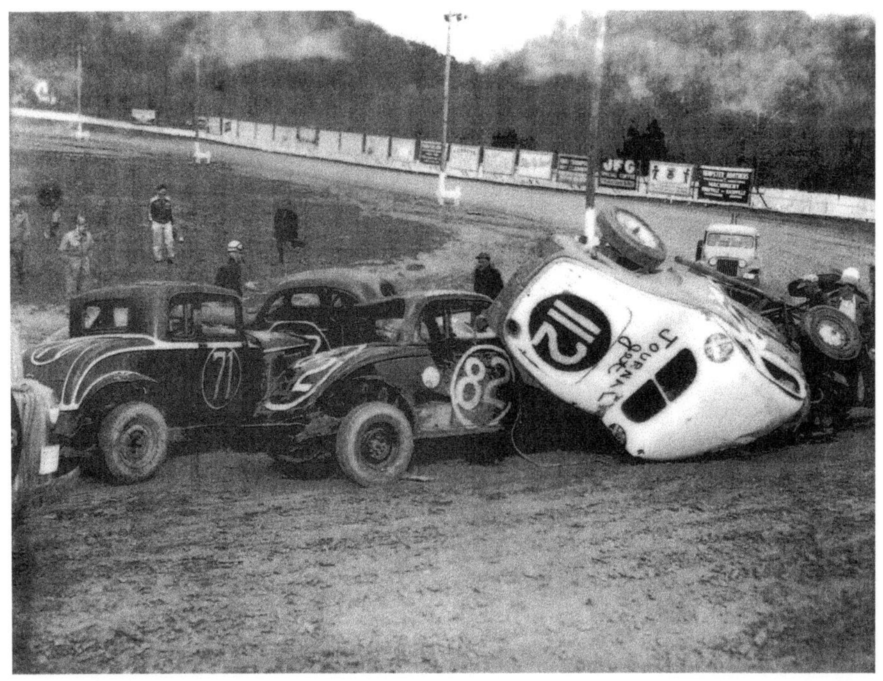

Drivers Phil Monaghan (82) and Johnny Phillips (71) were collected when car No. 112 got on its roof at Broadway Speedway. *Melvin Corum collection.*

Together they won eight of that season's twelve races, including a sweep of all three held at Broadway.

In the series-opening race in late April, Mundy started on the front row and outran fast qualifier Les Snow for the win. AAA returned to Tennessee on Fourth of July weekend, and Mundy remained undefeated for that season, winning over teammate Tony Bettenhausen. A month later, Mundy again outran Bettenhausen at Broadway to claim his seventh victory of the year and all but assured himself of the championship.

Teague, who drove the factory-supported "Fabulous Hudson Hornet" to seven NASCAR wins, including two on Daytona's Beach & Road Course, also counted a Broadway victory toward a championship. Teague had five wins in 1954, including Broadway, to capture the AAA title.

AAA left racing due to a large number of racing-related fatalities in the United States and abroad, but the series was taken over by the United States Auto Club, a group formed by Indianapolis Motor Speedway owner Tony Hulman.

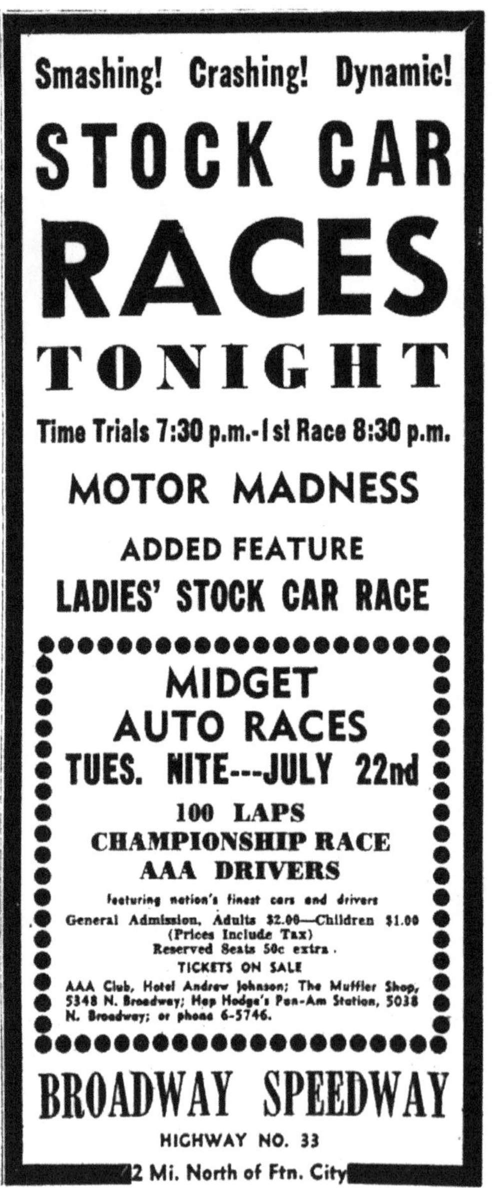

Broadway Speedway promoted a wide variety of auto racing events from 1948 to 1957. *Author's collection.*

Three different drivers tasted victory when USAC visited Broadway in 1956: Nelson Stacy, a war hero from Kentucky; Marshall Teague; and midwestern standout Les "Tiger" Snow.

Broadway also welcomed the MARC Circuit of Stars in late October 1956 as Russ Hepler picked up the last of his ten career series wins in the one-hundred-lap show. Georgia native Roz Howard won the 1957 MARC series race at Broadway and went on to capture that season's MARC Southern division championship.

USAC stock cars returned one last time in 1957 as Tennessean Sherman Utsman of Bluff City drove a Ford past Whitey Johnson for a $640 payday in the one-hundred-lapper. Utsman's uncle William "Dub" Utsman finished third, and future NASCAR national champion Gene Glover was ninth.

Broadway closed after that season amid competition from other area tracks.

5

Border Bash

The racetrack was right there," the old-timer said, pausing from his regular stroll around Newport's Cocke County A&I Fairgrounds.

"It was a big half mile—like Bristol—the track was all in here," he said, gesturing toward the gently curved, grass-covered ground that was once turn four of the Tennessee-Carolina Speedway. "Turns one and two were over there," pointing toward a horseshoe-shaped spot now filled with trees. "The grandstands were all along that hillside."

Tall with a headful of wiry, gray hair, the man was surely an athlete in his prime, but like the old speedway, that time was long since past.

Built for a reported $250,000, the track was originally named the Newport Fairgrounds Speedway and operated by the nonprofit Tennessee-Carolina Fair. It was scheduled to open on May 2, 1956, with Joie Chitwood and his "Congress of Canadian Daredevils" auto thrill show, but rains postponed the program. So the new dual-purpose facility's first event featured three days of trotter horse racing.

Chitwood and his thrill show returned on May 13 to generate Newport's initial mechanical horsepower. The following month, the track's first auto race was a Sprint Car affair sanctioned by the International Motor Contest Association and won by Jud Larson.

But the fairgrounds' most significant moment occurred on October 7, 1956, when it hosted Tennessee's first NASCAR Grand National stock car race.

The two-hundred-lap contest was the fifty-first of fifty-six races NASCAR president Bill France Sr. conducted that season in seventeen states, from

Tennessee-Carolina Speedway

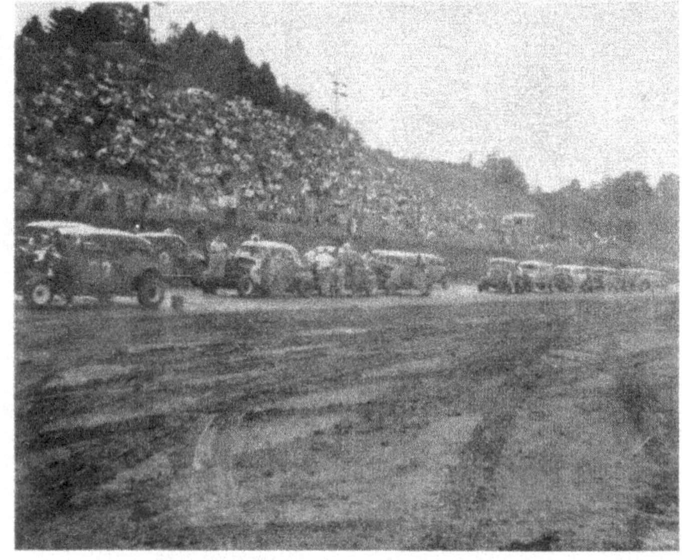

Racing Every Friday

NEWPORT, TENNESSEE

The Tennessee-Carolina Speedway souvenir program shows a large crowd in its sizable grandstands. *Melvin Corum collection.*

Florida to California and Oregon to New York. More than five decades later, a breeze blowing across the fairgrounds reverently whispered the names of Petty, Baker, Flock, Roberts, Myers, Lund and Weatherly.

Those legendary drivers battled before a crowd of six thousand who filled the grandstands along the western hillside and perched in nearby trees.

When the dust settled, Glenn "Fireball" Roberts, a rising star from Daytona Beach, Florida, captured the trophy and $850 top prize.

Buck Baker started his Carl Kiekhaefer–owned white No. 300-B Chrysler on the outside of the front row and led the race's first 149 laps. But the day belonged to Roberts, who steered his No. 22 Depaolo Engineering Ford past Baker on lap 150 and led to the checkered flag, in a race run without a single accident or caution flag.

Baker settled for second place but gained ground on points leader Herb Thomas, who started third but finished fifth. Roberts's teammate Bill Amick ran third, Joe Weatherly was fourth and Lee Petty finished a disappointing ninth.

South Carolinian Joe Eubanks, always a threat for a top-ten finish, started on the pole for the third time in his career by circling the track at 65.597 miles per hour. He never led a lap and finished sixth. Brownie King and George Green, both from nearby Johnson City, finished twelfth and fourteenth, respectively.

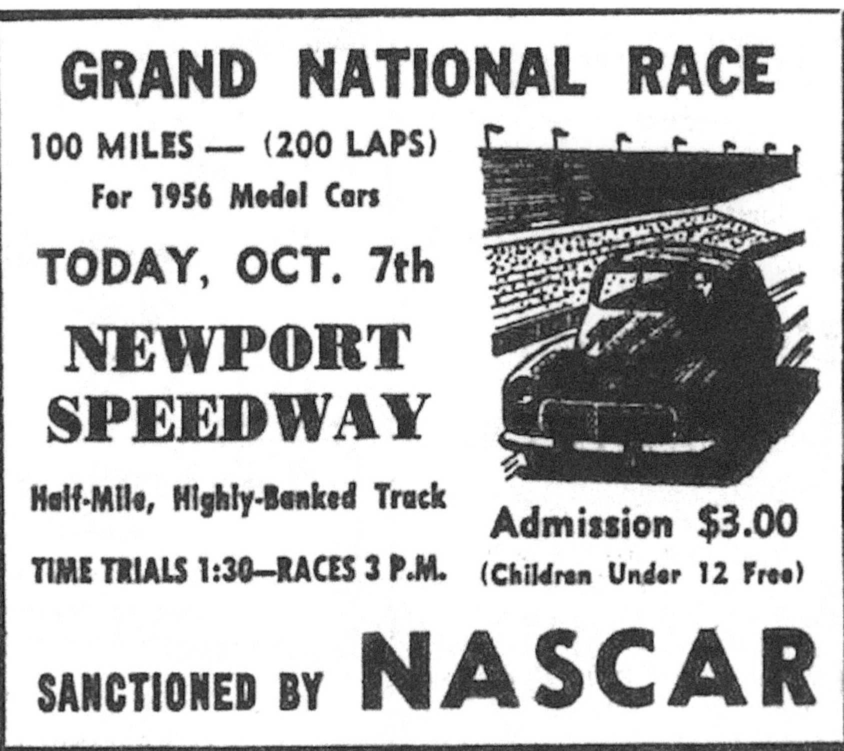

The Newport fairgrounds oval hosted Tennessee's first NASCAR Grand National race in 1956. *Author's collection.*

Fireball Roberts collected his second straight victory at Tennessee-Carolina when the Grand National series returned on June 15, 1957. That race was significant because it marked NASCAR's first eastern appearance after the Automobile Manufacturers Association unanimously agreed to withdraw support from all forms of racing.

The vote occurred on June 6, less than three weeks after a Grand National Mercury driven by Billy Myers flew over a retaining wall at Martinsville Speedway, injuring seven spectators who had slipped into a restricted area.

The manufacturers' sudden withdrawal sent shockwaves through the sport and forced many drivers to scramble to find cars, teams and any semblance of sponsorship. To help soften the impact, France convinced promoters to pay more, and NASCAR began offering "travel" or "appearance" money to its series regulars. Only seventeen cars rolled through the gates for that Saturday contest on Father's Day weekend.

Speedy Thompson, one of those former factory-sponsored drivers, qualified his Chevrolet on the pole, but the lap was nearly four miles per hour off the previous year's pace. Marvin Panch started his Ford on the front row, followed by the Chevrolet of Buck Baker and Tiny Lund's Pontiac. Roberts pocketed $1,000 for his sixth win of that season, holding off Panch and points leader Baker, all on the lead lap.

The series never returned, and Newport's spot on the 1958 schedule was filled by northern swing races in Bradford and Reading, Pennsylvania. NASCAR did race in Tennessee in 1958, moving to a newly paved oval at the Nashville Fairgrounds, the state's oldest race track.

With Broadway Speedway closed, the Tennessee-Carolina Speedway became the region's premier oval, hosting regional stock car races and the occasional touring series. The Ohio-based Midwest Automobile Racing Club visited on October 28, 1962. Jack Bowsher put his Ford on the pole with a lap of 26.14 seconds, but veteran Ignatius "Iggy" Katona foiled Bowsher's bid for his first series victory. Katona, fresh off winning his fourth championship, wheeled a Ford to his thirty-fifth series triumph while Bowsher finished second.

Katona prevailed again when the rebranded ARCA series returned on April 7, 1963. While ARCA didn't return, the track continued drawing large crowds to watch locals Tootle Estes, Paul Gose and L.D. Ottinger compete until a dispute between the promoter, fairgrounds board and adjacent property owner prompted its closure.

"I watched many a race here," the old-timer said. "It didn't close from a lack of fans."

6

Not Bad for Country Boys

Charging northward at one hundred miles per hour across the hard-packed sands of Daytona Beach, Herman "Brownie" King quickly discovered he couldn't see where he was going.

That startling revelation happened midway through the opening lap of the 1957 NASCAR Grand National Series race on Daytona's famed Beach & Road Course while surrounded by fifty-six of the world's best drivers. His near-zero visibility was partly the result of a heavy-duty spring designed by car owner and crew chief Jess Potter to control the car's windshield wipers, which failed its first test.

"We were in the south turn. They dropped that green flag, and we took off up that beach," King said. "I was back about the middle of the pack and all that salt water came up out of that sand, went all over that windshield, and those windshield wipers stood straight up in the air and just quivered. They didn't even touch the windshield."

In addition to the wipers, Potter had rigged a contraption under King's left foot to pump water onto his windshield. It worked fine in the pits but proved useless at high speed.

"I couldn't see where I was going. I looked on both sides of me and there were cars on both sides. I stuck my head out the window a little bit, and it was still a long way up to the north turn," he said. "That's the way I drove until we got to the turn. The windshield wipers started working once we slowed down and wiped the windshield off. After a lap or two, all the water evidently got out of the sand, and I didn't have any more problems seeing the rest of the day."

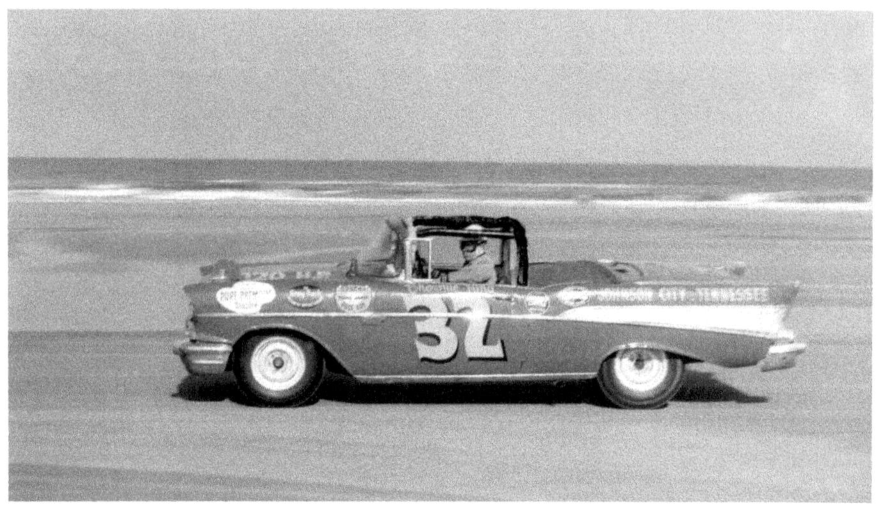

Brownie King drives Jess Potter's 1957 Chevrolet on Daytona Beach during a 1958 NASCAR race. *Courtesy Brownie King.*

In the decade before NASCAR founder Bill France Sr. built the mammoth Daytona International Speedway, he held organized races on the 4.1-mile Beach & Road Course that included a real beach and a real road. Each February, a section of U.S. Highway A1A normally used by snowbirds bound for a winter refuge provided a narrow, bumpy, two-lane backstretch.

But King, a fearless twenty-three-year-old from the hills of East Tennessee, found little glamour in his first competitive trip to the world center of racing.

"That was a thrill," he said. "Man, you would race forever. And the backstretch down A1A, those humps and bumps would about jerk you in two."

The course included a pair of two-mile-long straightaways terminating in corners that transitioned from asphalt to soft sand in the south turn and sand to pavement in the north turn. After that thrilling start, King's first time racing on the beach ended unceremoniously. He dropped out after burning up the Chevrolet's clutch and was credited with a fiftieth-place finish.

That season, King and car owner Potter finished ninth in the final Grand National points. They ran thirty-six of fifty-three races and were officially credited with sixteen top-ten finishes. Had they competed in that year's northern and western races, they likely could have finished in the top five. King even disputes the records, believing he had eighteen top tens.

"Somebody who had eighteen top tens and finished ninth in points today would make a couple million dollars," King said. "That wasn't too bad for country boys."

King also competed in both the Convertible and Grand National beach races in 1958, the final year before Daytona's speedway opened.

He finished twenty-first out of twenty-nine cars in the convertible race, bolted the roof on and drove the same Chevrolet to thirty-fifth on Sunday. His day ended when the engine failed. King took home $60 for his Saturday showing and $25 for Sunday—vast improvements over 1957, when he was among sixteen drivers who received no money.

One of the sport's true pioneers, King competed alongside its first generation of superstars—Tim Flock, Lee Petty, Fireball Roberts, Jack Smith, Curtis Turner, Joe Weatherly and Rex White—during six seasons in NASCAR's Grand National division and four seasons racing convertibles.

"Brownie was a charger," said White, the 1960 Grand National champion. "I remember racing with Brownie a lot. He's a good racer."

In addition to competing in the last beach race, King raced in the first two Daytona 500s and was in the starting fields when three of the sport's all-time greatest drivers—Richard Petty, David Pearson and Cale Yarborough—made their first NASCAR starts.

Nicknamed for his brown eyes, King became enthralled with racing as a youngster. He quickly went from "hanging out" at Jess Potter's garage to working on the cars and helping build his first machine—a 1932 Ford coach designed to run in the old Sportsman class. In the summer of 1954, King and Potter towed the new car to North Carolina's Asheville-Weaverville Speedway. The wide-eyed twenty-year-old didn't even have a competitor's license, but he didn't let a NASCAR age rule slow him down.

"You were supposed to be twenty-one, but I told a little fib. I said I was twenty-one and paid them ten dollars for my license," he said.

He stepped up to the Grand National ranks in 1956 driving a Chevrolet prepared by Potter and Joe George.

For their first start, they towed to Columbia, South Carolina, where King finished eighteenth on the half-mile dirt oval. After making repairs, the new team traveled to Concord, North Carolina, to race the following night. Later in the week, they went to the Greenville-Pickens Speedway in Greenville, South Carolina, and raced again. One week and four starts into his Grand National career, King finished eleventh on the fabled bullring at Hickory, North Carolina.

After racing primarily on smaller dirt ovals, King made his first start on asphalt in the 1956 Southern 500 on the imposing 1.375-mile superspeedway in Darlington, South Carolina.

"I went out and tried to get my speed up, up against the rail. But the car wanted to go down to the inside," King said. "So I pulled in the pits and asked Bobby Johns, 'How do you keep the car against the rail?' He told me you had to keep cutting the car to the right all the time. So I went back out and tried it, and it worked."

King qualified for the seventy-car field but had to start in the middle of the seventeenth row.

"That many cars starting—and they started three abreast—you didn't know what was going to happen when they got to the turn because there was only room to run two abreast around the turns. Everybody was trying to get into those two lanes," he said. "The morning before the race, everybody was down there eating breakfast, but I couldn't eat a bite. I was about sick to my stomach wondering what was going to happen. But once they dropped the green flag, all the butterflies went away."

King avoided that day's mishaps and posted a respectable thirty-second-place finish. His payday for completing 306 laps in the sweltering South Carolina heat was $50, the same as last-place finisher Arden Mounts. Winner Curtis Turner pocketed $11,750.

The 1957 season actually began in late 1956, and King finished eleventh behind fellow East Tennessean Bill Morton and a spot ahead of Ralph Earnhardt at Concord, North Carolina. Their second 1957 start was that harrowing ride on Daytona Beach, but things improved decidedly from there.

They posted four top-ten finishes in their next five starts. In May, King finished eighth at the Richmond, Virginia fairgrounds, ahead of Ralph Earnhardt, Buck Baker and Tiny Lund. He scored another top-ten finish at Charlotte, followed by a fifteenth-place effort on "the biggest dirt track" King ever saw, the treacherous 1.5-mile tri-oval at Lehi, Arkansas.

Driving a lone 1956 Chevrolet maintained in Potter's humble Johnson City garage, they raced on every imaginable surface from the beach to the hardscrabble half-mile North Carolina dirt tracks at Concord, Weaverville, Charlotte, Shelby and Wilson, to one-mile ovals at Raleigh, North Carolina, and Langhorne, Pennsylvania, plus the newly paved Martinsville Speedway in Virginia. They unveiled a new 1957 Chevrolet during Labor Day weekend at Darlington, South Carolina, and it nearly proved King's undoing.

"We was doing real good, running in eighth-place late in the race. Jess put two recaps [tires] on the left side, and we'd run about twenty laps [before] one of them blew out. It sent me sailing against the wall. It did one complete flip and landed on its side with the top facing the traffic. I didn't know whether to unbuckle that seat belt or not, but I knew I was lying right in the groove. The cars were really flying by. I stuck my head up out of the car and saw them coming toward me. I jumped out and ran across the fence on the

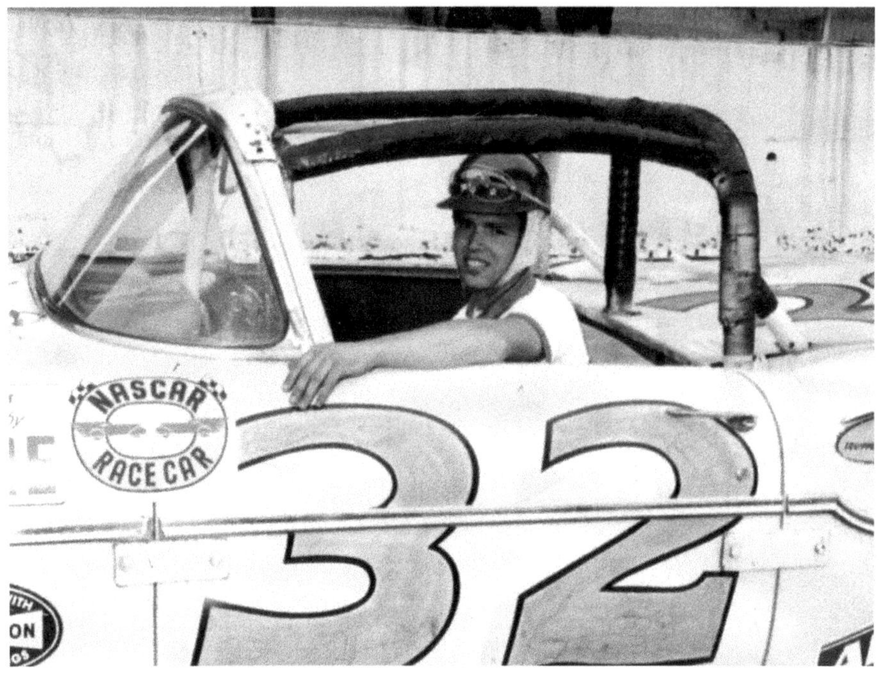

Brownie King of Johnson City finished fifth in NASCAR's national Convertible division points in 1959. *Courtesy Brownie King.*

upper side. [Race leader] Speedy Thompson tried to get slowed down, but he clipped my rear bumper and turned it around sideways."

After righting the car and making repairs, King returned to finish twenty-first on an afternoon when Bobby Myers was killed and rookie Joe Caspolich critically injured in separate crashes. King posted his best Grand National finish a few weeks later, when he was fifth at Columbia, South Carolina.

His best finish in any NASCAR race was third place in a 1958 Convertible division race at Wilson, North Carolina. After starting fourteenth, King finished a lap down to winner Bob Welborn and runner-up Herb "Tootle" Estes from Knoxville.

A few weeks prior, King finished eighth in a Convertible race in Columbia on July 12, 1958. Richard Petty brought the family Oldsmobile home in sixth that night in his first ever NASCAR race.

In 1959, King and Potter finished fifth in the final Convertible division points—behind Richard Petty—while dividing their time between the Grand National and Convertible divisions. They recorded one top-five finish and five top-tens in eighteen Grand National starts.

At the immense new two-and-a-half-mile Daytona Speedway in 1959, King finished fourteenth in a Saturday Convertible division race that was the first ever run there. A day later, King finished thirty-third in the same car, in the first Daytona 500.

King and Potter split in 1960, with King opting to build a 1960 Chevrolet. His plan included buying a new car from the local Chevrolet dealer for $2,800 and converting it into a race car.

"I financed that car through GMAC. But the guy at the dealership agreed to buy back the stuff I took out of the car to make it a race car. So when it was ready, I owed GMAC $1,800," King said. "That was a lot of money back then." After qualifying for his second Daytona 500, King encountered mechanical problems that put him seventeen laps down and nearly got him collected in a massive wreck.

"There was a fifteen-car pileup that demolished a lot of cars. Well I ran through that and hit a driveshaft," he recalled. "I didn't have a pit crew, so I pulled in and asked Jess Potter to look at my tires. He said they were OK, but they never felt right. After the race, I looked up under there, and the right front tire had the inner tube bulged out. If that had blown, I would have wrecked that car."

King returned home, sold the car and paid off his loan. At age twenty-six, King suddenly found himself out of NASCAR racing. He would make only one more Grand National start, driving a Ford Thunderbird at the brand-new Bristol International Speedway in 1961. In ninety-seven Grand National starts during six seasons, King was officially credited with twenty-seven top-ten finishes.

Some of King's best memories and greatest success came after leaving the Grand National ranks to concentrate on his hometown dirt bullring, the three-eighths-mile Sportsman Speedway in Johnson City. The track has produced more than its share of NASCAR regulars, and nearly every week in 1960, King wound up battling one of racing's future stars: South Carolina driver Tiny Lund.

An accident cut short his 1961 season, but King returned to racing in 1962 and won the Bristol Speedway's weekly Sportsman championship. Bristol subsequently stopped running weekly events, and after a few more races at Sportsman Speedway, King hung up his helmet for good because "it was time."

7

World's Finest Speedway

Winnie Moore Carter was a strong, independent woman with three sons to raise and a Tennessee dairy farm to manage after her husband, Joseph, died before she turned thirty.

She and her sons, John, Stanley—who friends called "Bud"—and Landon, spent years rising before dawn to milk cows, tend to corn, pick blackberries and scratch out a living on land at the confluence of Beaver and Back Creeks, about five miles south of Bristol. But the years of unrelenting work took a toll, and by the fall of 1960, her sons were grown, and she'd decided to sell.

One day, there was a knock at the door.

Larry Carrier, a tall, good-looking homebuilder, stood on the front porch of her farmhouse, inquiring about buying the property. No, he didn't want to get into the dairy business, and no, he wasn't a farmer, although he did fancy horses. Carrier and business partner Carl Moore envisioned a far different activity on the rolling land, especially between those two hills on the rear of the property.

Just a few weeks before, Carrier and Moore were among twenty-nine thousand in the grandstands of North Carolina's Charlotte Motor Speedway. Unlike fans who dreamed of racing into victory lane and kissing the trophy queen, they were much more interested in the day's attendance, gate receipts and the vision of a potential windfall. It was Carrier's first trip to a racetrack, and he was amazed people would spend hard-earned money to watch stock cars drive in circles for hours.

That journey was soon followed by another, to Daytona Beach, Florida, where Bill France Sr., the president of something called the National

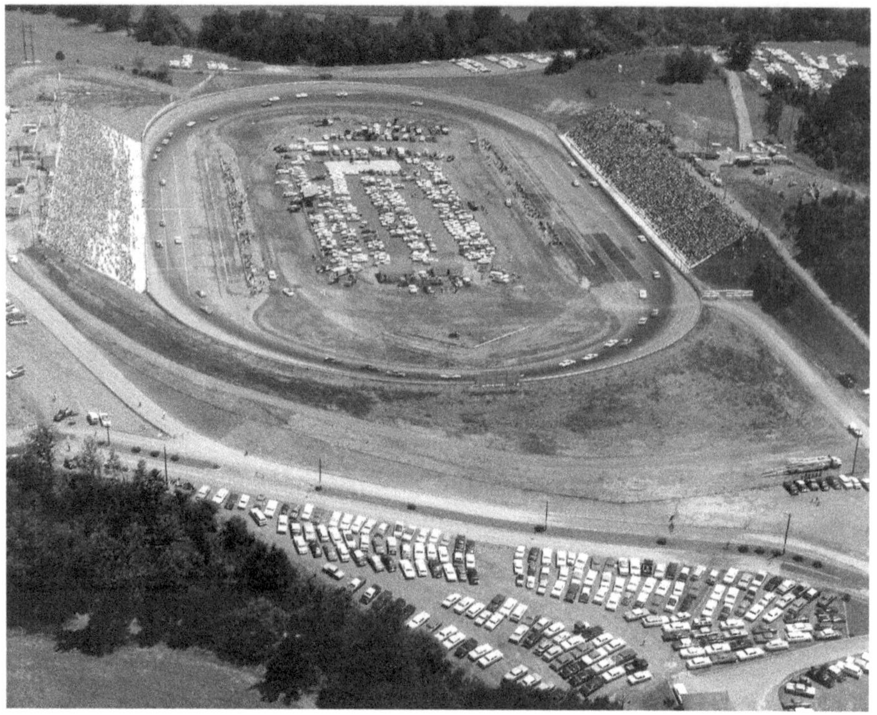

Originally known as Bristol International Speedway, the half-mile oval opened in 1961. This aerial photo was taken in 1963. *Bristol Motor Speedway collection.*

Association of Stock Car Automobile Racing, *gave* them two races on his 1961 Grand National schedule. There were a few problems with their plan, not the least of which was that they owned neither a racetrack nor the property on which to build one.

No, this wouldn't be like that dusty little Avoca Speedway that operated one summer a few miles up the road, Carrier told Carter. It would be larger with permanent grandstands and a paved racing surface, and it would attract large crowds of people from all over.

None of that really mattered. What did was the color of their money. It was green and loaned at a high interest rate from the Berlow Vending Company, a Philadelphia-based sports concessionaire recommended by France after Carrier, Moore and contractor-partner R.G. Pope failed to even gain an audience with bankers around East Tennessee.

Both sides agreed on a price, and on January 16, 1961, the partners publicly unveiled plans to build the "world's finest speedway." Originally

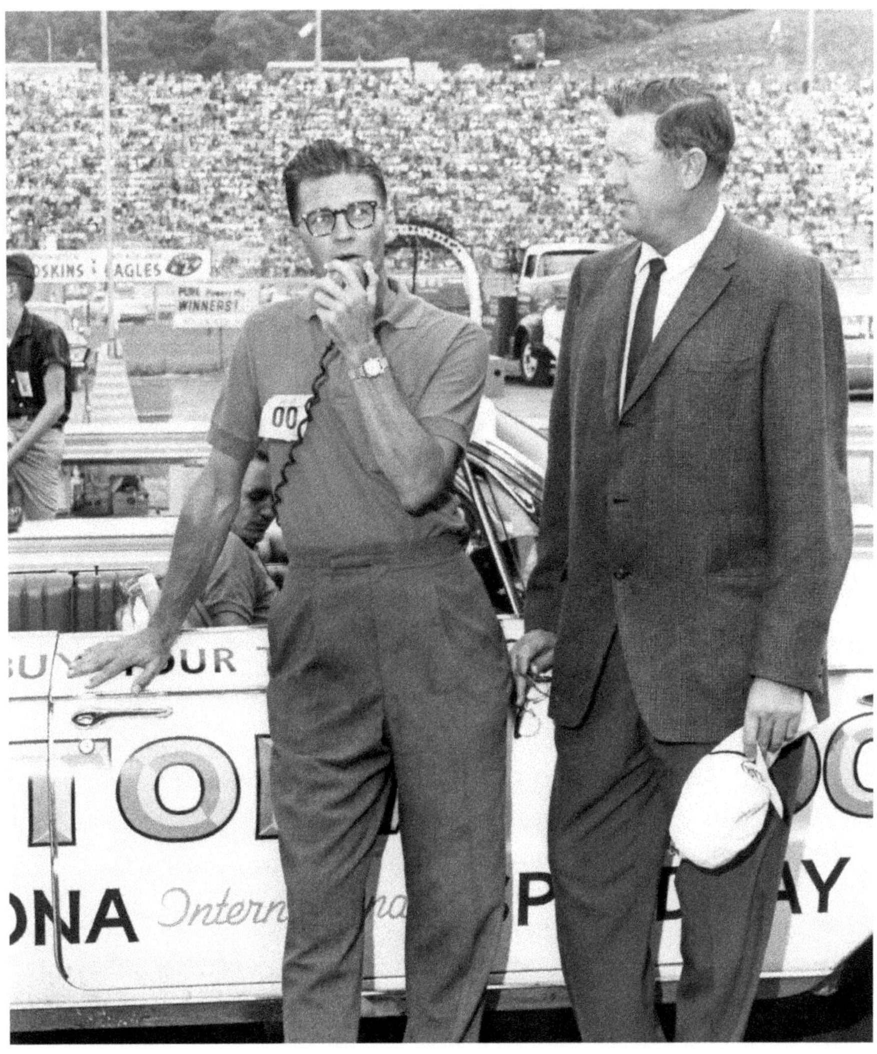

Bristol track cofounder Larry Carrier (left) speaks to the crowd during the 1961 Volunteer 500 as NASCAR president Bill France looks on. *Carl Moore collection.*

called Bristol International Speedway, it would be a paved half-mile oval with corners banked twenty-five degrees and eighteen thousand permanent seats. Work began the following week and was somehow completed in six months, just in time for that first race on July 30.

Carter and some members of her family were in the stands for the first Volunteer 500, thanks to some complimentary tickets from the new owners.

Temperatures soared to ninety degrees that Sunday afternoon, and the Carters left before the race was over. While they never returned, countless others have in the decades since.

The banking was made steeper in 1969, and Bristol claimed its title of "World's Fastest Half-Mile."

Bristol's first NASCAR night race happened in August 1978, a desperation move by new owners Gary Baker and Lanny Hester to try to rejuvenate attendance that sagged due to withering summer heat and a lack of on-track competition. The experiment became a spectacle, contributing greatly to a fifty-five-event sellout streak that began in 1982 concurrent with a rapid increase in seating capacity.

Ironically, the original Bristol was built with lights, and Carrier ran weekly Saturday night Sportsman and Modified races in the summers of 1961, 1962 and part of 1963.

Through a series of events, Carrier reacquired the facility in 1985 and initiated improvements that sparked attendance growth unlike any other track. NASCAR's popularity was also booming, and Bristol played a vital role—both in person and on television—as Darrell Waltrip, Dale Earnardt, Rusty Wallace and Alan Kulwicki made Bristol their personal playground.

Pavement became concrete in 1992, a controversial move by Carrier after high speeds on the track's high-banked corners ruined repeated attempts to keep the asphalt intact. The result was another zenith of popularity as Bristol's slam-bang action came to personify everything fans enjoy about short-track racing. That attention attracted potential suitors.

In January 1996, Bruton Smith, who also created the Charlotte track that provided Carrier and Moore's initial inspiration, agreed to the asking price. After writing checks totaling more than $25 million, which he calls a steal, Smith has invested many times that amount to expand and improve every square inch to the point that all that remains of the original facility is the land on which it sits.

Today, Bristol Motor Speedway is one of the world's largest sports palaces; its 160,000 gleaming aluminum grandstand seats fully encircle the bowl that bills itself as the "Last Great Colosseum." Paved parking lots spread out in every direction, and the nearby farms, businesses and front yards become temporary campgrounds and parking lots for those still making the twice-annual pilgrimage from across the United States and overseas.

For all of the transformation, one thing remains constant: guests come first at Bristol, much like when family and friends gathered for dinner around Winnie Carter's table.

8

Tennessee's Big Bill

When Bill Morton left for a race, he usually took just enough money to get there, figuring the need for money to buy gas to get home would inspire him behind the wheel. And Bill Morton always made it home.

Known as one of the sport's toughest characters, Morton was a millwright who spent years knocking around on Bill France's NASCAR Grand National circuit during the 1950s and 1960s. But much of his legacy was established on dirt tracks in and around East Tennessee, where he won about four hundred feature races against some of the sport's all-time greats.

"He was a hardcore race car driver. He wasn't rough with the race car, and he didn't like for you [to disrespect] his race car. That's how he earned his reputation of being kind of rough in the pit area," Morton's son, Tony Morton, recalled. "At one time, he was probably barred from every racetrack he ever raced at. He didn't like finger-pointing, and he didn't like you shaking your fist at him. He went out there to race, and that's what he intended to do. He looked at it as more of a challenge to pass someone without wrecking them. Now bumping, shoving and tire marks, that's going to happen."

While Morton collected plenty of checkered flags and trophies, he also endured more than his share of crashes. He visited hospital emergency rooms from Bristol to Chattanooga and spent thirty days in an Atlanta hospital after his Ford flipped multiple times during the final NASCAR Grand National race of the 1958 season.

"I was right ahead of him at the time he wrecked," friend and competitor Brownie King recalled of that day at Georgia's old Lakewood Speedway.

"The No. 55 [Jimmy Massey] Pontiac hit the bank and flipped over on its side. I barely missed him, almost clipped him with the right rear but didn't. Bill was beside me and Bill hit him.

"It turned him sideways, and he hit that bank on the inside [which is] what started doing all those flips. He rolled that thing; I don't know how many flips he turned. His arm stretched out with him upside down. He was knocked unconscious. His roll bars held, but it hurt his hands."

Rookie driver Fred Harb watched the crash and stopped his Mercury on the track to shield Morton from the oncoming cars. He was extricated and transported to the hospital.

Besides his injuries, the crash ruined a potential big break for a string of good showings in the Convertible division.

"He was offered factory help from Ford in 1958. He came close to quitting work and racing full time, but then he had that bad wreck at Lakewood Speedway," Tony Morton said. His father missed much of the following season but returned to make three Grand National starts in late 1959.

Morton's NASCAR career actually got off to a bumpy start in October 1955, with an accident in his first race at the Memphis-Arkansas Speedway in Lehi, Arkansas.

"He and my mother drove a 1955 Buick Roadmaster down there, took the headlights out of it, took the hubcaps off it, and he raced it," Tony Morton said. "He blew a tire, went through the fence and turned it over. It was a four-door, and they couldn't get the doors open. So they had to crawl through the windows and drive it all the way back from Arkansas to Kingsport without windows. They got it beat back out so they could get the doors open; he went to Columbia, South Carolina, the following week and wrecked it again."

Morton received sixty dollars for his twenty-fourth place finish in the forty-one-car Arkansas field and pocketed fifty dollars for finishing thirteenth in Columbia's twenty-one-car field.

An Ohio native who moved to Church Hill just west of Kingsport, Morton first tried driving at Morristown in 1953 and the old Tri-City Speedway in 1954. The ensuing years were a mixture of racing locally and in NASCAR's Grand National and Convertible divisions.

"He bought a real race car and ran NASCAR again. He mostly ran around Asheville-Weaverville, Bristol, Atlanta and Martinsville," Tony Morton said. "He always had to be back at work Monday morning."

Morton welcomed the new Bristol International Speedway in 1961. After running its first Grand National race in July, he returned to compete in the track's weekly Modified division races. Morton captured back-to-back track titles in 1961 and 1962, the only full seasons the racetrack ran weekly NASCAR points.

He continued racing Grand National, but that all changed in June 1965 when a new track opened close to home. Morton drove to Atlanta on Friday to qualify Curtis Larimer's Ford for the Dixie 400. He then drove home Friday night, raced at the all-new Kingsport Speedway on Saturday night, loaded up and drove all night to Atlanta to race on Sunday. The Ford's engine broke after ninety-seven laps, his fifth consecutive early exit due to mechanical problems. Morton drove back to Tennessee, went to work the next morning and never returned to NASCAR.

"Dirt was his first love," Tony Morton said.

Bill became a regular at Kingsport, which began as dirt; Sportsman Speedway in Johnson City; and Appalachian Speedway when it opened in 1969. He also frequently traveled to Chattanooga and Knoxville and won numerous times at tracks in Virginia. For much of that time, he raced out of the same shop as eventual NASCAR champions Gene Glover and Ken Hunley but later drove for car owners Bud Rambo of Johnson City and Don Gray of Kingsport.

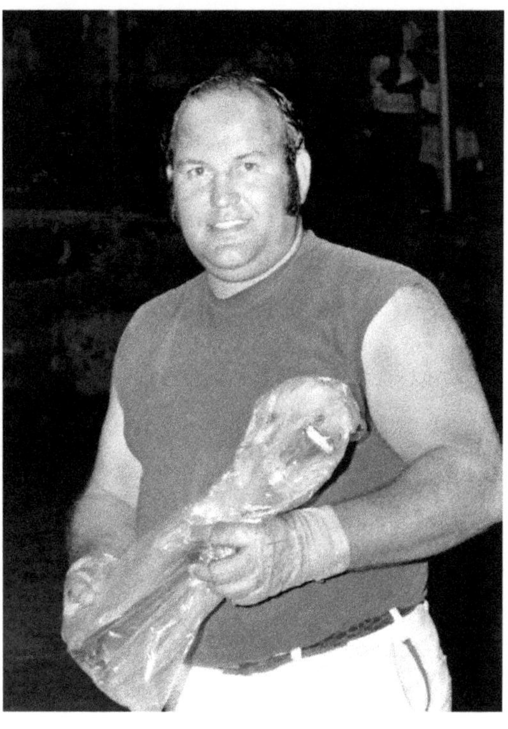

Muscular Bill Morton collected a number of trophies and championships during a lengthy career. *Courtesy Ernie Collins.*

"We went to Chattanooga in the early '60s and couldn't win as often because the competition was so tough. You had a lot of guys coming out of Georgia and Alabama, and it turns out he was racing against Bobby and Donnie Allison, Friday Hassler, Joe Lee Johnson and Freddy and Harold Fryar. They turned out to be some of the best short-track drivers in the country, but you just didn't know it at that time," Tony Morton recalled.

It wasn't much easier close to home.

"You had a lot of guys come out of Georgia like Buck Simmons. And you had locals like Walter Ball and the Corums—Bill and Melvin—H.E. Vineyard, Tootle Estes, Herman Goddard, Ronnie Johnson was getting started, Gene Glover and the Utsman family. There was just a lot of competition," Morton said of the region's standouts.

From the late 1960s through the 1970s, Morton averaged about twenty wins per season and claimed track championships at Kingsport, Sportsman, Appalachian and Newport Speedways. His best season was 1978, when he picked up twenty-eight victories in forty-one starts racing primarily at Newport, Bulls Gap and Atomic Speedways.

"There were ten tracks within a two-hour drive. That's why a lot of guys stayed home to race because there was no need to travel four or five hours down the road," Tony Morton said. "And back then you didn't just go out and hit the interstate; you traveled on two-lane roads and then turned off onto a dirt road to get to the racetrack. Those old tracks could be kind of rough, and sometimes if you won, you might have to get ugly to get your money."

On the lighter side, Morton shared the same name as a successful Nashville driver, which prompted more than a little confusion during his NASCAR driving days.

When East Tennessee's Morton won his first track championship at Bristol in 1961, NASCAR shipped the trophy to Nashville. Another year, Nashville's Morton won a championship and series sponsor Permatex shipped his trophy to Church Hill. Their championship jackets got switched once, which was a real problem since the East Tennessee Morton wore a size 46 short and his Nashville counterpart a 38 long.

"In 1962, the NASCAR newsletter listed Bill Morton in the top three of the national standings. They were combining their points," Tony Morton recalled. "Daddy called the other Bill—and he was going to call NASCAR—and Daddy tried to convince him not to so they could split the points money."

It was equally entertaining at the racetrack, like the time in 1962 when both men went to Daytona International Speedway to run the Sportsman race.

"Back then, if you were a rookie, NASCAR painted your bumper yellow," Tony Morton said. "Well, Daddy had raced the Grand National circuit for years and run all kinds of speedways, but he walked in the garage and NASCAR was putting yellow paint on his bumper. He told them it was supposed to be the other one, but they both had the same car number. It's always been a lot of confusion, but they had a good time with it."

Morton continued racing until 1981 but stopped after his health declined. He died in 2001.

9

Chattanooga's Champion

Joe Lee Johnson's NASCAR racing success came in bunches, but he ended a promising career prematurely, haunted by the tragic circumstances of losing a close friend.

Driving a white 1957 Chevrolet sponsored by Chattanooga's iconic Honest Charley Speed Shop, Johnson took charge of NASCAR's Convertible division in 1959. Early in the season, he captured back-to-back wins in Fayetteville, North Carolina, and Richmond, Virginia, by defeating Glen Wood, Marvin Panch, Joe Weatherly, Curtis Turner and a twenty-one-year-old Richard Petty.

That August, NASCAR staged one of eight "sweepstakes" races at Nashville, with Convertibles and Grand National cars racing together. Johnson was the points leader and collected his third series win, followed closely by Larry Frank, Elmo Langley and eventual Grand National champ Lee Petty.

Frank soon began cutting into Johnson's points lead, which stood at forty-eight entering the season finale, another sweepstakes race at Martinsville, Virginia. When the dust settled, NASCAR declared Frank the champion by finishing two spots ahead of Johnson. But Johnson sought and received a recount and was later awarded the title by twenty points.

The lanky Johnson, who once dominated short tracks around East Tennessee, was the talk of NASCAR in 1960. Fresh off winning the Convertible title, he claimed victory in the inaugural World 600 at the all-new Charlotte Motor Speedway. Making his first start in a Chevrolet

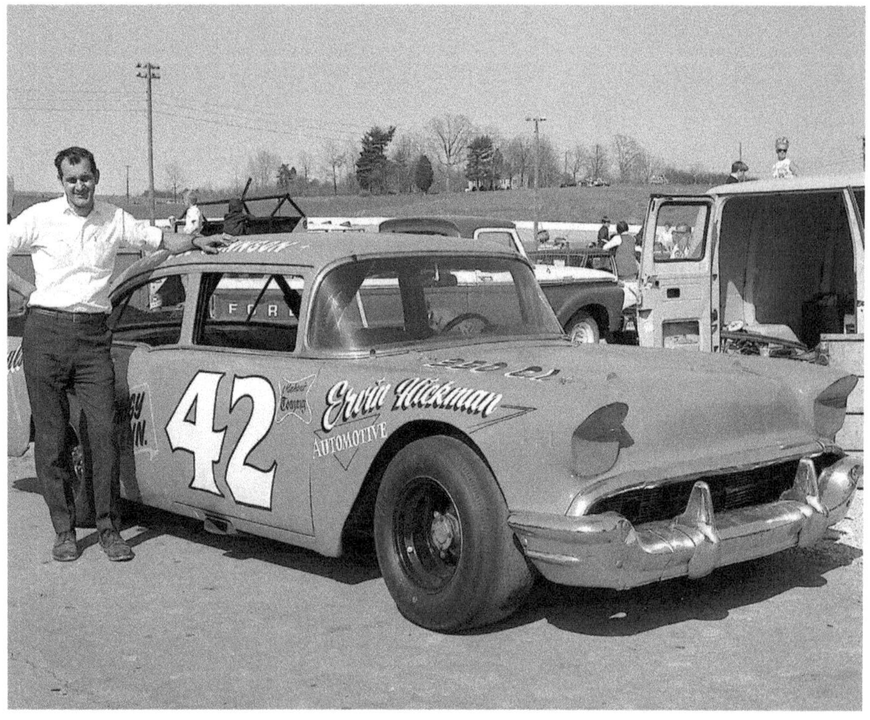

Joe Lee Johnson of Chattanooga won the 1959 Convertible championship and 1960 World 600. *Ray Taylor photo.*

prepared by Paul McDuffie, Johnson won by four laps over second-place Johnny Beauchamp.

Charlotte and the 600 are now regarded among the sport's crown jewels, but that first one is primarily remembered for the track's asphalt surface coming apart in large chunks that cut tires, damaged fuel tanks and caused crashes aplenty. Johnson drove a conservative pace that day, avoided trouble and took the lead with just forty-eight laps remaining.

The win was worth $27,150 and seemed to signal that he and McDuffie were an instant force to be reckoned with. That all changed in a ghastly instant three months later during the Southern 500 in Darlington. Johnson brought McDuffie's Chevrolet into the backstretch pits for service on lap ninety-five. At that instant on the track, Bobby Johns and Roy Tyner made contact exiting turn two, and Johns's Pontiac careened and flipped into Darlington's unprotected pit area.

McDuffie, mechanic Paul Sweatland and NASCAR official Joe Taylor were struck by flying debris and died of their injuries. Three other members of Johnson's crew were also injured, and a distraught Johnson withdrew from the event.

"Paul was my friend, not just my mechanic," Johnson told interviewers years later. "After that, my heart just wasn't there."

Johnson returned to the track only once more that season but couldn't recapture the Charlotte magic in that track's fall race. He entered nine races in 1961, with support from car dealer Herb Adcox, but his only respectable runs were a ninth in the Daytona 500, eighth at Charlotte and ninth at Greenville-Pickens Speedway in South Carolina.

"Joe Lee was the champion, and he was from Chattanooga. So we were quite proud of him," Adcox reflected. "He was an excellent driver."

Johnson tried again in 1962, but mechanical failures spelled mediocre finishes every time out. His final Grand National race came at Nashville, but he parked the car after just two laps. It was a stark contrast to just four short years before when the same fairgrounds oval produced one of Johnson's biggest wins.

Johnson quit racing NASCAR Grand National but still competed around East Tennessee. After he stopped driving, Johnson bought and operated the Cleveland Speedway and supported son Ronnie's driving career.

10

The Turtle

In a sport built on speed, Herman "Turtle" Beam was one of a kind.

An engineer from Johnson City, Beam was a highly regarded innovator and mechanic who found an unusual way to post some remarkable statistics during a decade behind the wheel in NASCAR's Grand National division.

The bespectacled Beam was the very antithesis of the sport's hard chargers whose dash and daring won the adoration of fans but frequently relegated them to the sidelines before the checkers flew. In a primitive era where finishing involved taking care of the equipment, Beam developed his own solution: drive slower. Staying out of the way allowed Beam to finish eighty-four consecutive races entered through the 1961, 1962 and 1963 seasons—unheard of then and a record that still stands.

Beginning on April 30, 1961, at Martinsville, Virginia, Herman finished his last twenty-six starts that season, all fifty-one races entered the next year and his first seven outings of 1963. The streak finally ended nearly two years later on March 17, 1963, when the clutch of his Ford failed midway through the Atlanta 500.

Those fifty-one starts in 1962 represented Beam's most ambitious season, as he scored eighteen top-ten finishes and ranked eleventh in the championship standings. The Turtle never won a pole but did start out front once—on April Fool's Day 1962. Qualifying was rained out at the Richmond fairgrounds, so drivers drew for positions. Beam drew first place. On the pace lap, he pulled to the inside and let the entire field go by, saying later he didn't feel right about being out front. He finished twelfth.

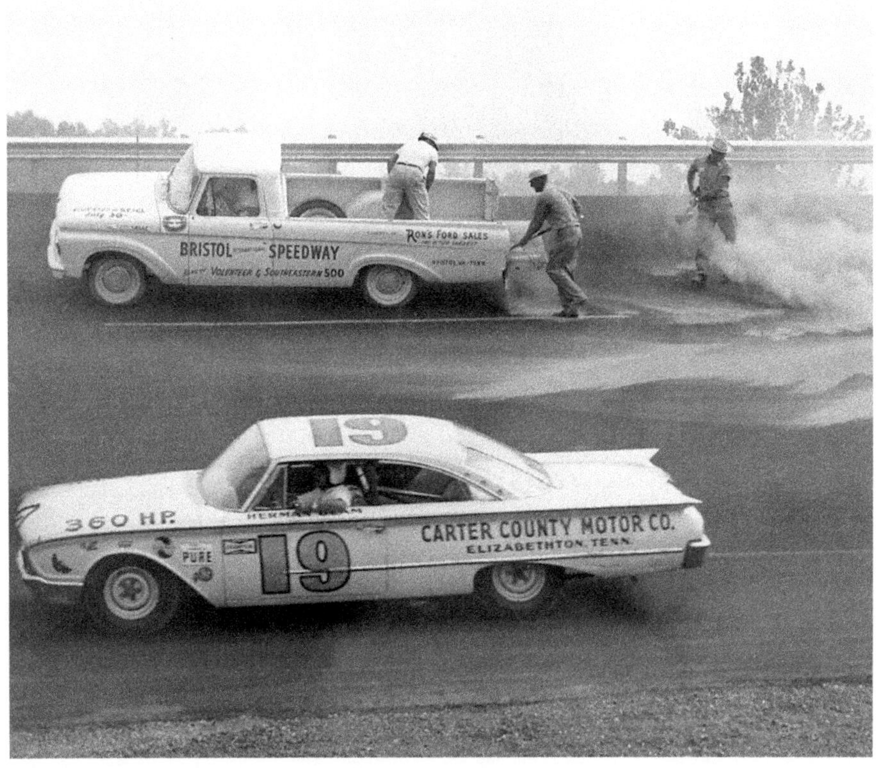

Herman "Turtle" Beam (19) spent much of his career driving slower than others but still assembled some impressive credentials. *Carl Moore collection.*

Beam's Grand National driving career began late in 1957, as he finished twentieth at Greensboro, North Carolina. He started twenty races the following year, primarily in the Carolinas and Virginia, and was running at the finish of an amazing seventeen. His best finish that year was tenth at Asheville-Weaverville Speedway, which paid $130.

In 1959, Beam finished twenty-first out of fifty-nine starters in the first Daytona 500. It would prove a breakthrough season as he finished a career-best fourth in the final Grand National standings, trailing champion Lee Petty, Cotton Owens and Speedy Thompson. He also placed third in the season's final car owner standings after running, at the finish, all but one of thirty races entered.

On the day Junior Johnson discovered drafting and drove an underpowered Chevrolet to victory in the 1960 Daytona 500, Beam finished thirty-second. But he was lucky to start the race at all. Three days before, Beam became the first driver black-flagged at the massive Daytona Speedway because he forgot to wear his crash helmet! It took eight laps and John Rostek crashing on lap five before officials recognized what happened. He spent the remainder of that qualifying race parked as punishment.

By dropping out of just one race in 1960, Beam finished twelfth in the championship standings, one spot ahead of World 600 winner Joe Lee Johnson.

Beam's 194th and final Grand National start occurred on July 11, 1963, at Dog Track Speedway in Moyock, North Carolina. He registered a seventh-place finish, but his Ford was the last car still running. Four days prior, the car finished fifth at the Speed-O-Rama 200 at the Rambi Speedway, later known as Myrtle Beach Speedway, with young South Carolina hotshot Cale Yarborough behind the wheel.

That signaled the start of what may be the most unique relationship in motorsports history. The quiet, reserved, bookish Beam paired with Yarborough, a hellcat trying to scorch his tire tracks into racing history. It was a marriage partially arranged by Ford Motor Company, whose officials recognized both Yarborough's raw talent and Beam's mechanical prowess.

Beam's methodical approach helped the former football star and boxer learn to manage his equipment and aggression, as the duo posted six top-tens in thirteen races together. For 1964, Ford provided a new car and assistance with better parts.

Their deal ended in June after Yarborough crashed late in the running at the Piedmont Interstate Fairgrounds in Spartanburg, South Carolina. A front wheel bearing failed, sending the car into the wall with just twenty-one laps remaining. Yarborough says Jacque Passino, the head of Ford racing, became upset after learning Beam put a used bearing in the car instead of a new one and ended the company's relationship. Beam's account was that he fired Yarborough after the accident, telling others the future Hall of Famer would never amount to anything.

Either way, Larry Thomas replaced Yarborough in Beam's car and posted five top-five finishes and four more top-tens, including a second-place finish at Hickory, North Carolina.

"We try to run pretty good and make our stuff last too," Beam said that October. "There has never been such a gap between the factory and independent cars. It's just like there's two races. My car has the same motor as it did at Daytona in February. You think that's true of the factory cars?"

J.T. Putney drove for Beam in 1965 and finished seventh in the championship standings.

Beam's last race as a car owner occurred on November 14, 1965, in Augusta, Georgia. He entered Fords for Putney and Gil Hearne, but both fell out with mechanical problems. He later worked as crew chief for Paul Lewis, and his mechanical expertise helped many, including Brad Teague.

A vacant lot on Johnson City's west side is all that remains of the rented two-bay service station where the Turtle once performed his mechanical magic.

11

Fiercely Independent

NASCAR racing reached an uncomfortable crossroads in the early 1960s with a widening gap between its haves and have-nots. The U.S. automakers brought money, technology and national visibility to a primarily regional enterprise now competing on larger, paved tracks near major cities like Charlotte and Atlanta. Factory-supported teams had superior equipment and more of every imaginable resource, so those drivers typically won most of the races, effectively choking the life out of underfunded independents who still viewed racing as a sport.

Paul Lewis became a fixture in NASCAR's Grand National division during that era, wearing the independent label like a badge of honor. Although not a boxer, the Johnson City resident wasn't afraid to stand toe-to-toe with the sport's heavyweights, refusing to back down from NASCAR officials, auto manufacturers or racing's greatest drivers.

"There were two divisions running in NASCAR. You had the factory-backed cars, and you had the independents. We had to race among ourselves because we couldn't really race with the factory-backed cars. Not bragging, but I did accomplish that," Lewis said. "The factories gave them everything they needed plus gave money to the owners. You couldn't do it on what you were winning, even those big teams. They had so many people working for them; they had so many race cars, equipment and the garages. And the factories were just uncooperative with the independents. I had trouble with Ford, Chevrolet and Chrysler. I've battled with just about everybody."

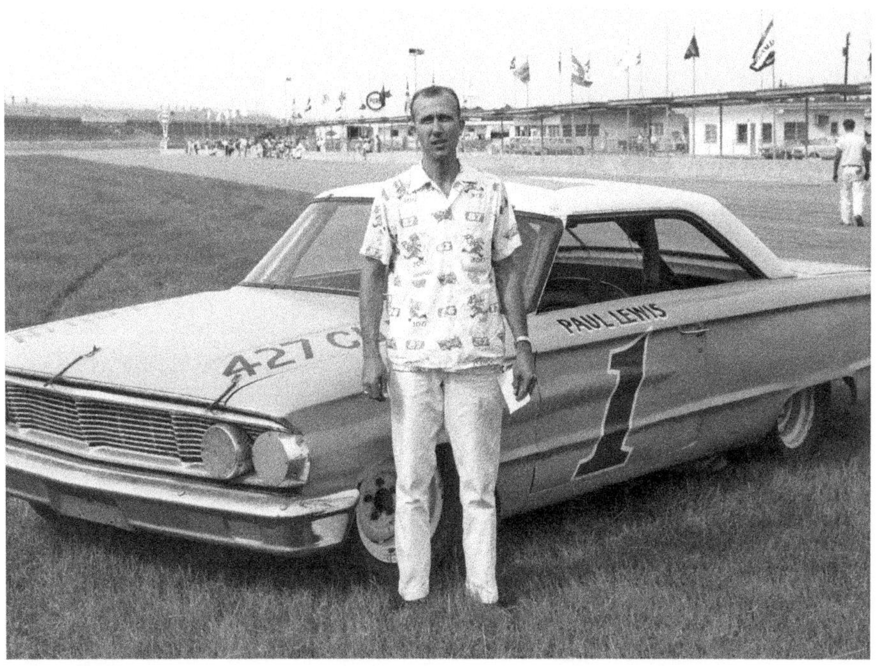

Paul Lewis of Johnson City raced this Ford, formerly raced by Cale Yarborough and Herman Beam, during the 1965 NASCAR Grand National season. *Paul Lewis collection.*

A standout on East Tennessee dirt tracks before moving to NASCAR in 1960, Lewis drove cars owned and prepared by Jess Potter. In that era, engines were to be assembled only with parts supplied by the automakers. Lewis and other independents long contended that factory-supported teams had better, more durable components, so a frustrated Lewis took his case to NASCAR and manufacturer Chevrolet at the biggest race of his rookie season in Darlington, South Carolina.

"All us independents had been raising cane with Norris Friel, the NASCAR technical director," Lewis said. "At the Southern 500, I went to Norris and told him the independents were fed up. We couldn't get the parts that the factory teams could. We couldn't even get a sheet that had the part numbers to order them."

Lewis proposed the independents boycott the race, but after a series of meetings between drivers and the manufacturer, new parts lists were distributed. He went on to finish fourteenth that weekend but lost an engine utilizing the very parts he predicted couldn't survive. Looking back, Lewis never worried such actions might impede his career.

"Norris was a fair man," Lewis said. "He knew there was a lot of disenchantment among the independents. And Bill France Sr. wanted to make it work. He had to romance the factories, because they would bring the financial support and more publicity. He was a smart man."

Lewis made his first NASCAR start a few months before, in a one-hundred-mile race at North Wilkesboro, North Carolina. He started Jess Potter's 1958 Chevrolet twentieth and finished twelfth in what proved a humbling afternoon.

"That was the first time I'd raced on asphalt," he recalled. "We went over there with dirt-track tires on that 4,400-pound car. It was a bulldozer. Those dirt-track tires would get hot, and they wouldn't grip at all. I spun out five or six times. The last couple times, I just sat in the car laughing, thinking how stupid I was."

A near riot broke out after the finish as angry fans threw rocks and bottles at race winner Lee Petty, who bumped hometown hero Junior Johnson from the lead with fourteen laps remaining. A few weeks later, Lewis scored his first top-ten finish with a sixth-place run at North Carolina's Asheville-Weaverville Speedway. Lewis competed twenty-seven times that season,

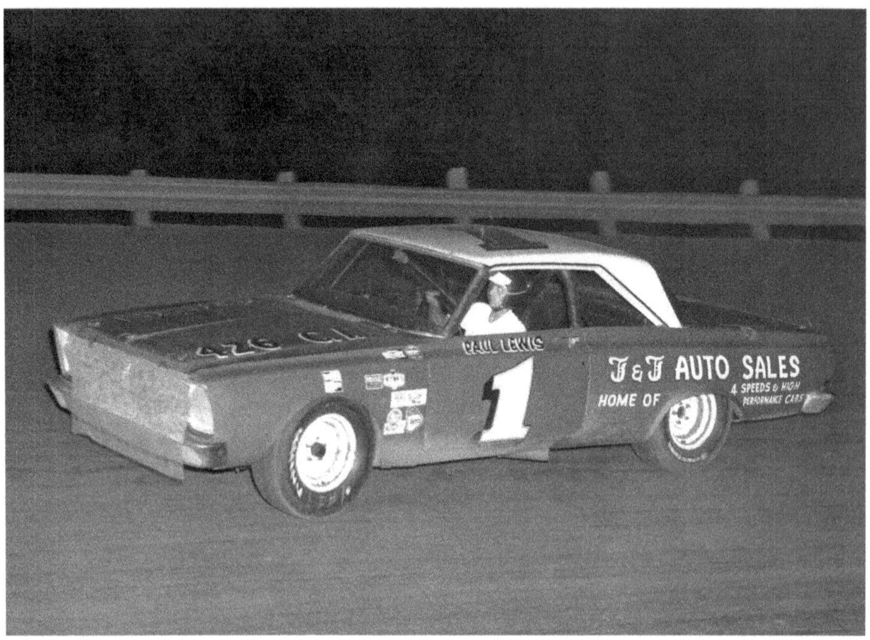

Paul Lewis wheeled this Plymouth to a NASCAR Grand National win over David Pearson in 1966 at Smoky Mountain Raceway. *Ray Taylor photo.*

alternating between Potter's two-year-old Chevrolet on dirt and a nearly new 1960 Chevrolet purchased from fellow Johnson Citian Brownie King on the larger speedways.

Among his starts was the inaugural World 600 at the all-new Charlotte Motor Speedway. Originally scheduled for Memorial Day weekend, the race was reset to late June because the track's virgin asphalt surface was breaking apart.

"Charlotte was horrendous. Trying to drive the race car and keep the front wheels on asphalt and the rear wheels on asphalt and still straddle all the holes was almost impossible," Lewis said. "They worked on it that week, and we didn't get to practice much on it."

Lewis was one of six drivers—including Junior Johnson and Richard Petty—stripped of his finishing position that day for entering pit road improperly. "There was a wreck right in front of me, and I got a piece of it. I was in the infield grass and just trying to get back to my pit to change a flat tire. I wasn't trying to improve my position," Lewis said decades later, as if still arguing his case.

He was also part of one of the most infamous races in NASCAR history, the shortened 1960 North Carolina 500 at Asheville-Weaverville. The race was concluded early because the track surface came apart, but a mob of angry fans held drivers hostage in the infield for about four hours after the race.

"The problem didn't show up during practice and qualifying, but when you put all those cars out there, that thing started coming apart. There were big holes in it, and we were trying to dodge all that stuff and trying to race," Lewis recalled.

"One piece broke my windshield, and when it did, all that glass came in on me. It got down my back and down in my seat. I couldn't lean back because my seat was full of glass. When I got done, there were cuts all over my back."

NASCAR stopped the race to try to clean up the asphalt and told the drivers, but not the crowd, it would be called complete just past the halfway point. The red and checkered flags flew at lap 258 with Junior Johnson the winner.

"The people were pretty inebriated by then. NASCAR stopped the race, but the fans weren't going to go for that, so they went down and blocked the pit entrance. We all got caught inside and couldn't go home because they had a pickup truck backed across the pit entrance with eight or ten drunks in the bed of that thing," Lewis recalled.

The standoff continued for some time until Pops Eargel—a football lineman–sized crewmember for Bud Moore—used a large piece of wood to knock members of the mob out of the way. Police then moved in and made numerous arrests.

Lewis made 114 Grand National starts but, like many independent drivers and mechanics, balanced racing with a full-time job. He operated an auto trim and glass shop in Johnson City but lacked the funds, time and manpower to run up to fifty races annually.

"We'd run sometimes two and three times a week. We worked all day at the business and half the night working on the race car to get ready for the weekend. Then you'd drive all night long and try to drive a race car the next day. And if you tore it up, you worked on it almost right up to race time," he said.

In 1965, Lewis purchased a proven year-old Ford from fellow Johnson City driver-owner Herman Beam; the same car the factory supplied to help further the career of Cale Yarborough. Lewis claimed a pole, three top-fives and thirteen top-tens in twenty-four starts, but parts durability issues continued. So Lewis put in a call to Jacque Passino, who directed Ford's racing program.

"I'm sure you've heard some static about my complaining about these parts and these engines we're trying to run," Lewis told Passino. "These stock, street high-performance engines will not stand NASCAR racing. I'm calling because I'd like to buy a short-block assembly like you all are running."

Passino expressed surprise, Lewis said, and then instructed him to drive to the Holman-Moody race shop in Charlotte, North Carolina—ground zero for Ford's racing efforts—where he could purchase the engine. The next morning, Lewis did as instructed and, after convincing John Holman, left with the fully prepared 427-cubic-inch engine he'd been promised. The price was a whopping $400.

"We tore that thing down as soon as we got it home, and it was all different. It had a steel crankshaft, lightweight rods and domed pistons. It was a super trick racing engine," Lewis said. His persistence and investment paid immediate dividends.

"We stopped blowing engines, and I sat on a pole about the first time I ran it. That car was a top-ten car, both qualifying and running, unless something happened. I ran that engine for a long time. When I sold that car, I believe most of that short-block assembly was still in the car from that original purchase."

Beneath the hood wasn't the only place stock cars received extra attention, as mechanics often massaged the aerodynamics of the boxy sedans to improve high-speed handling.

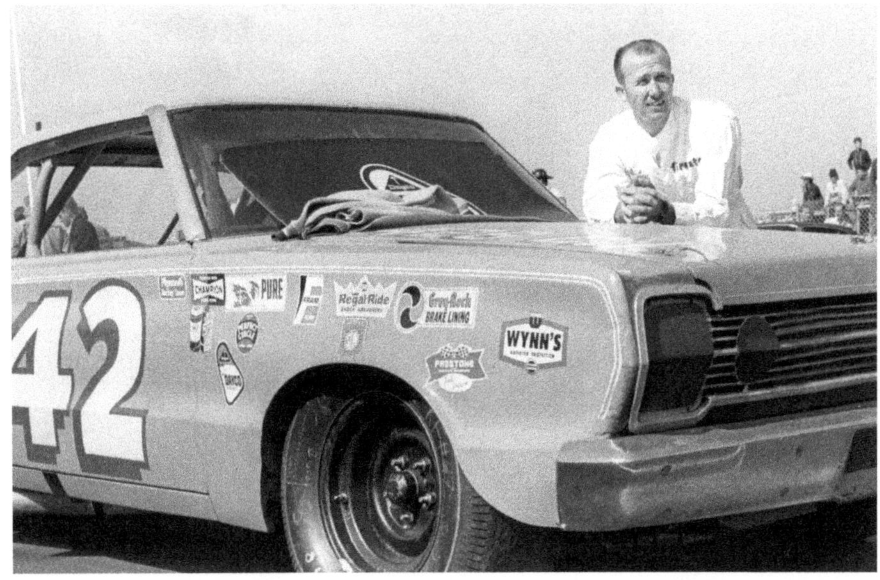

Paul Lewis made one start in a Plymouth prepared by Petty Enterprises. *Paul Lewis collection.*

"Height-wise, the sheet metal was stock. The guys that had the money and engineering from the factories did some swollen quarter panels, bowed the front fenders and dropped the front end. They could carry a lot more speed into the corner than I could, and my car would just dance around. They weren't supposed to, but NASCAR didn't have templates back then," Lewis said.

After examining other cars, Lewis returned home and began cutting and welding the Ford's frame and radiator supports to lower the front end over the chassis. "We went to Charlotte, and I was the fastest Ford there," he said.

Lewis sold that car to former NASCAR Late Model Sportsman champion Rene Charland and bought a year-old Plymouth from the Petty organization.

"Very few people were running the Chrysler product back then, so I had this foolish idea that if I ran a Chrysler instead of a Ford or Chevrolet, I might get some factory help," he said,

Without assistance, Lewis posted a win, nine top-fives and fourteen top-tens in twenty-one starts in 1966, with Herman Beam stepping in as crew chief. Despite running fewer than half of that season's forty-nine races, Lewis finished sixteenth in the final points standings. Had he run those other races and maintained that performance level, Lewis could have battled David Pearson for the championship.

His greatest highlight occurred that season during a Grand National race at Tennessee's Smoky Mountain Raceway. The Thursday night contest was wedged between the Volunteer 500 at Bristol and an upcoming Saturday night show at Nashville.

"We got down there a little late, as usual," Lewis said. "The boys jacked the car up, the car slipped off the jack and knocked a cooler fitting off the rear-end housing. We worked all the time we had trying to get that thing fixed by race time. I didn't practice, didn't time trial, didn't anything; I just fell in on the rear of the field as they dropped that flag.

"We'd run fifty or seventy-five laps, and I worked my way up to the factory cars. Those guys were beatin' and bangin' around on each other, so I backed off because I thought something was gonna happen. They were really getting wild. A couple of them spun out, and I missed them. I was as fast as any of them down there, so I just let them keep on having their problems. I'd pick my time and get them one at a time. When I finally got the lead, I never looked back."

David Pearson led one hundred laps in his Cotton Owens–owned Dodge that night but couldn't catch Lewis and his Plymouth in the race's final stages.

"I just worked traffic and kept Pearson back there," Lewis said. Unlike today's choreographed victory lane celebrations, this one was brief and uneventful.

"It wasn't no big deal. There wasn't the feeling then as you'd get now," Lewis said. "Nobody made a big deal out of it. You pull in, there was a big trophy sitting there, they had a track queen and they made a few pictures. A few reporters talked to you, and in ten or fifteen minutes, it was over because everybody wanted to go home, and you had another race to get to."

Lewis made his lone start in a factory-supported race car that year, driving the No. 42 Petty Engineering Plymouth in the season-ending American 500 at Rockingham, North Carolina.

"It was superior horsepower-wise. I don't believe it handled any better than my car, but that horsepower," he said. In an ironic twist, Lewis finished twenty-ninth while Buddy Arrington qualified Lewis' Plymouth and raced to a fourteenth-place finish.

The 1967 Grand National season began in November 1966, with a three-hundred-lap race on a half-mile oval in Augusta, Georgia. Richard Petty collected the first of that season's record twenty-seven victories, while Lewis finished a solid second with Petty's team providing pit service. It appeared for a time Petty might offer Lewis a job driving the No. 42, but the team opted instead to run the second car only a handful of times.

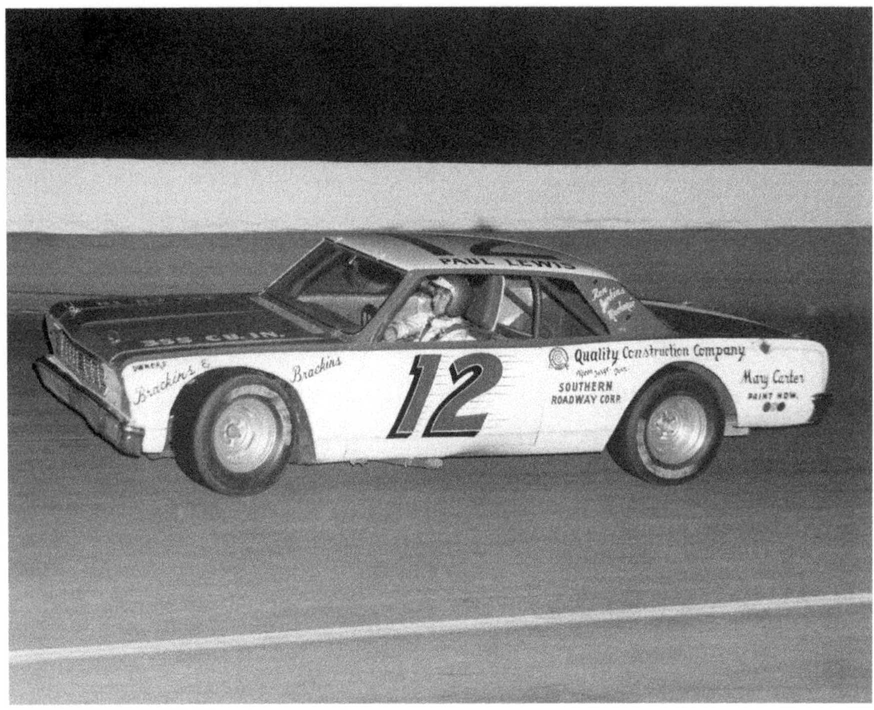

Paul Lewis won a number of NASCAR Late Model Sportsman races in the former Bobby Allison Chevelle owned by the Brackins brothers of Sevierville. *Paul Lewis collection.*

Amid the uncertainty of Petty's plans, Lewis accepted an offer to drive a Dodge Charger built by Cotton Owens and owned by Tennessean A.J. King of Sevierville. The car was well financed, but the flamboyant King was new to NASCAR. The relationship soured quickly.

"That car was fast. It was a good car, but it had the wrong people working on it. I had no control over that," Lewis said. He made eight starts, posting one top-five and four top-tens before splitting up. Bobby Isaac, "Little" Bud Moore, Sam McQuagg and Pete Hamilton took turns wheeling the car, but only Moore was able to match Lewis's single fifth-place finish.

Lewis made a smattering of Grand National starts in Emory Gilliam's Dodge before landing in one of the most recognizable cars of the era, a Chevelle formerly piloted by Bobby Allison. Owned by Tennessean J.D. Brackins, the car featured a small-block Chevrolet engine that often ran competitively with the larger, more powerful engines in other cars. With Donnie Allison serving as crew chief, Lewis made five starts, posting a fifth-place finish in Montgomery, Alabama.

"We intended to run the whole two-hundred-lap race with one tank of fuel. I wasn't trying to outrun anybody because I knew they had to stop, and the last fifty laps were going to be mine," Lewis said. "Well it got down to fifteen or twenty laps to go, and they had a caution flag. They wanted me to come in for fuel, but I'd been conserving gas all day. I came in, they jacked the car up and the cylinder on the jack burst." A second jack also proved faulty, and the prolonged pit stop dashed his chance for another victory.

After a brief hiatus, Lewis returned with the same Chevelle, only this time running in NASCAR's Late Model Sportsman division.

The combination proved potent as the team set a track qualifying record at Bristol and won multiple Late Model Sportsman races at tracks across the Southeast. Exactly how many remains in doubt, since records from that era are elusive.

Lewis was named to the North Carolina Auto Racing Hall of Fame in 2005 and was a 2009 inductee into the Racer's Reunion Memory Lane Hall of Fame for stock car independents at the Memory Lane Museum in Mooresville, North Carolina.

12

Dirt-Floor Garage

Men who drove Jess Potter's stock cars express only admiration for a man who devoted his life to racing.

"He was one of the hardest working guys I've ever seen. And he would help anybody that had a problem," recalled Brownie King. "If I wasn't in the pits and somebody pulled in next to us with a problem, he'd run over there and help them. He done that to the day he died."

In the late 1950s, King drove Potter-prepared Chevrolets in eighty-one NASCAR Grand National races and twenty-three starts in the old Convertible division. A high-water mark was when Potter finished third in the 1959 Convertible owner standings.

"He could fix anything. He didn't have the money to experiment on stuff like the factory teams did, and by the time we found out what they was doing, they was doing something different to make theirs even better," King said.

He and fellow Johnson City drivers Paul Lewis and the late George Green were regulars for Potter, who also counted Buddy Baker and E.J. Trivette among his drivers. Racing out of a primitive, cramped garage, Potter sometimes entered two cars even though he could barely afford one.

"Jess and his brother, Clyde, had a garage on Market Street. It had a wooden floor about halfway. So if you were working on the race car, you had to work in the dirt," Lewis said. "Just picture an old-style garage with stuff lying everywhere and workbenches, warped boards and engines lying everywhere. And here you've got a brand-new 1961 Chevrolet that you're making a race car out of on the dirt floor."

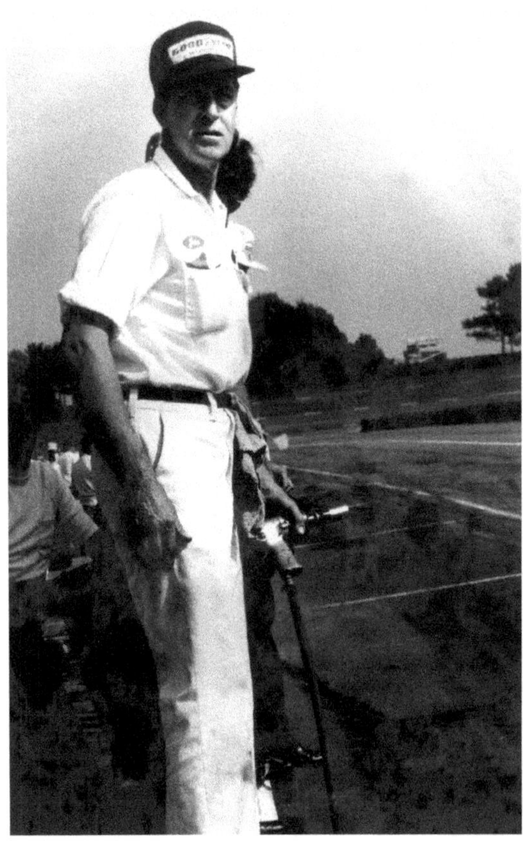

Jess Potter stands on pit wall to service a car. Potter fielded cars in NASCAR for a decade and later served as a mechanic. *Mike Potter collection.*

Orphaned at a young age, Potter came to Johnson City from rural Unicoi County. When he was twelve, he began hanging around with some moonshine runners and helping them soup up their cars until one day he got caught behind the wheel. A judge gave him two choices: jail or join the army. Once his tour with Uncle Sam was complete, Potter returned to Johnson City, began repairing cars and figuring out how to make them go faster.

"Daddy was very innovative," his son Mike Potter recalled. Employing some tricks learned on liquor cars, Potter built some fast race cars, including a bright yellow Nash that carried Sherman Utsman to his first stock car win at Tri-City Speedway.

Potter wanted to go NASCAR racing, but the family garage didn't generate enough money. Much to the delight of his wife, Florence, Potter got a full-time job with a steady paycheck servicing Honey Crust Bakery delivery trucks during the day. He then spent most nights in the garage working on race cars.

Potter made his Grand National owner's debut on May 5, 1956, at Columbia, South Carolina, where King finished eighteenth. They ran fourteen races that season, posting a best finish of eleventh in Hickory, North Carolina. King equaled that showing in the first race of the 1957 season, at the half-mile Concord Speedway in North Carolina.

The duo's next outing was on the famed Daytona Beach and Road Course, where King survived his first adventure of beach racing. Over the rest of that season, they captured sixteen top tens in thirty-six races and finished ninth in the final Grand National standings. Potter and King remained together through 1958 and 1959, with King dividing his time between the Convertible and Grand National divisions. They finished eighth and fifth in points during the final two Convertible series seasons.

Paved tracks were few and far between in the late 1950s, and Potter's homebuilt Chevrolets were ideal for the rough-and-tumble action that normally ensued on dirt.

"We ran a lot of old dirt tracks back then like Martinsville, Hillsboro, Hickory and the old Charlotte fairgrounds. But that thing was a hog. It was unbelievable how heavy it was, but it was an advantage in a sense because it didn't have enough horsepower to break its [tires] loose," Lewis said. "The guys with all the horsepower would get in trouble coming off the corners because they'd run so fast down the straightaways they'd break loose. But that old car was so heavy it would get grip, and I could run pretty good against a lot of cars. At that time, a Grand National car had to weigh 4,000 pounds, and that thing was something like 4,480 with a full load of fuel."

Lewis became Potter's primary driver in 1960 and 1961, posting nine top-ten finishes in forty races.

Travel sometimes proved as interesting as the race itself. Potter would toss a creeper, a jack and some tools into the race car, hitch the tow bar to the back of his 1941 Cadillac and head off down the highway. Sometimes his wife and kids piled up in the car, or sometimes it was just him, the driver and a volunteer crew member or two.

"I always worried about him. He worked all week at his job, worked all night on the race car and didn't get enough sleep at all," Lewis said. "But he'd always drive to the race track. We'd be on those trips, he'd be nodding off and it would scare me to death. I'd ask him to let me drive, and he'd say 'No, you need your rest. You've got to race.' He never would let anybody else drive."

One night, an errant cow nearly made the ultimate sacrifice.

"We were going to Charlotte, and there were six of us in that old Cadillac towing that '56 Chevrolet," King recalled. "We were going down Linville Ridge towards Marion, North Carolina, and there was a cow. I said, 'Jess, you better slow down; there's a cow.'"

But roaring downhill at sixty miles per hour in a loaded, two-ton vehicle flat-towing another two-ton vehicle made stopping all but impossible.

"Jess hit that cow in the back end, knocked it down and we went over the bank on the left side. The only thing that kept us from turning over was the

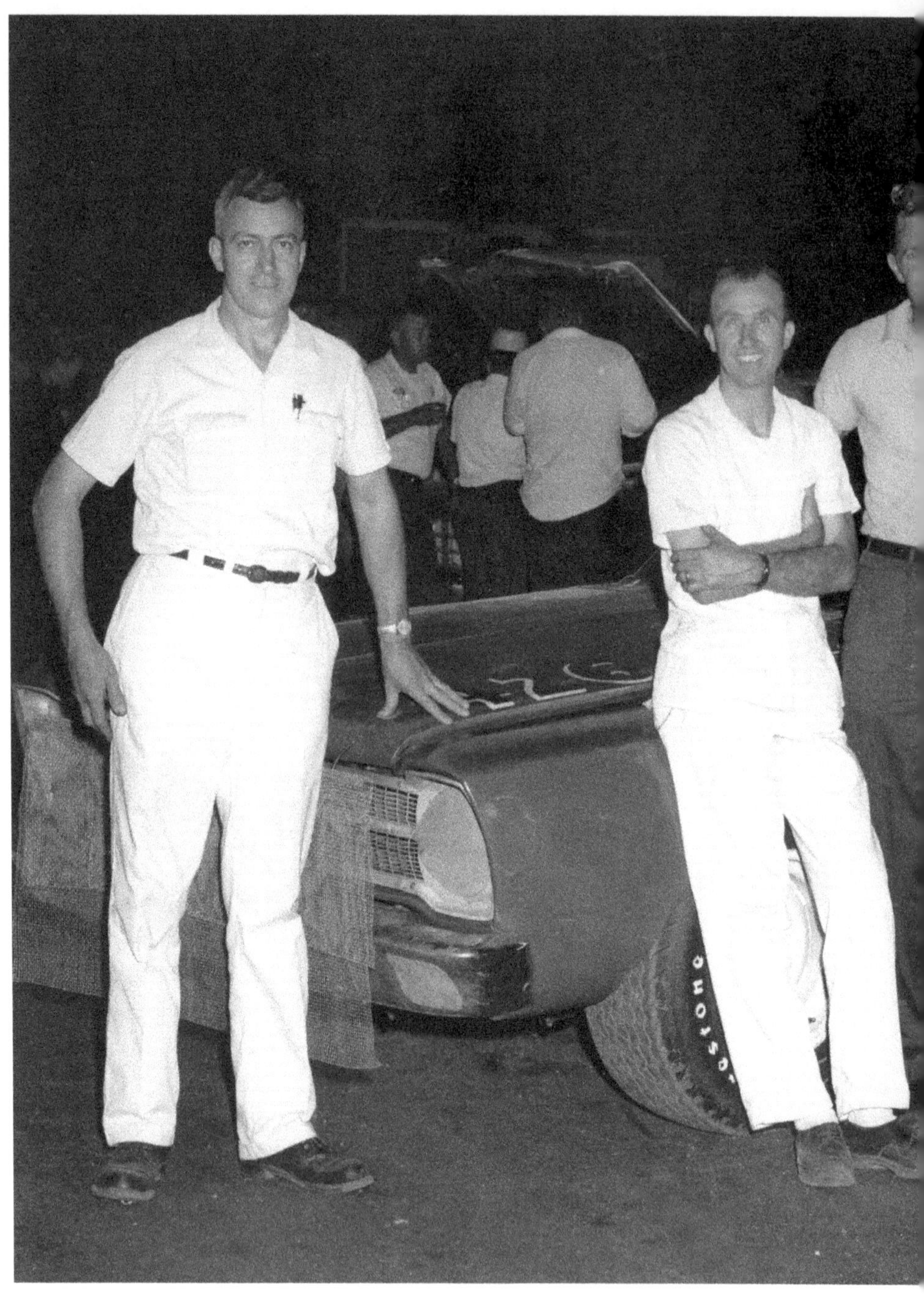

At Smoky Mountain Raceway. *Pictured left to right:* Jess Potter, Paul Lewis, Clell Anthony, Herman Beam, John Roberts and Jerry Elliott. *Ray Taylor photo, courtesy Mike Potter.*

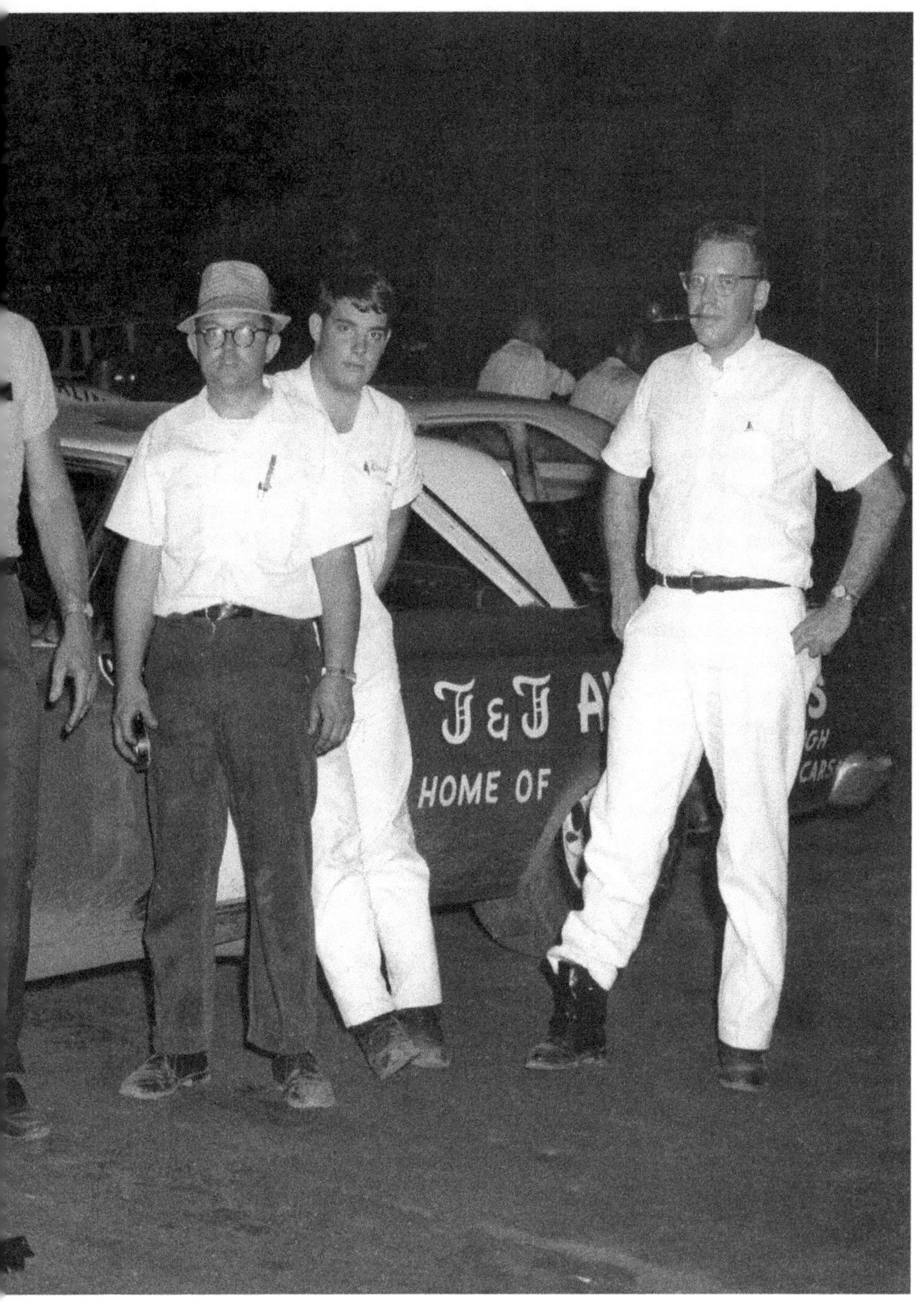
HOME OF
CARS

tow bar hooked to the race car," King said. "Jess got out and picked that cow up and set it over on the other side of a barbed wire fence. I thought it was dead, but it got up and ran away. We got the race car and Cadillac back up on the road, and one of us drove the race car ten miles or so into Marion.

"Jess pulled into the service station and asked the guy for a welder. He said a cow had pulled out in front of him. Joe George started laughing, and he laughed all the way to Charlotte," King recalled. "Well, Jess was tired of listening to him. We got over there, Jess was unhooking the tow bar and Joe started telling George Green about Jess saying the cow pulled out in front of him. Jess dropped that tow bar on Joe's big toe. That's the only time I ever saw him get mad."

Green started thirty-nine Grand National races in Potter's cars between 1957 and 1961, racing around his service in the U.S. Army, before becoming his primary driver.

In 1962, Green drove Potter's No. 1 Chevrolet in forty-six Grand National races. Despite going winless, they still put together fifteen top-ten finishes and wound up sixteenth in the final standings. Potter's cars ran only eleven races in 1963, and Green made three starts. Despite two top-ten finishes, they parted ways, and Green, age thirty-five at the time, never drove in another Grand National race.

Potter remained with the Grand National circuit through the 1965 season and then devoted his time to helping others, including his sons Mike, Gary and Ronnie, get into racing. He died of a heart attack in 1981 at the age of fifty-eight.

"He'd always help people. He gave a lot of drivers chances," King recalled. "He devoted his whole life to racing and helping others."

13

G Is for Gypsy

You just have to smile. G.C. Spencer's bronze military grave marker lies first in a double-file row near the entrance of Johnson City's Monte Vista Memorial Park, and the adjacent driveway forms a quarter-mile loop around the cemetery's first section. G.C. always did love a good short-track race, and now he's on the pole for eternity.

Spencer was among the last of a generation of NASCAR independents—resilient blue-collar men obsessed with competition and speed—who sacrificed mightily to help forge stock car racing into one of America's premier sports. He was a colorful, fun-loving swatch woven into the sport's patchwork quilt and a proud man who utilized every means at his disposal to keep pace with generations of Hall of Famers from Lee and Richard Petty to David Pearson, Buck Baker, Cale Yarborough and the Wood brothers.

Freshly discharged from the U.S. Navy, Spencer's odyssey began on the short tracks near his hometown of Owensboro, Kentucky. After moving across the Ohio River to Evansville, Indiana, to work at a Chrysler plant, he was soon driving Modified coupes on tracks in Kentucky, Tennessee, Indiana and Illinois. Teaming with master mechanics Louis and Crawford Clements, Spencer enjoyed his greatest success with a series of cars known as the "Flying Saucer."

He won fifty times at Bowling Green, Kentucky, and recalled fourteen straight at a track in Metropolis, Illinois, driving the competition away and putting the promoter out of business. Homecomings meant a trip to victory

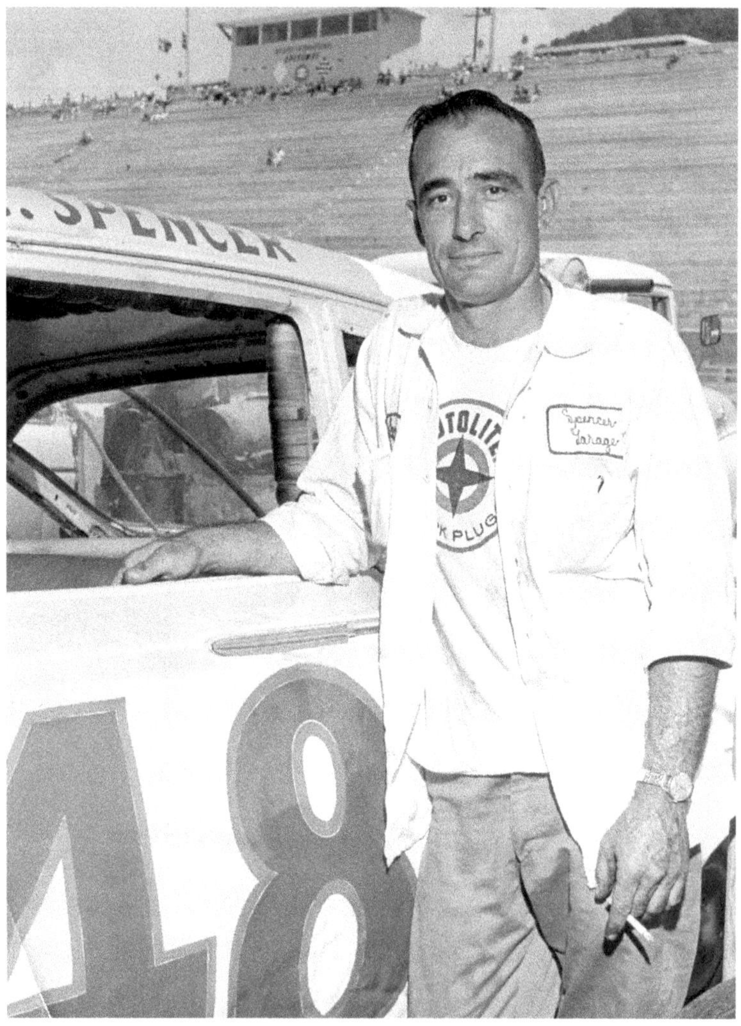

Grover Clifton (G.C.) Spencer dominated midwestern short tracks before becoming a NASCAR independent. *John Beach photo, courtesy Carl Moore collection.*

lane at the old Legion Field in Owensboro, where a wide-eyed, six-year-old Darrell Waltrip found an idol and a life's ambition.

"G.C. Spencer was my hero. I would go to the races with my grandmother. She was a fan of G.C., so I was too," Waltrip said. "Sometimes after the race, we would go to the pits to look at the cars, and I got to meet G.C. He knew my grandmother because my grandfather was a deputy sheriff in

Owensboro. G.C. was real nice to me. I told my grandmother [that] I was going to drive race cars one day."

Between 1948 and 1951, Spencer and the Clements brothers won so much their combination was finally outlawed. For the next six years, Spencer continued winning, driving everything from Modified and Sportsman cars to Midgets and dirt Sprint cars, ultimately totaling some two hundred victories.

In 1957, the Clements brothers relocated to South Carolina to work for NASCAR team owner Bud Moore preparing cars for Buck Baker and Speedy Thompson. Spencer soon followed. He entered his first Grand National race at age thirty-three, driving a 1957 Chevrolet owned by Baker, in the 1958 Southern 500 in Darlington, South Carolina. Spencer qualified twelfth fastest and, despite having never run any race of more than one hundred laps, finished a respectable sixteenth. He earned $315.

Spencer put together his own Chevrolet for the 1959 season and ran twenty-eight of forty-four races. His first top-five finish came on the half-mile dirt Hub City Speedway in Spartanburg, South Carolina, and he earned four top-ten finishes that year.

While the talent level in NASCAR far exceeded anything he'd experienced in the Midwest, Spencer had a breakthrough year in 1965. Ford offered him the assistance needed to contend for a championship and then promptly pulled that offer after rival Chrysler withdrew from the sport, amid a dispute over its Hemi engine. G.C. did receive a race car from the Wood brothers and promptly took full advantage.

He scored his first pole, recorded fourteen top-five finishes and twenty-five top tens. He ran second three times—all to eventual champion Ned Jarrett and his factory-backed Ford. Spencer finished fourth in the final standings behind Jarrett, Dick Hutcherson and Darel Dieringer. That season also included one of his greatest disappointments: watching certain victory slip away.

Racing on the half-mile dirt oval at Valdosta, Georgia, Spencer had the field covered when the water hose came loose and the engine began overheating. Cale Yarborough passed him for the lead with eighteen laps remaining and scored his first Grand National win. With steam billowing, Spencer continued limping around the track until the engine blew and was still credited with a third-place finish.

The gypsy moved to Jonesborough in East Tennessee that same year, after finalizing a divorce from his first wife. He married again two years later and relocated to nearby Bluff City.

Spencer declined an offer to drive for car owner Nord Krauskopf and crew chief Harry Hyde in the 1966 World 600 at Charlotte. Instead, he nearly won the race in his own year-old Plymouth. Race leader David Pearson wrecked, and second-place Spencer cut down his left side tires running over some debris. A mix-up by his crew cost him two laps in the pits, which was the margin he finished behind Richard Petty, who came on in relief of teammate Marvin Panch.

Spencer made a handful of starts for others, including Cliff Stewart, Jack Smith and three for Petty Enterprises. Late in the 1967 season, he drove a No. 42 Petty Plymouth to third place in the Southern 500 in Darlington. He also ran fifth in the National 500 in Charlotte and was collected in a grinding four-car crash in Rockingham, North Carolina.

Good finishes came less often during the 1970s, and Spencer sometimes resorted to some creative engineering, according to friend, competitor and fellow independent Blackie Wangerin.

"He knew how to blow the rules," Wangerin said. "G.C. had his nitrous oxide bottle hid up under the firewall. After we'd go through inspection back then, we'd put the bottle up under the firewall. Well, we were at Talladega, and he had his car sitting out in the sun. Well his bottle let loose, so I threw my jacket over it so NASCAR wouldn't see it. When he came back, I told him, 'We aren't going to go very fast today because your bottle went off.'"

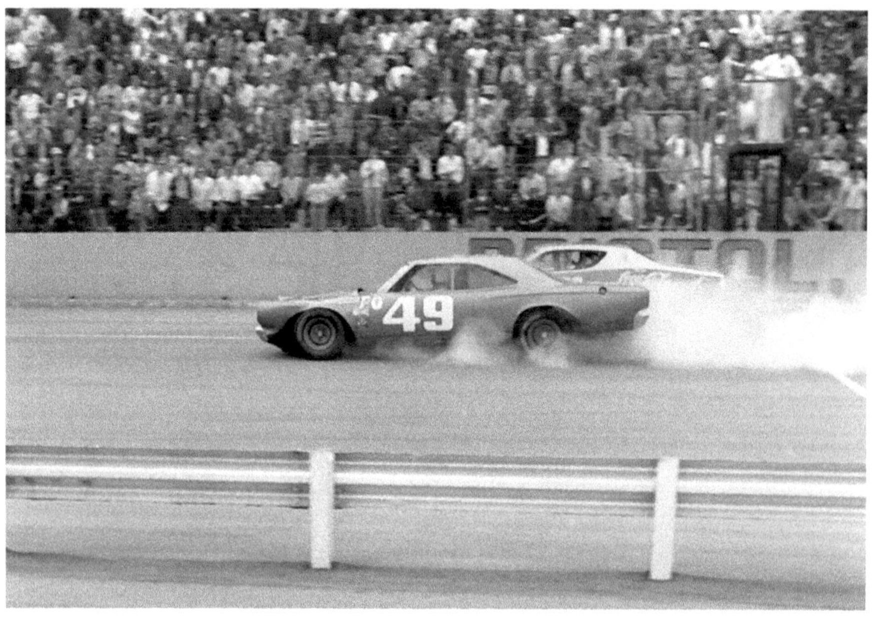

G.C. Spencer blows the engine in his Roadrunner at Bristol as Bobby Allison goes by. *John Beach photo, courtesy Carl Moore collection.*

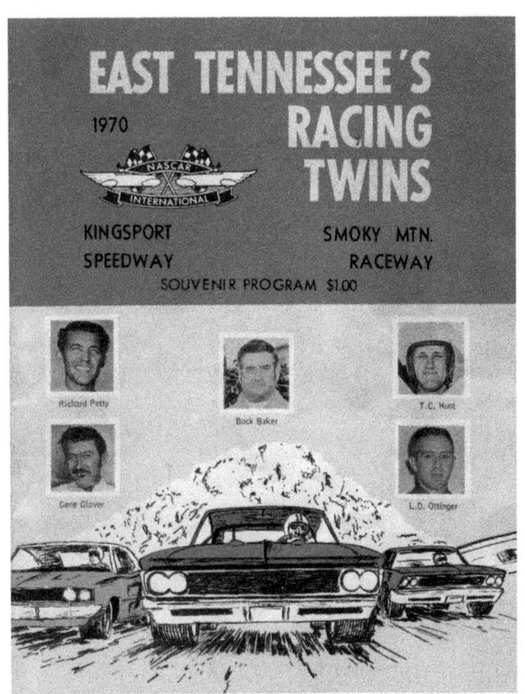

This program cover illustrates how East Tennessee tracks Kingsport and Smoky Mountain worked together hosting NASCAR Late Model Sportsman division races in the 1970s. *Courtesy Tony Morton.*

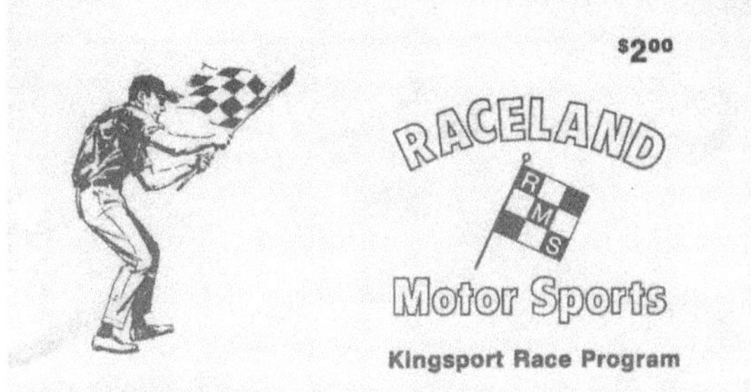

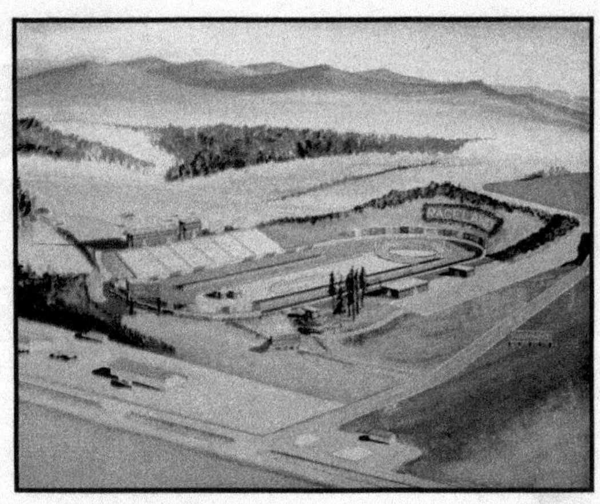

This 1984 program marked J.D. Stacy's purchase of Kingsport Speedway, returning it to a dirt surface and his short-lived plans to revolutionize dirt racing. *Author's collection.*

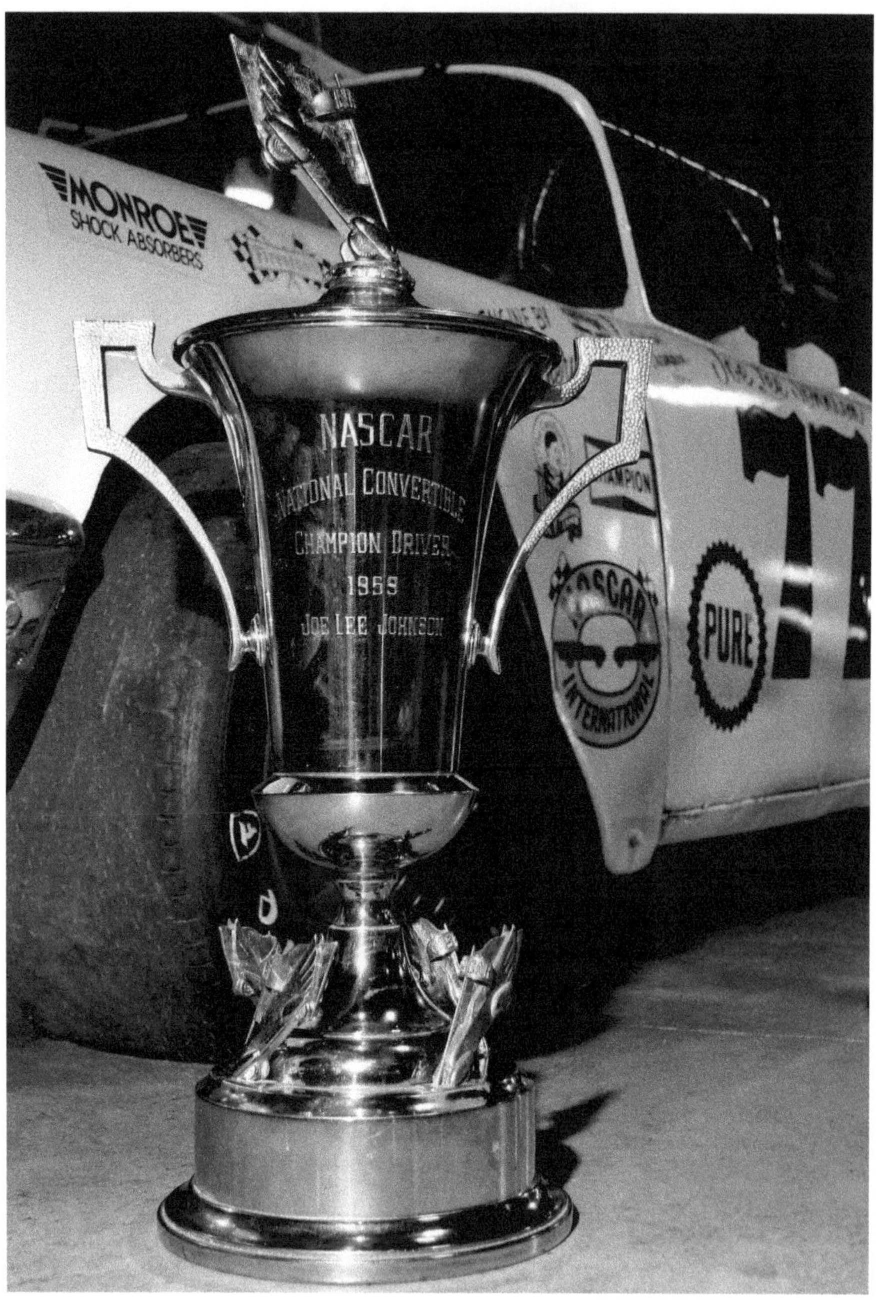

Joe Lee Johnson of Chattanooga earned this trophy for winning the 1959 NASCAR Convertible division championship. *Author photo.*

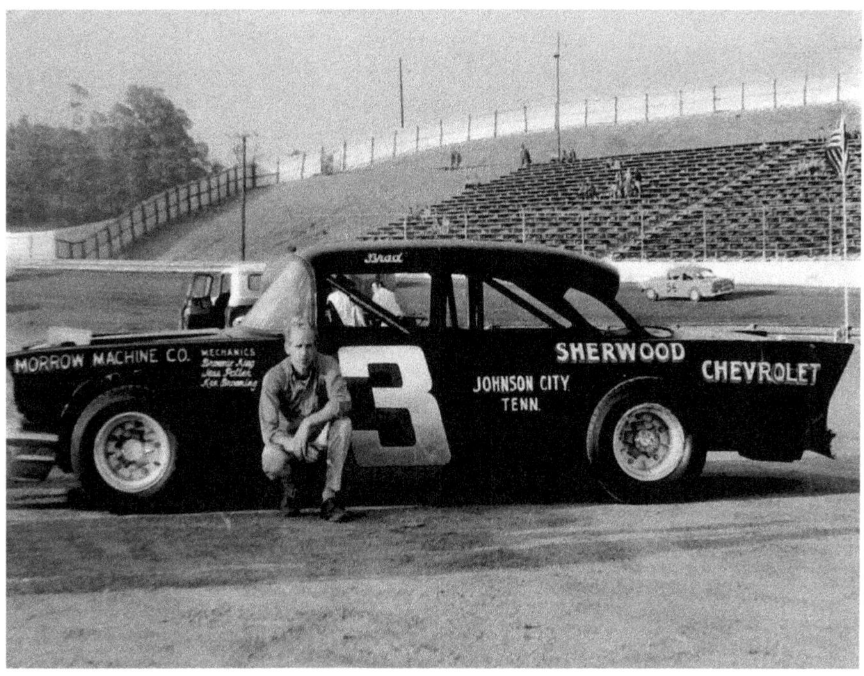

Brad Teague began racing on the dirt tracks of East Tennessee, including the old Appalachian and Sportsman Speedways. *Courtesy Robert Walden.*

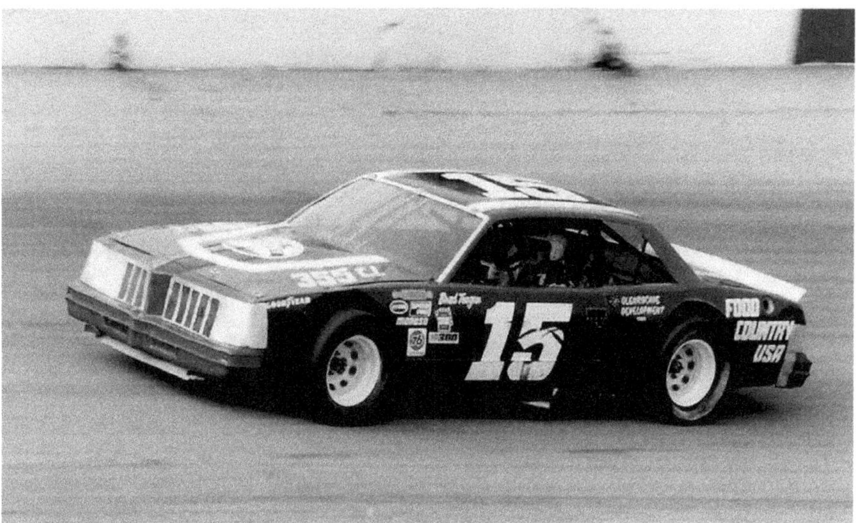

Brad Teague became one of the drivers to beat in the NASCAR Late Model Sportsman series in cars owned by Charlie Henderson. *Chris Haverly photo.*

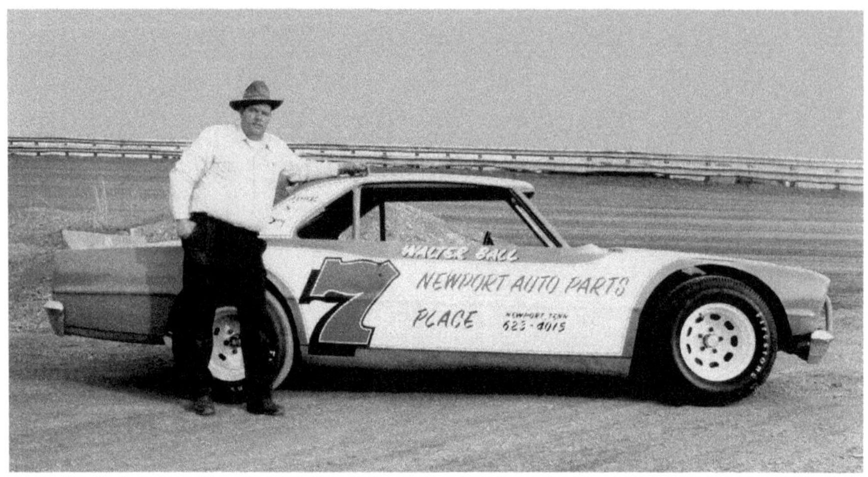

Walter Ball was one of the most successful dirt-track racers in East Tennessee history, with four hundred feature wins and championships at six tracks. *Courtesy Walter Ball family.*

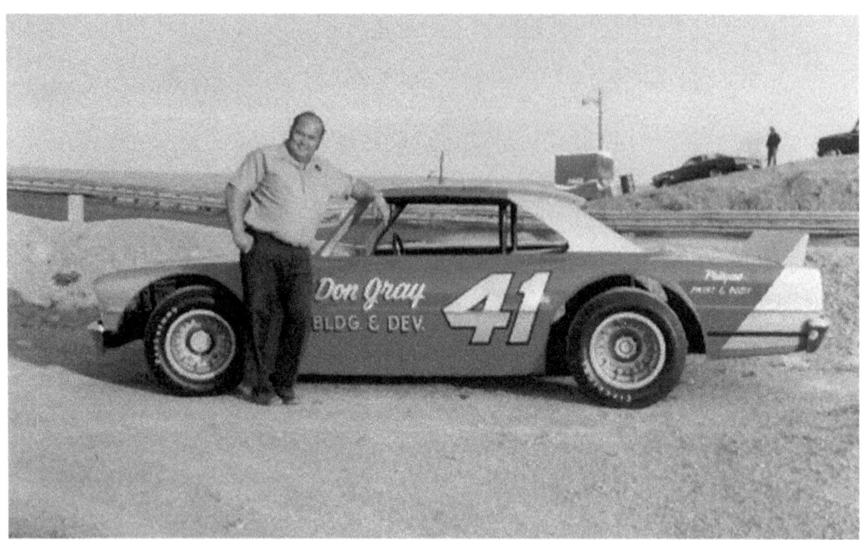

Bill Morton raced in NASCAR before winning some four hundred short-track races in and around East Tennessee. *Tony Morton collection.*

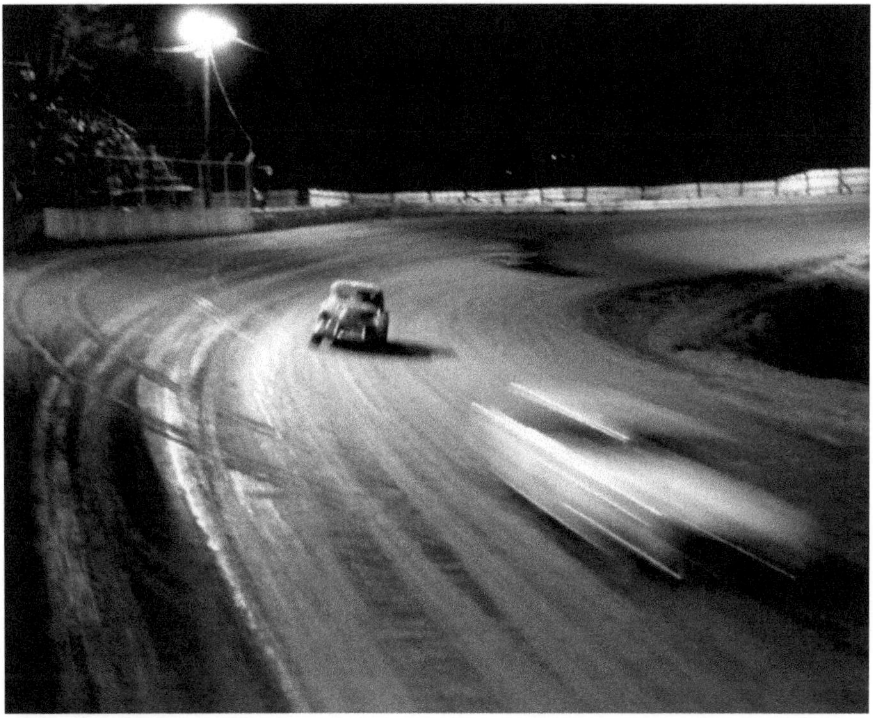

Sportsman Speedway provided great entertainment for fans around Johnson City from 1959 until 1974. *Courtesy Ernie Collins/Bob Dotson.*

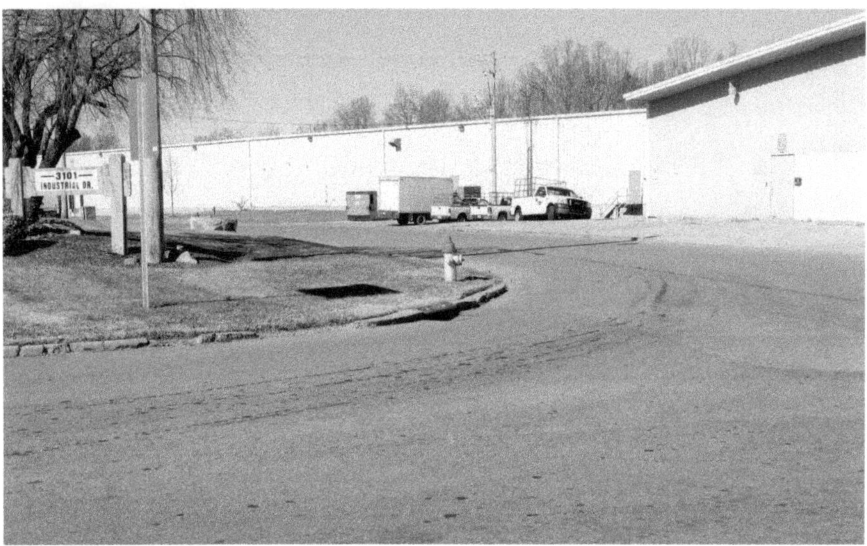

This corner of Industrial Drive in Johnson City is roughly where Sportsman Speedway's turn two was until the track closed in 1974. *Author photo.*

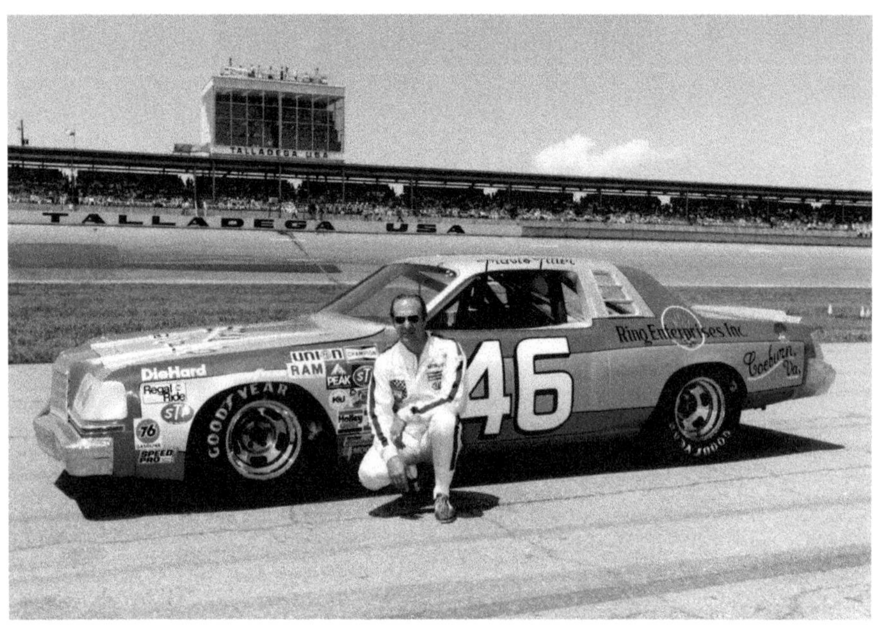

Travis Tiller was a regular in the NASCAR Winston Cup Series for ten seasons. *Courtesy Travis Tiller.*

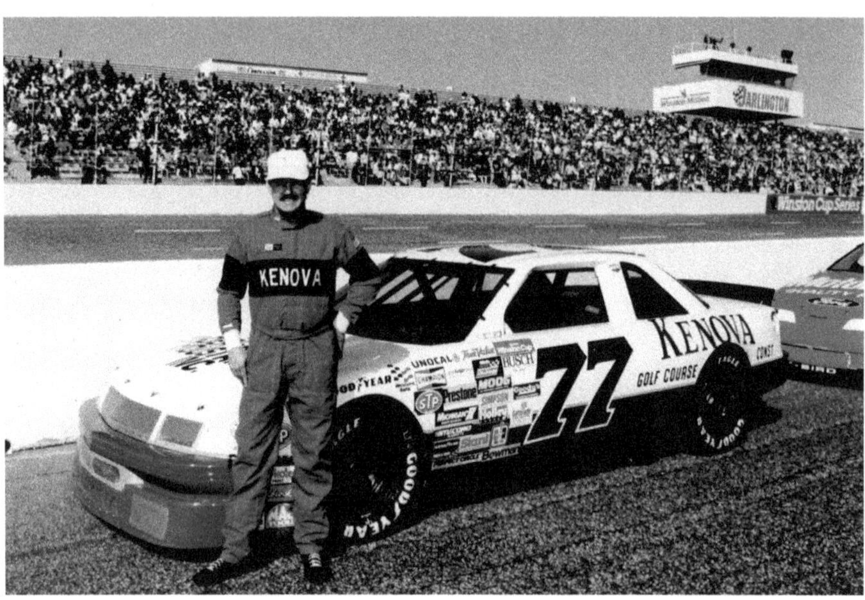

Mike Potter made a combined seventy-five starts in the NASCAR Winston Cup and Busch series. *Courtesy Mike Potter.*

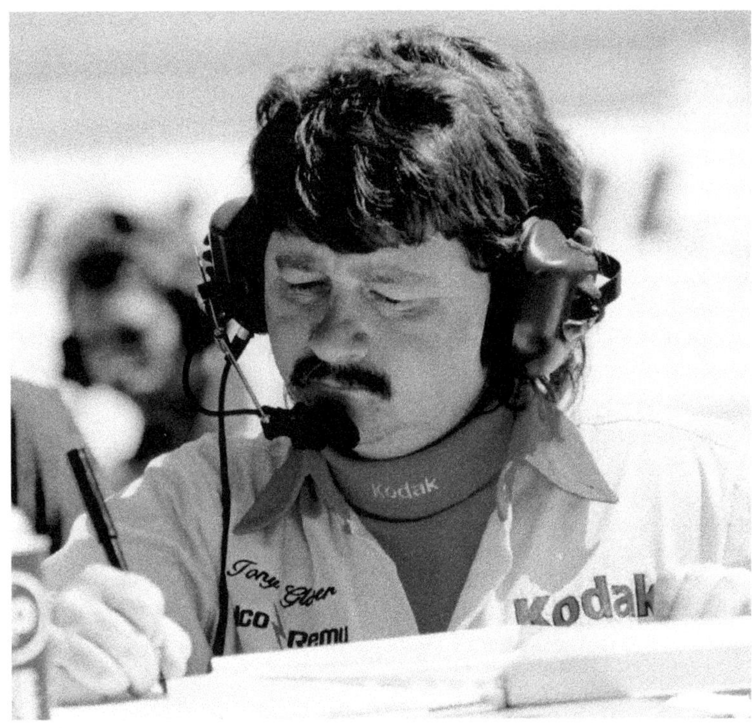

After working for his father, Tony Glover became a successful NASCAR crew chief, winning twelve races, including three Daytona 500s. *Author photo.*

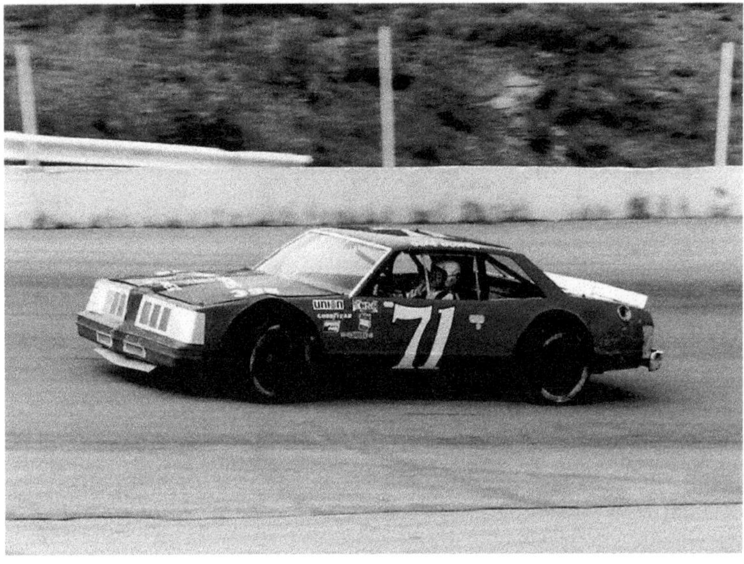

Gene Glover capped a successful short-track career by winning the 1979 NASCAR Late Model Sportsman championship. *Chris Haverly photo.*

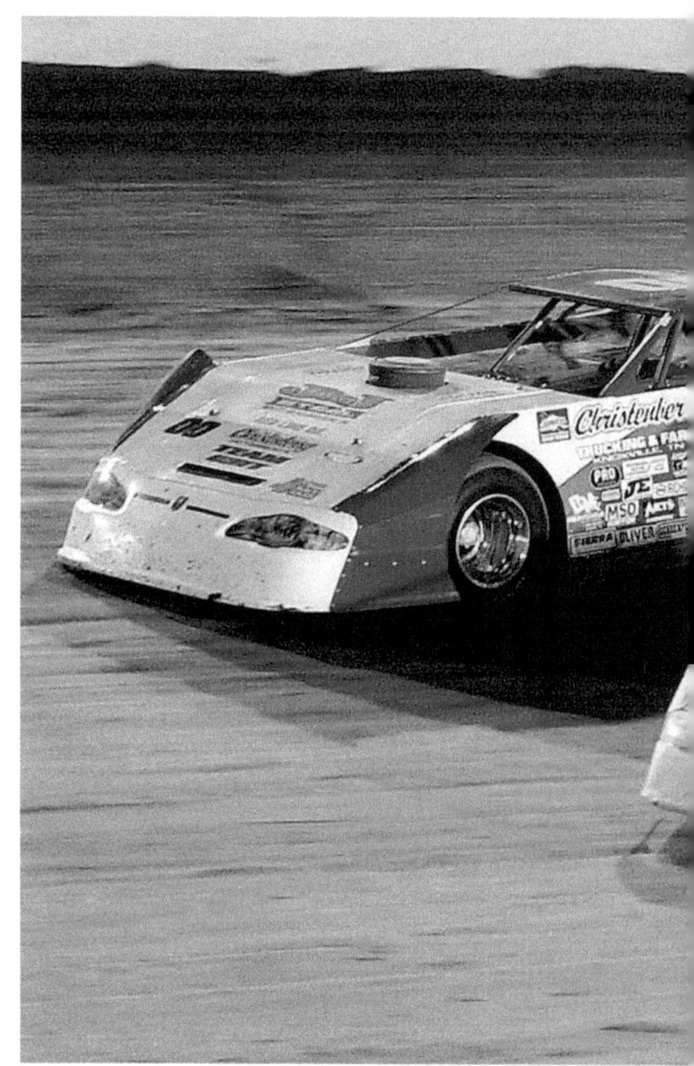

Dirt racing legends Scott Bloomquist (0) and Freddy Smith (00) race during the 2001 Dirt Weeks at Bristol Motor Speedway. *Bristol Herald Courier.*

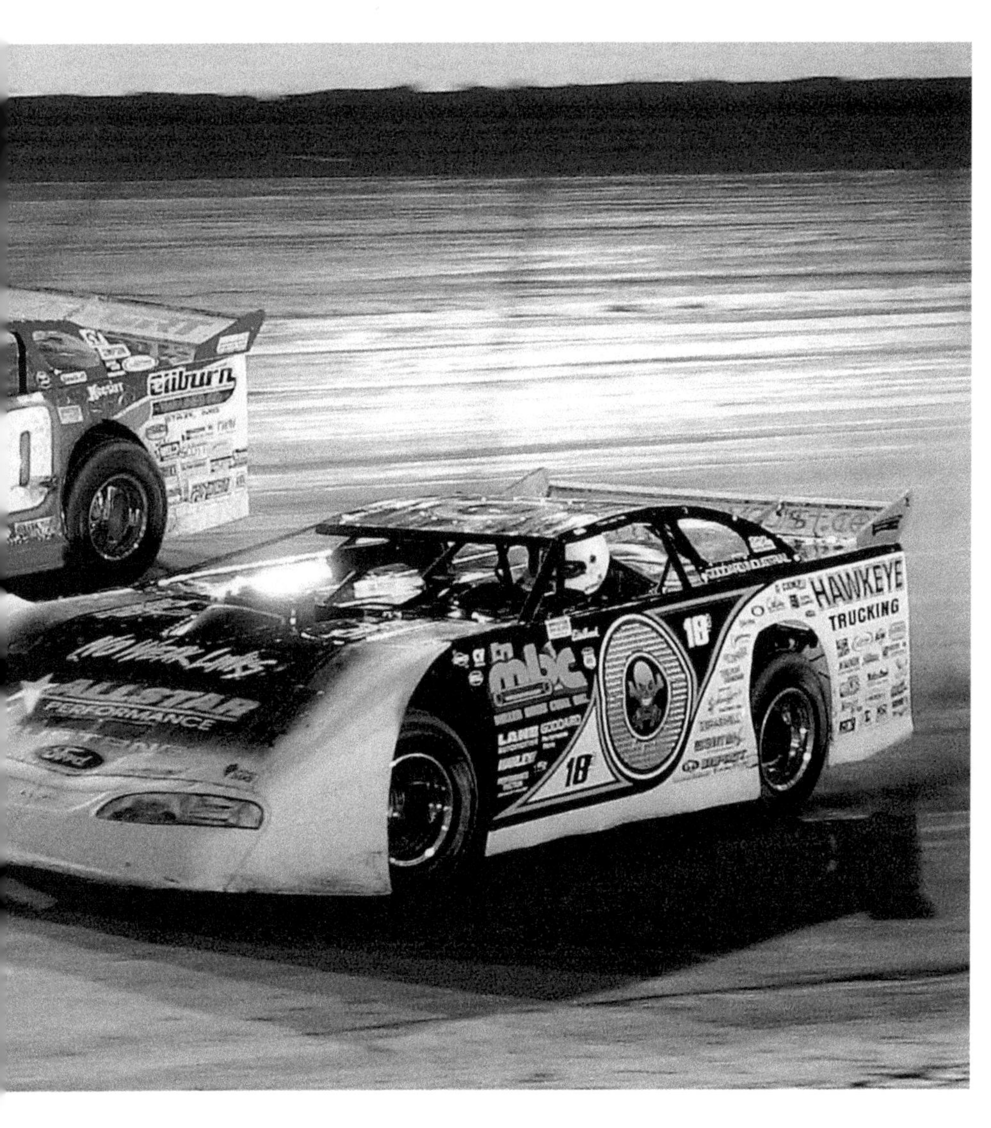
HAWKEYE
TRUCKING
ALLSTAR
PERFORMANCE
18
Ford

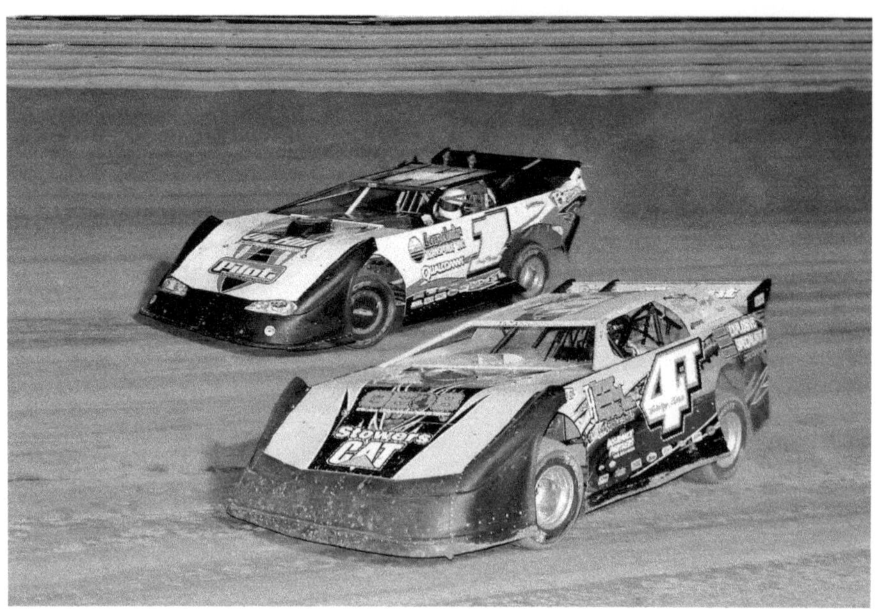

Vic Hill (1) and Tommy Kerr (4T) race their dirt Late Models side by side at Volunteer Speedway. *Joey Millard photo.*

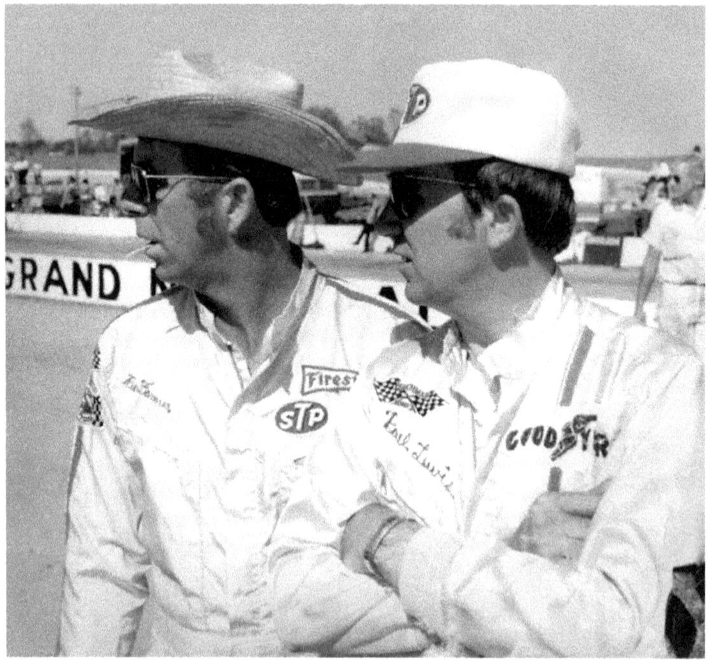

Legendary Red Farmer from Nashville (left) and Paul Lewis of Johnson City observe qualifying. *Courtesy Paul Lewis.*

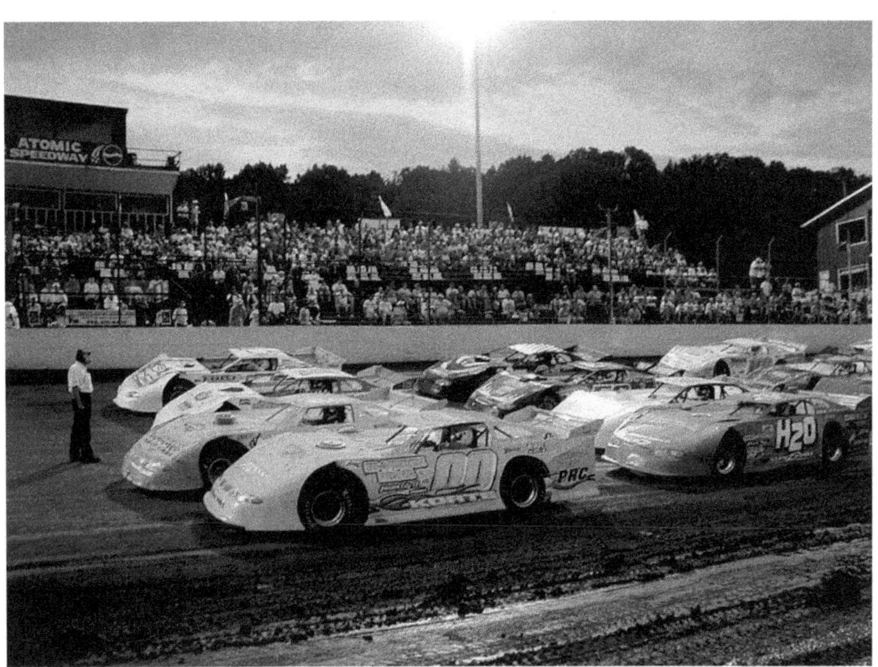

Above: A field of Late Models lines up four wide to salute fans at iconic Atomic Speedway. It was one of the nation's premier dirt tracks before closing after the 2006 season. *Michael Moats photo.*

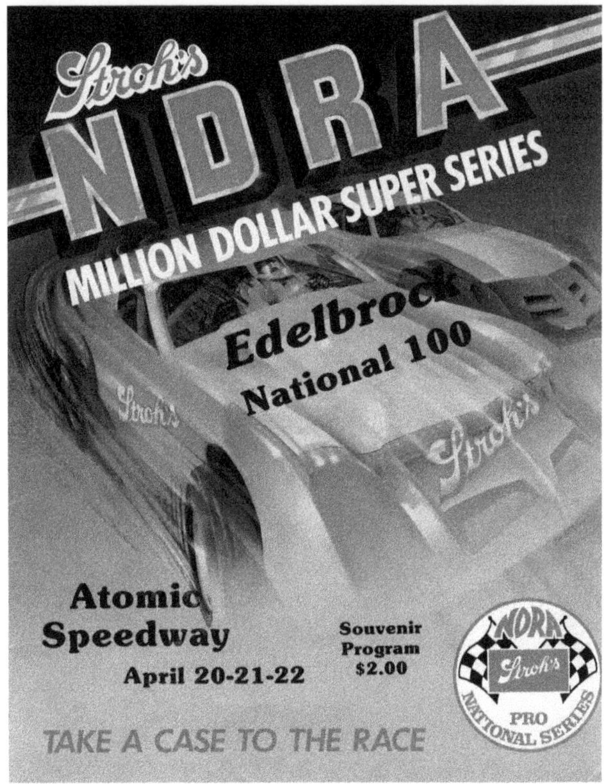

Right: As this program cover illustrates, Atomic Speedway was one of many East Tennessee ovals to host the trend-setting National Dirt Racing Association. *Author's collection.*

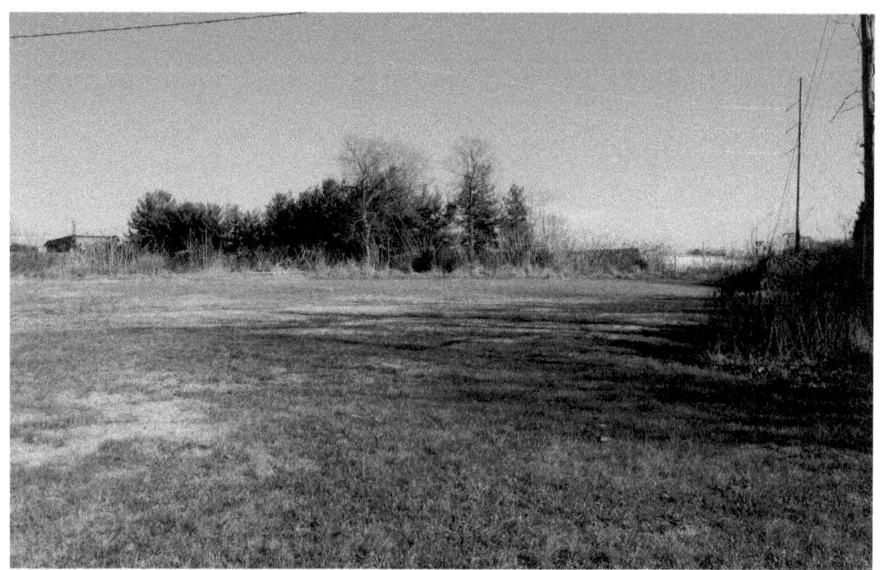

The outline of turn two of the former Tennessee Carolina Speedway is still evident at the Cocke County fairgrounds in Newport, the site of Tennessee's first NASCAR race. *Author photo.*

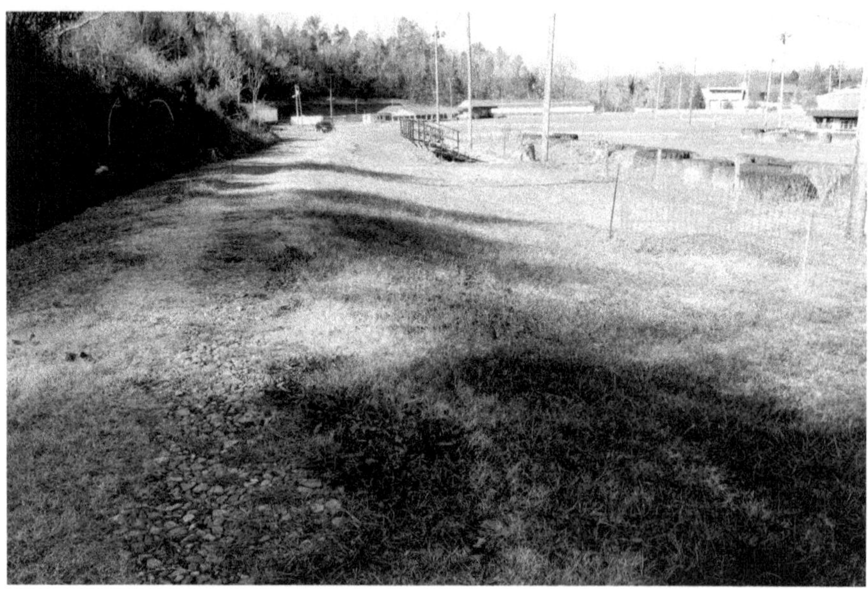

This was the front straightaway of the former Tennessee Carolina Speedway, which operated in Newport from 1956 to 1967. *Author photo.*

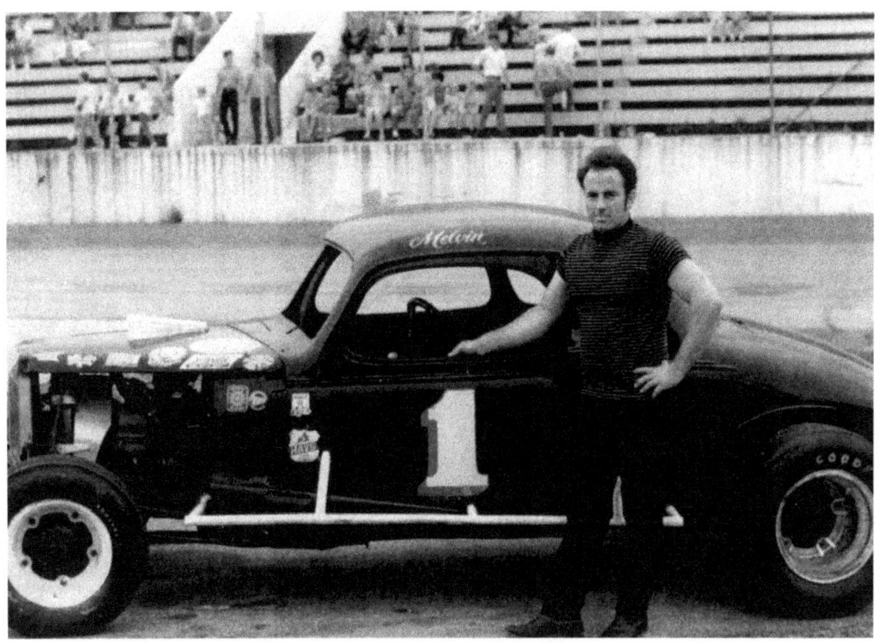

Melvin Corum of Maynardville poses with his Chevrolet coupe at the former Knoxville Raceway. *Courtesy Melvin Corum.*

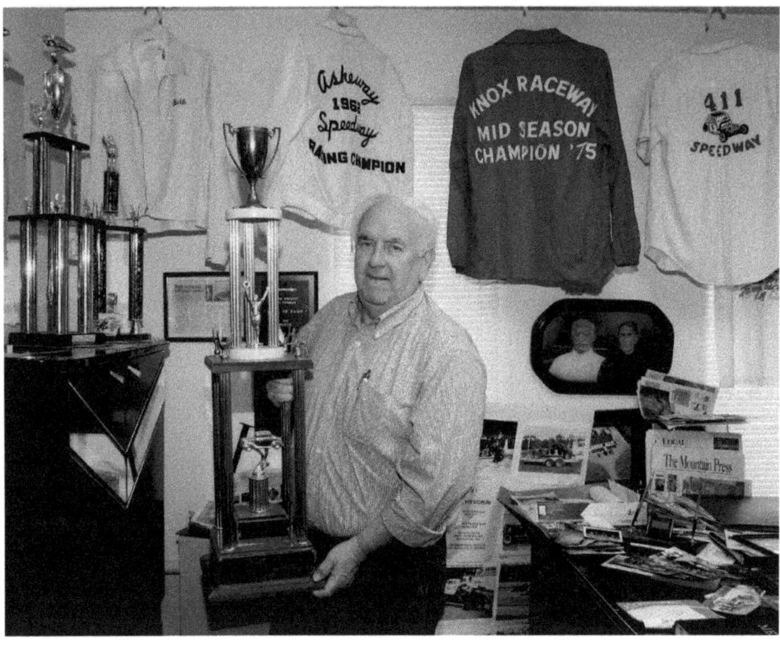

Melvin Corum proudly displays mementos of a career that included more than three hundred short-track wins. *Author photo.*

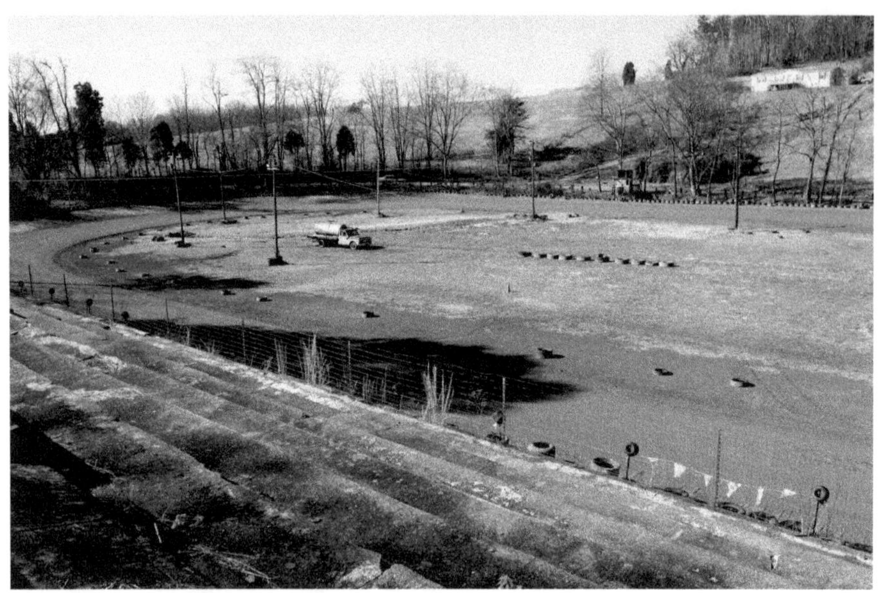

Ashway Speedway still operates as a go-kart track, but decades ago, many of East Tennessee's legendary racers competed there. *Author photo.*

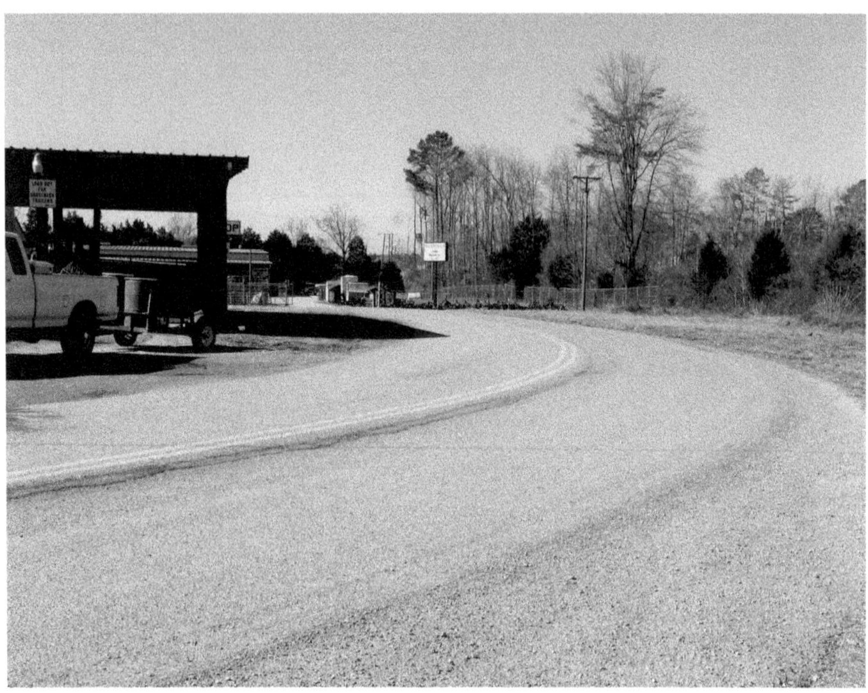

Fountain Valley Road circles the Halls Stockyards near Knoxville, offering one of the few clues to the former Broadway Speedway. *Author photo.*

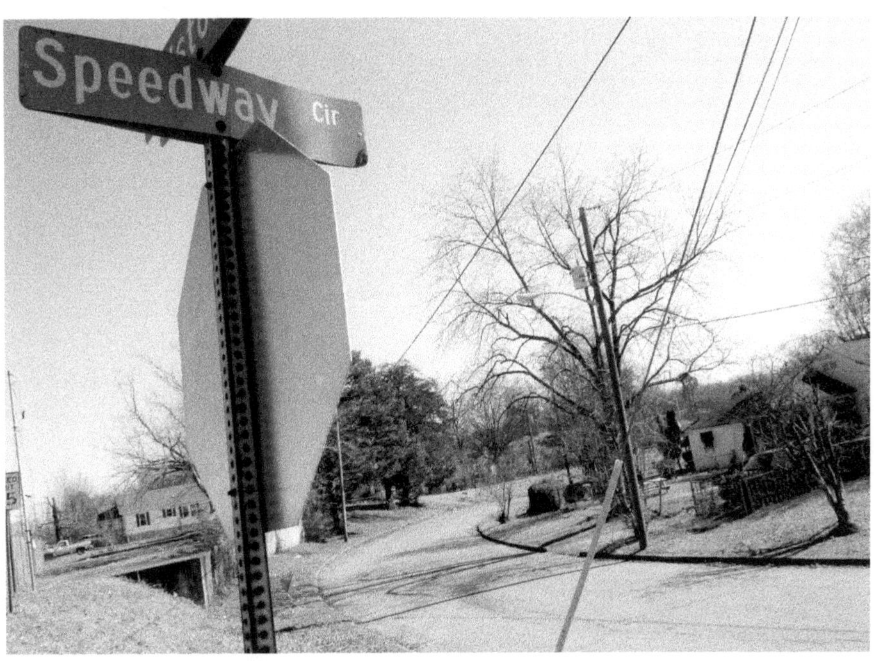

Speedway Circle in east Knoxville is a residential street that maintains the exact oval configuration of the old Johnson's Race Track. *Author photo.*

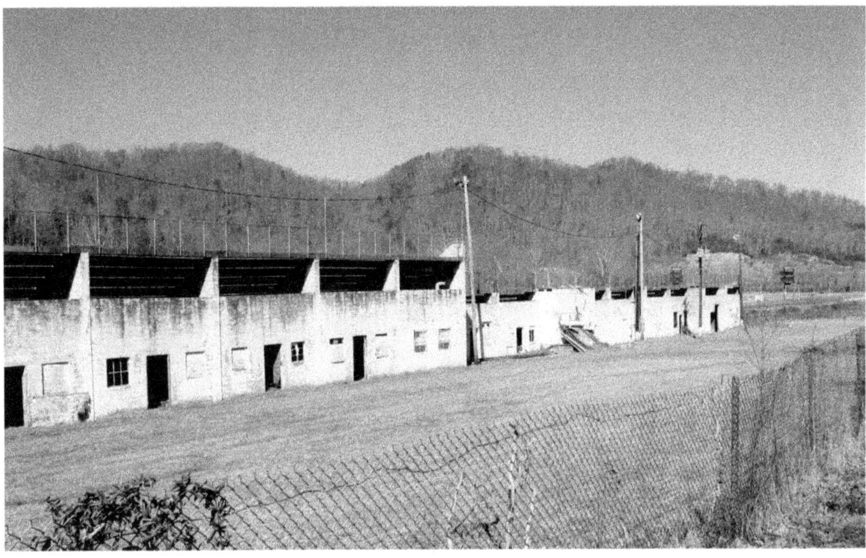

Large concrete grandstands at the Knoxville Dragway were part of the Knoxville Raceway oval that once operated on the site. *Author photo.*

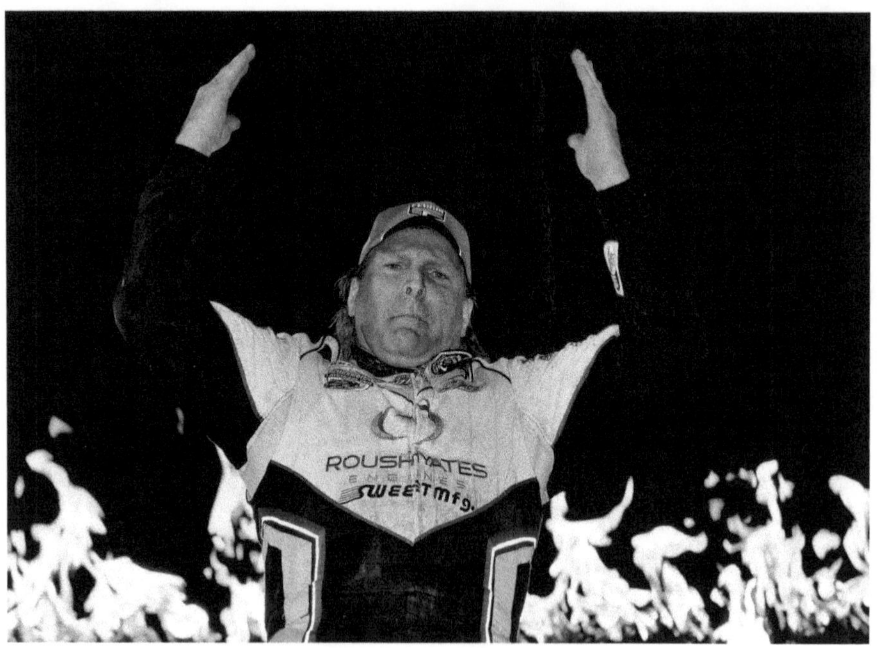

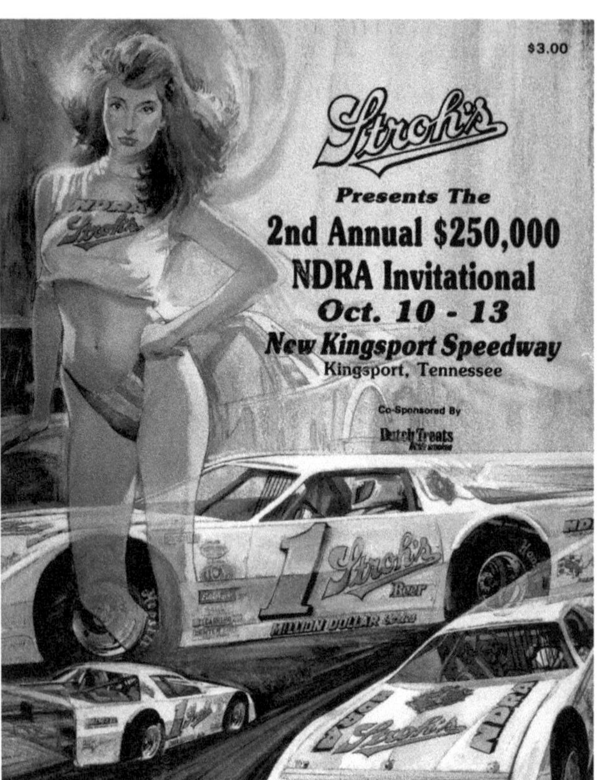

Above: Scott Bloomquist of Mooresburg celebrates winning the 2013 $100,000 Eldora Dream. He has dominated the nation's dirt Late Model racing for decades. *Joey Millard photo.*

Left: This program is from the 1985 NDRA Invitational at Kingsport Speedway, one of the organization's final events. *Courtesy Tony Morton.*

The independents shared a common bond, racing primarily with their own money.

"We all borrowed back and forth off each other," Wangerin said. "We borrowed everything from transmissions to rear ends, driveshafts, shocks. We had to. None of us had any money. We were just having fun."

Spencer made 415 NASCAR starts without a victory and ran only a partial schedule during the last decade of his driving career. He stopped in 1977, at the age of fifty-one, after finishing twenty-fifth in the Atlanta 500. He fielded cars for others until the expenses became overwhelming, later admitting he'd stayed too long.

"I would never have gotten to drive in the Daytona 500 if it wasn't for G.C. He was a great guy," John A. Utsman said. "Running on that big track was one of the greatest thrills of my life. And G.C. let me drive Bristol in 1973, and we ran tenth."

That performance caught the attention of Benny Parsons, who, later that same year, utilized Utsman as a relief driver to help win Bristol's Volunteer 500.

Spencer sold his team's assets to Larry McClure in 1983 and went to work for the new Morgan-McClure Motorsports team in nearby Abingdon, Virginia. He retired after three seasons but returned briefly in 1988 to assist a team owned by Bob Clark for drivers Brad Teague and Joe Ruttman.

Arguably Spencer's greatest accomplishment had nothing to do with winning. During a 1964 NASCAR Modified race at Daytona, he was involved in a multicar crash in which his Studebaker caught fire. Driver Lee Roy Yarbrough was also involved and knocked unconscious. Spencer and drivers Fred Lorenzen and Larry Frank braved the blaze to rescue Yarbrough, and all were later honored by NASCAR.

The gypsy's journey ended in 2007.

14

Billy Graham, Richard Nixon and Don Naman

Don Naman must be out of his mind. That was the consensus in NASCAR's Daytona Beach, Florida headquarters after officials there failed to convince the colorful promoter to reschedule his Smoky Mountain 200 Grand National race.

There was nothing wrong with the facility. Smoky Mountain Raceway had been hosting Grand National races since 1965. While maybe not ideal, the Thursday, May 28, 1970 date wasn't uncommon either. No, their concern centered about a half hour to the north in Knoxville, where renowned evangelist Billy Graham was in the midst of a ten-night crusade at the University of Tennessee's Neyland Stadium. Sanctioning officials feared the massive crowds attending the nightly crusades would snarl traffic for fans headed to the race.

Those concerns hit overdrive on May 27, when crusade organizers announced President Richard Nixon would speak in Knoxville the following night. It would be the president's first appearance on a college campus since four students were shot and killed during an antiwar protest at Kent State in Ohio. Undeterred, Naman kept his date despite their objections, artfully mapping and marking alternative routes to the track and telling anyone who would listen that the race would occur.

That evening in Knoxville, hundreds of city buses helped transport an estimated 100,000 people to Graham's crusade. Published accounts say 75,000 jammed into the stadium—some to cheer and others to protest—while an estimated 25,000 stood outside as Nixon's helicopter landed on the field and the president spoke briefly.

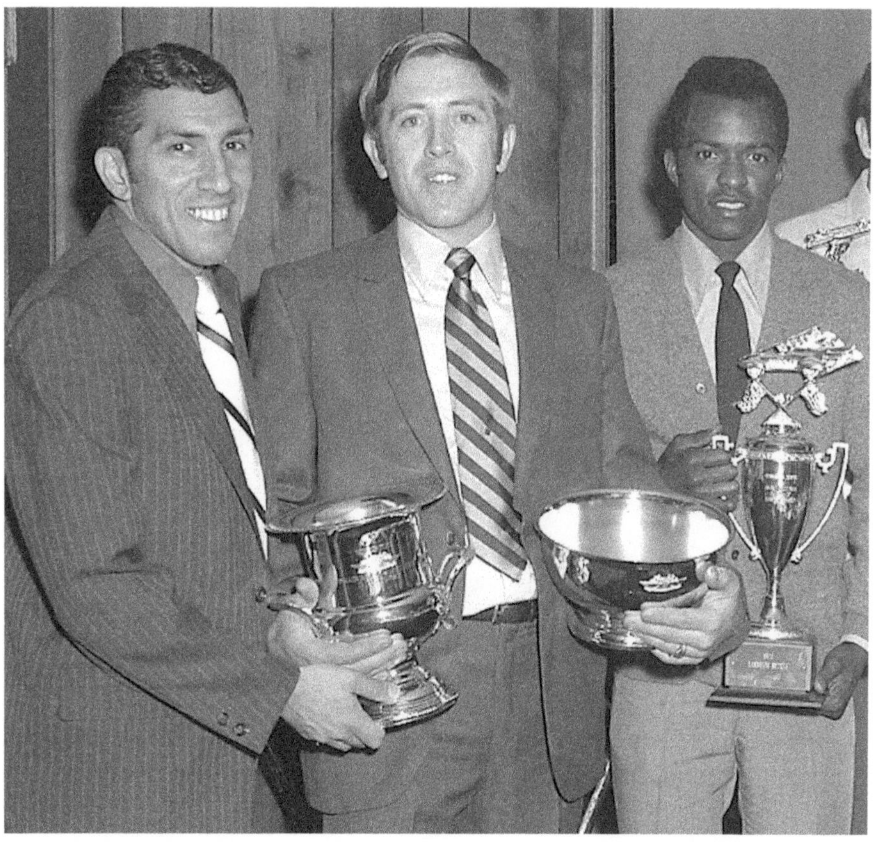

Promoter Don Naman (left) presents trophies to 1970 Tennessee state champion L.D. Ottinger (center) and Smoky Mountain Raceway Hobby champion Randy Bethea. *Ray Taylor photo.*

Twenty-seven miles away, Bobby Isaac let his race car do the talking, recording a dominant performance on the Smoky Mountain half mile before a grandstand filled with 7,300 race fans. Isaac started on the front row and led all two hundred laps, finishing a lap ahead of second-place James Hylton and third-place Neil Castles.

"We had a sellout for that race," Naman said years later. "We had cars lined up Highway 411 for miles trying to get into the track. It was an amazing experience."

A Brooklyn, New York native, Naman was introduced to stock car racing in 1960 while serving in the air force. He later moved to Tennessee to work as a photographer and began attending races at the Smoky Mountain track when

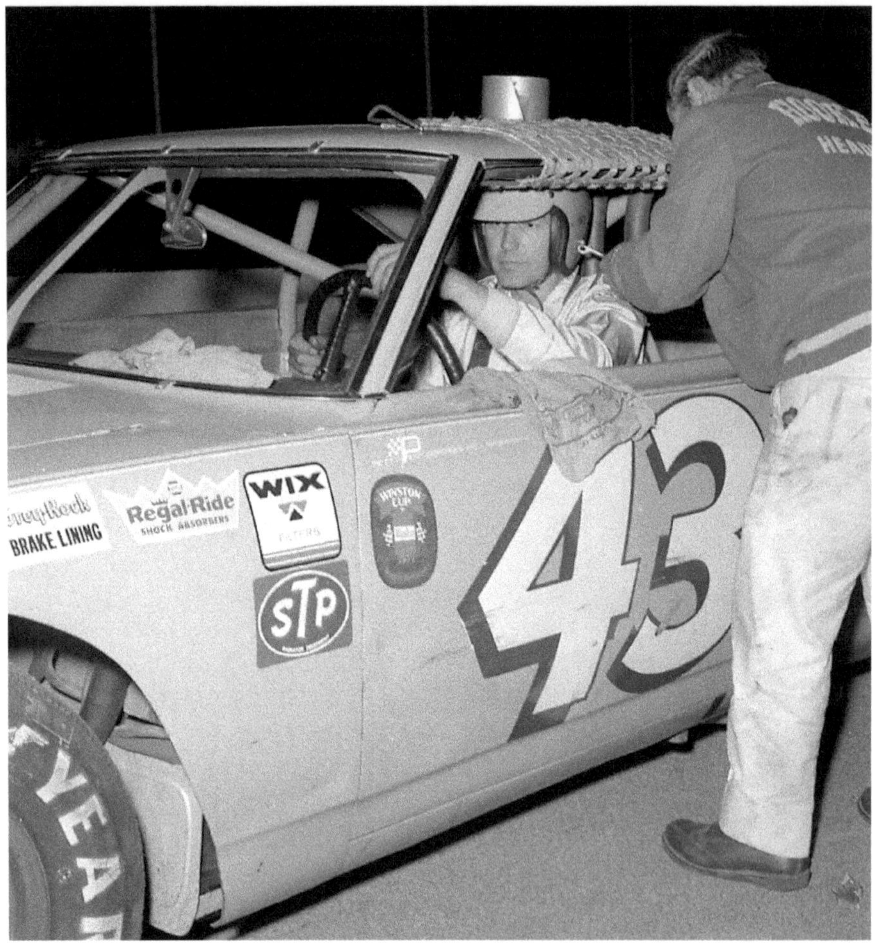

Richard Petty prepares to race his Plymouth in a NASCAR Grand National race at Smoky Mountain Raceway, where he won six times. *Ray Taylor photo.*

it opened in 1964. Quickly enamored, he became its promoter in 1965 and secured NASCAR sanction and a date on that season's Grand National schedule.

That first race couldn't have been worse, as heavy rains forced a one-day postponement and left the dirt surface rough and rutted. Dick Hutcherson survived to take the win, but only nine of twenty-four cars were running at the end. Two more Grand National races were run on dirt, with David Pearson and Paul Lewis picking up victories. The track was paved in 1967, and Richard Petty captured the first of his six Smoky Mountain trophies in June, as part of his twenty-seven-win season.

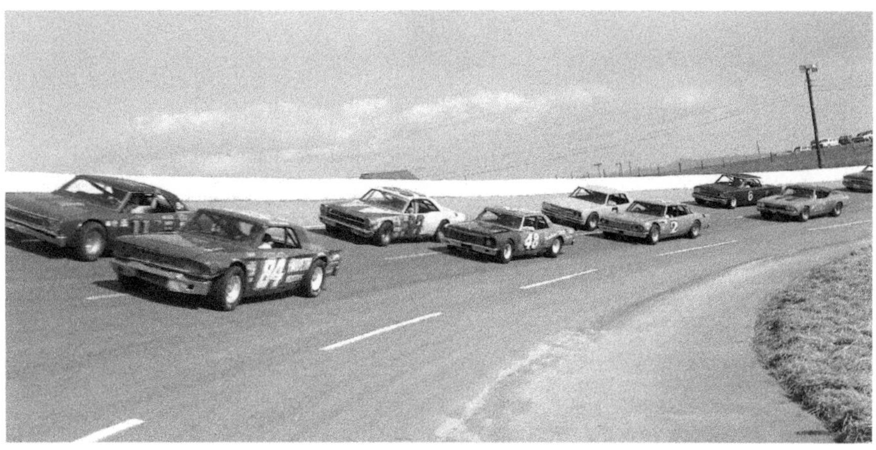

Flookie Buford (84), Hank Maxwell (11), Darrell Waltrip (48) and Red Farmer (97) lead the NASCAR Late Model Sportsman cars in a race won by L.D. Ottinger (2). *Ray Taylor photo.*

Likely the track's strangest, most widely known incident happened in 1968, after Buddy Baker blew a right front tire and his Ray Fox–owned Dodge slammed into the wall. Rescue workers got Baker out of the car, strapped him to a gurney and loaded him into the ambulance for a trip to Blount Memorial Hospital. After waiting for track workers to open a gate, the ambulance driver hit the gas, the back door flew open and Baker squirted out onto the track still strapped to the gurney. With race cars coming toward him, he slid down the track and tumbled into the infield, relatively unscathed.

As for Naman, NASCAR president Bill France Sr. flew to nearby McGhee-Tyson Airport after the 1970 sellout and offered him the general manager's job at France's new Alabama International Motor Speedway in Talladega. Naman accepted, holding that post for eighteen years and doing much to expand that track's popularity. He later served as executive director of the International Motorsports Hall of Fame, located on the speedway grounds.

"Don Naman was one of the nicest guys I ever met," said Herb Adcox, the Chattanooga auto dealer and father of driver Grant Adcox. "He really took care of Grant. We gave one of Grant's cars to the museum in Talladega just because of Don, and it's still there. He was good for racing. I don't believe he ever made an enemy of a driver."

15

Tragedy Times Two

Drivers accept the risk of dying every time they strap into a race car. It has been an unfortunate truth since auto racing began and, despite dramatic advances in safety, remains so today. That constant danger separates racing from traditional stick-and-ball sports is a topic most drivers refuse to discuss and, some might argue, provides an odd part of the sport's allure.

By sacrificing two of its favorite sons to the sport they dearly loved, the city of Chattanooga seems especially damned.

Raymond "Friday" Hassler built a reputation as a short-track superstar seemingly destined to repeat that success on stock car racing's biggest stages. Grant Adcox grew up around racing and enjoyed phenomenal success in the ARCA series but endured terrible tragedies during his NASCAR career. Both were lost amid the grinding report of metal against metal and metal against concrete.

Hassler's nickname "Friday" came from his work schedule at an auto body shop. He began racing in soap-box derbies and soon began to tackle the Modified class at Smoky Mountain Raceway, the Nashville Fairgrounds Speedway, Bristol International Speedway and Birmingham International Raceway in Alabama. Now in the 1960s, a regular Saturday night show at Birmingham regularly included national Modified champion Bobby Allison, his brother Donnie, Red Farmer, Freddy and Harold Fryar, Bob Burcham, Joe Lee Johnson and Charles Griffith.

Hassler and new car owner Red Sharp put together a 1955 Chevrolet that carried them to back-to-back Birmingham championships in 1965

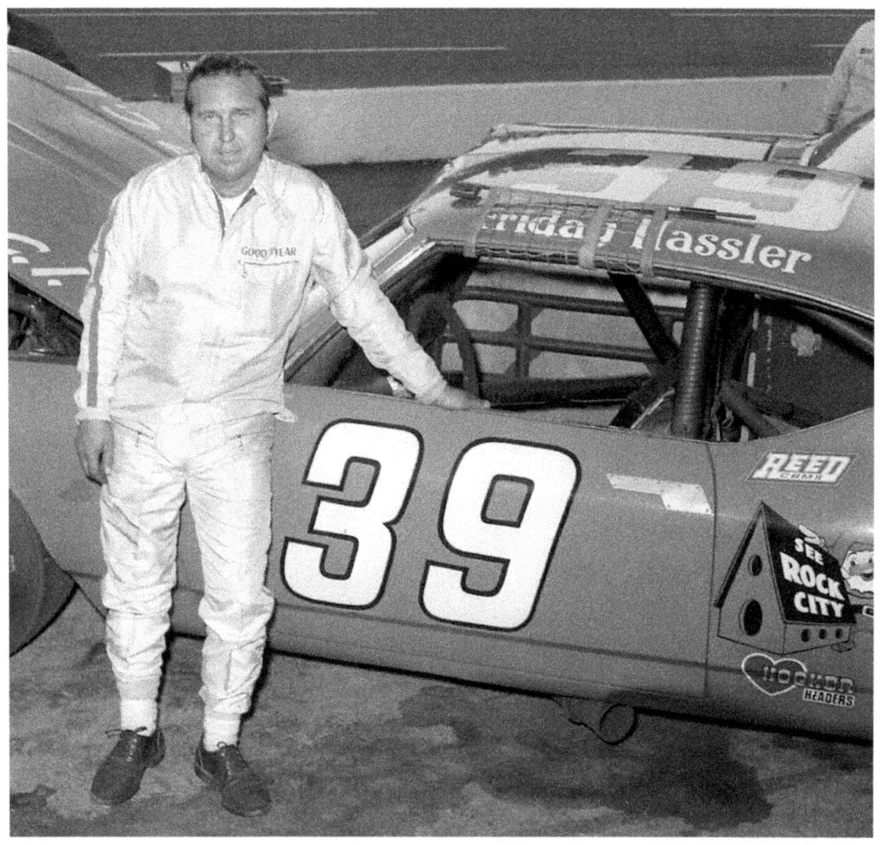

Raymond "Friday" Hassler was a terror on southeastern short tracks but had a solid NASCAR career ended by a tragic accident at Daytona in 1972. *Ray Taylor photo.*

and 1966. During one stretch—from July 4, 1965, to July 4, 1966—Hassler earned twenty-three consecutive victories.

How tough was it? Allison won NASCAR's 1965 championship, while Farmer and Hassler finished second and fourth in the national standings. Hassler won the 1966 Birmingham title, finished tenth at another Alabama track but only wound up in the top twenty nationally.

Sharp then built a 1966 Chevelle, and the duo advanced to the NASCAR Grand National circuit. Although wins eluded them, they posted multiple top-five and top-ten finishes during 1967 and 1968. After splitting up, Hassler enjoyed success in his own car.

In fact, Hassler's red 1969 Chevelle appeared on the cover of *Stock Car Racing* magazine's July 1971 issue beneath a headline branding him

"Chevy's Last Hope." The accompanying profile defined Hassler as the lone competitive General Motors driver on a NASCAR circuit dominated by the factory-supported Plymouth of Richard Petty, the Dodge of Bobby Isaac and the Ford of David Pearson.

With its three-month advance schedule, the magazine's editors weren't aware another Chevrolet—a white-and-red 1971 Monte Carlo prepared by Junior Johnson and driven by Charlie Glotzbach—was about to burst on the scene or that Hassler would play an integral role in Chevrolet's first Grand National triumph in a decade.

The magazine hit newsstands around Memorial Day weekend, just as Glotzbach and Johnson took the wraps off their new car and qualified fastest at the World 600. Now having a competitive Chevrolet made the turnstiles click because diehard fans flocked to see the new "Chevalay." Glotzbach led four times for eighty-seven laps that day, but a crash ended the party early.

Nearly lost in the shuffle was Hassler's solid top-ten finish in the debut of his new Chevelle.

Both were in the field a few weeks later when the tour arrived in Bristol for the Volunteer 500. Glotzbach lived up to his considerable prerace hype by qualifying on the front row alongside Richard Petty, while Hassler timed in eleventh quickest. In the race, Hassler fell out with wheel bearing failure after just 104 laps.

Glotzbach, meanwhile, took the lead from Petty on lap 44 and established a relentless pace that soon took a toll on his neck, which was still sore from the Charlotte accident. He radioed to ask for relief, and Hassler, who drove a few practice laps in the car earlier in the weekend, was ready when Glotzbach pitted on lap 255.

Bobby Allison inherited the lead during the driver exchange, but Hassler retook it on lap 281. The two swapped the top spot again before Allison pitted for relief from James Hylton. Hassler never relinquished the lead after lap 357, finishing three laps ahead of Allison's Ford in the fastest race ever run at Bristol—500 laps without a caution flag—at a 101.074-mile-per-hour average speed. Standing on the hood of that Monte Carlo, smiling for photographers and sharing the Bristol trophy would prove the penultimate moment in Hassler's career.

Automakers withdrew their support prior to the 1972 NASCAR season opener in Riverside, California. Independent Hassler responded with a ninth-place finish in his first visit to the road course. Buoyed by that success, Hassler headed to Florida for the Daytona 500.

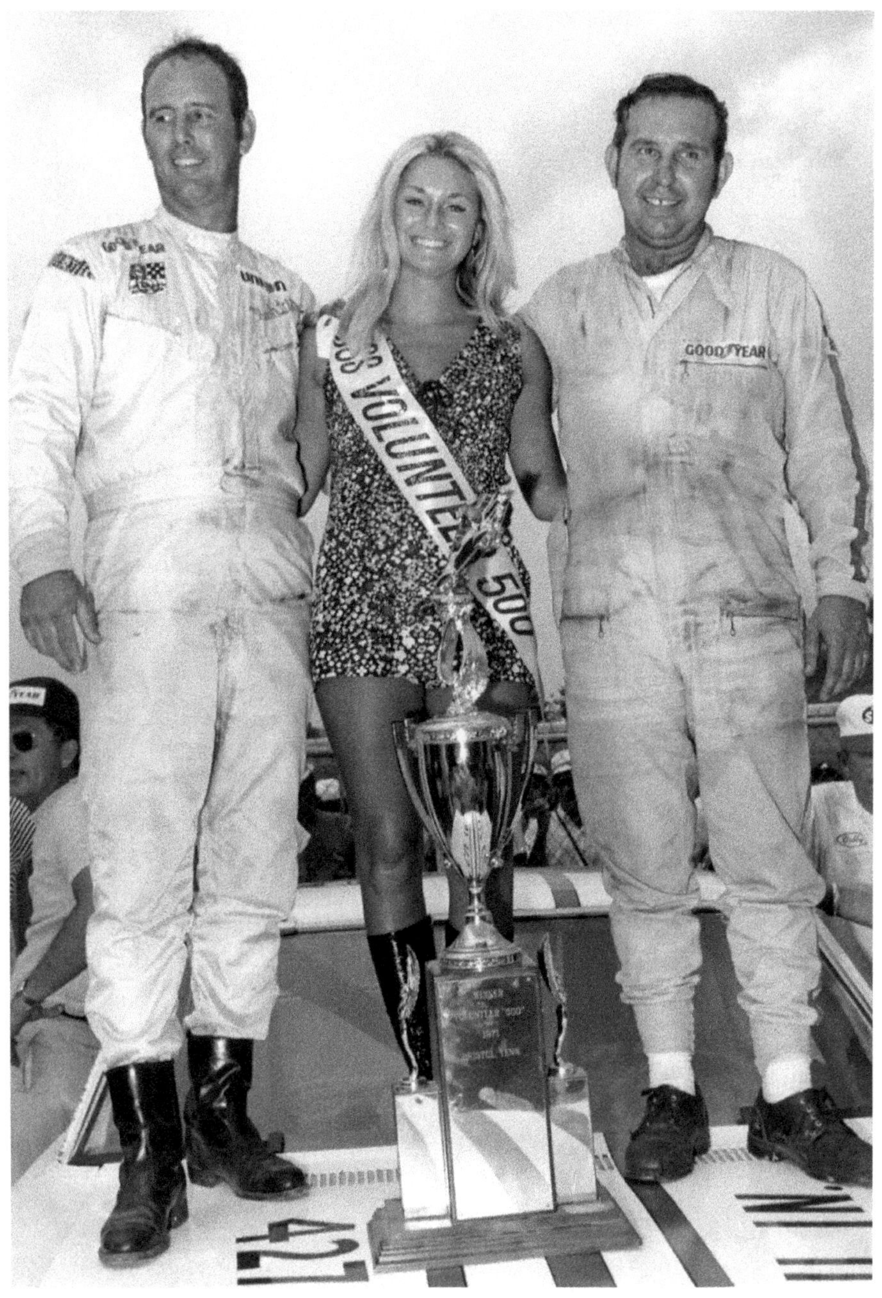

Friday Hassler (right) was a relief driver for Charlie Glotzbach (left) when they won the fastest race in Bristol history in July 1971. *John Beach photo.*

Hassler's wife, Joanne, would later say something was different, that her husband seemed apprehensive.

Running in the middle of a large pack of cars during the first of two 125-mile Thursday qualifying races, Hassler was collected in a thirteen-car crash. His Chevelle momentarily appeared in the clear as smoke billowed beneath it. The car abruptly turned right, struck the backstretch wall, spun around and was slammed by the Dodge of Jimmy Crawford.

G.C. Spencer thought he'd missed the wreck until another car knocked his Dodge into the infield grass. Dazed, Spencer looked up and saw his friend's mangled Chevrolet. He climbed from his own wreckage and ran onto the track toward Hassler, who was slumped over the steering wheel. Spencer began waving frantically for rescue workers, but it was too late. Hassler was dead at age thirty-six.

On a sunny Sunday afternoon, ninety-eight thousand watched five hundred miles of racing unfold in Florida while some five hundred miles to the north in Chattanooga, Joanne Hassler buried her husband.

Grant Adcox also grew up around the East Tennessee racing scene, thanks to his father, Herb, a successful auto dealer who loved racing and had sponsored Joe Lee Johnson, Freddy Fryar and others.

"I used to take Grant to the races when he was slightly larger than a baby," Herb Adcox recalled. "We would go to the dirt tracks around Knoxville on Friday and Saturday nights. Some of the drivers were very famous in that area. We'd come home, but we couldn't go to bed because Mama would make us take a bath because we'd be completely covered up with that dirt. So he got an early start."

A few years later, one of the dealership mechanics asked the senior Adcox to sponsor another race car.

"He and his father fooled around with racing. He asked me to help him, and I did. When they got it completed, he said come out and see the car run Friday night. Well who was the driver? My son. He was about sixteen at the time. I had no idea he was going to drive it," Adcox said.

Grant's early Late Model Sportsman career included racing against Friday Hassler at short tracks like Smoky Mountain, but Adcox ultimately found his greatest success on the sport's fastest tracks. He recorded eight of his nine ARCA series wins and four poles on the superspeedways of Daytona, Talladega, Michigan and Atlanta.

In 1986, Adcox established an ARCA record with four superspeedway wins in a single season. It began at Daytona, where he qualified third quickest and outran polesitter Ralph Jones, who was driving a Ford prepared by

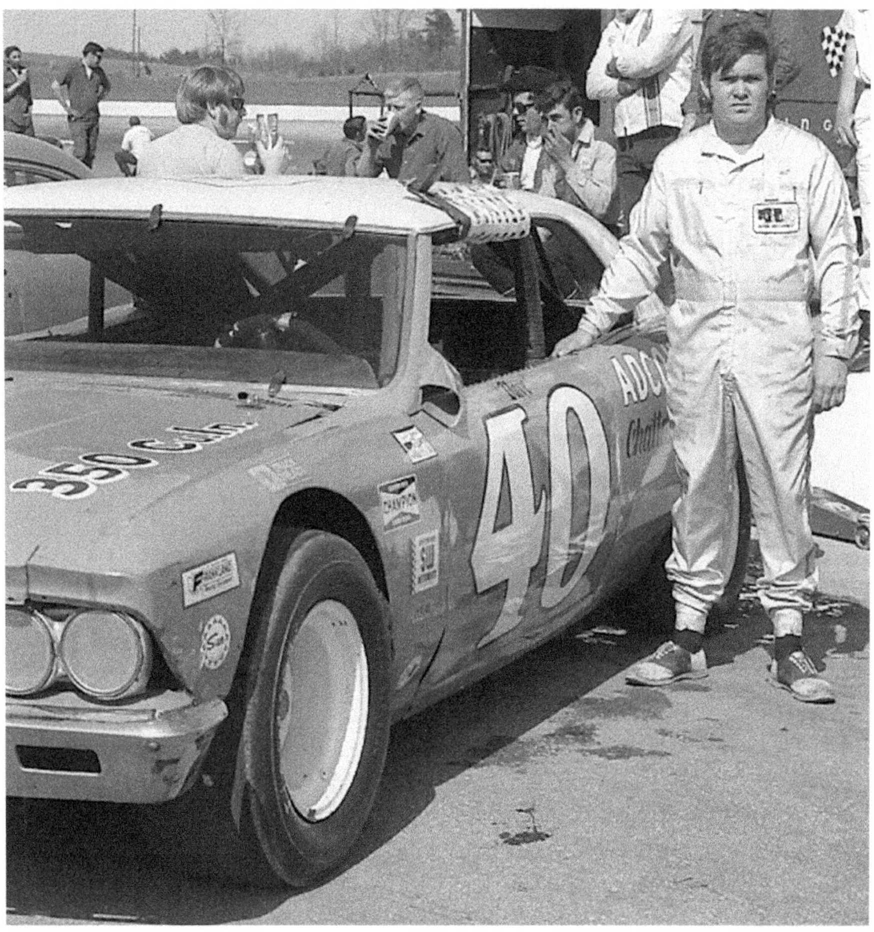

Grant Adcox attended races as a baby and began racing in the Late Model Sportsman class at Smoky Mountain Raceway. *Ray Taylor photo.*

NASCAR stars Bill and Ernie Elliott. In the season's first visit to Talladega, Adcox led 100 of 117 laps to defeat future NASCAR standout Davey Allison.

Adcox held off top qualifier David Simko's Chevrolet during ARCA's second stop at the 2.66-mile Talladega superspeedway and then captured the pole and win during that season's final race in Atlanta.

He reprised two of those victories in 1987, sweeping both races at Talladega. In May, he qualified second and led Charlie Glotzbach and Red Farmer to the checkered flag. Starting from the pole that July, Adcox led 87 of 117 circuits and again beat Simko.

Subsequent poles came at Daytona and Talladega, as did more wins at Talladega and Atlanta. Adcox collected his final checkered flag in August 1989 for his lone ARCA short-track victory at Michigan's Flat Rock Speedway.

Adcox remains ARCA's most successful driver at Talladega, with five wins, including those amazing four straight.

"I attribute that to friendships like Waddell Wilson and Robert Yates," Herb Adcox said. "You could take one of their used engines and usually beat about anybody else. Having the right connections and right friendships was important. I remember when we first started, tires were fifty dollars, and that was a hell of a lot of money in the 1970s. They [Cup teams] would go out and practice on them and then sell them to Grant."

In 1987 and '88, Adcox won ARCA's Bill France Four Crown Award for outstanding runs on the diverse range of tracks where the series competes.

Yet for all that success, tragedy stalked Adcox when he raced in NASCAR, beginning with his rookie season in 1974. In just his fourth Cup start—the Winston 500 in Talladega—Adcox came down pit road and braked to enter his pit just as his orange-and-white Chevrolet rolled across a patch of oil and water. The car veered left and slammed into the rear of Gary Bettenhausen's Matador, trapping catch-can man Don Miller between the two cars and injuring two other crew members on the Roger Penske–owned team.

Miller was taken to the hospital, where his right leg was amputated. A distraught Adcox withdrew and raced only once more that season.

Adcox scored the first of his six NASCAR top-ten finishes in his family-owned Chevrolet in the 1975 Winston 500 at Talladega. But a different kind of tragedy struck the Adcox team when it returned to Alabama in August. After qualifying nineteenth, crew chief Gene Lovell suffered a fatal heart attack in the team's garage area. They withdrew, as rain washed out the event.

The young driver's spot in the lineup went to former Daytona 500 winner Dwayne "Tiny" Lund, who was driving a Dodge owned by East Tennessean A.J. King. It was the first time King fielded a Cup series car since the late 1960s, when Paul Lewis, Bobby Isaac and Pete Hamilton were among his drivers.

The following weekend, racing from Adcox's starting spot, Lund was involved in a six-car crash on the backstretch. As he spun back up the racetrack, his car was violently struck in the driver's side door by rookie driver Terry Link. Lund died of massive chest injuries a short time later.

"Tiny and I raced the night before somewhere," NASCAR standout L.D. Ottinger recalled. "He said he didn't really want to run that race, but he needed the money. Dang if he didn't wind up getting killed."

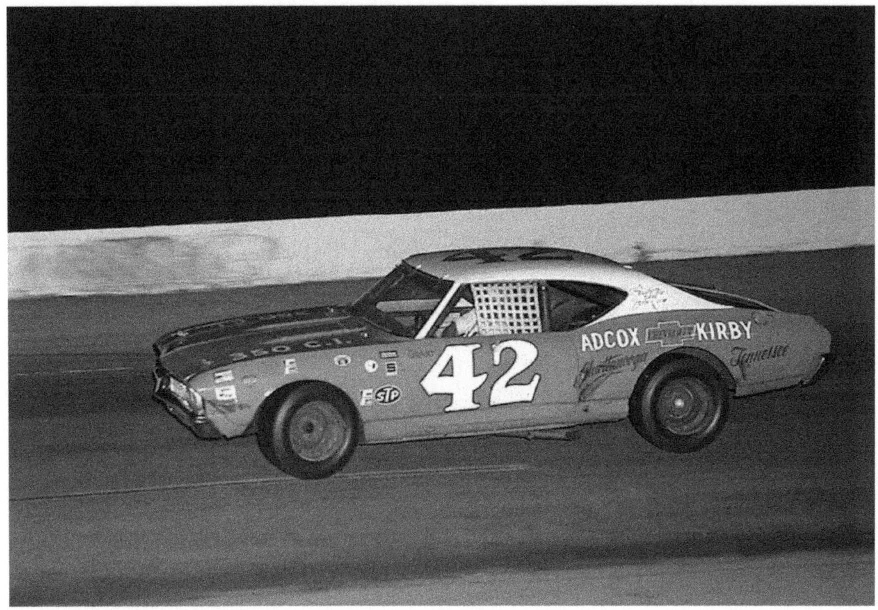

Chattanooga's Grant Adcox raced in both NASCAR and ARCA but lost his life in a tragic crash at Atlanta in 1989. *Ray Taylor photo.*

Adcox competed sparingly in NASCAR throughout the 1980s.

He was running four laps down in the 1989 NASCAR Atlanta Journal 500 when his orange-and-white Oldsmobile slammed the outer concrete wall. The impact damaged its suspension, ripped the passenger-side window from the car and fractured an oil line, sparking a fire as the car rolled down the track, across the apron and onto the infield grass.

Drivers who are OK after a crash lower their window net, but Adcox wasn't able. At the moment of impact, his racing seat ripped loose from its mounting brackets, and he was thrown into the steering wheel at 150 miles per hour. He suffered significant head and upper chest trauma and, after being extricated from the car, was flown to Georgia Baptist Hospital in Atlanta, where he was pronounced dead.

Grant Adcox was thirty-nine, the same as the number Hassler ran on his cars for much of his career.

ARCA named its Sportsman of the Year Award to honor him.

Through it all, Herb Adcox still attends races at Daytona, Talladega and, yes, Atlanta.

"Racing has been good to me. It was good to him except when we lost him," Herb said. "I enjoyed it so much because he enjoyed it so much. I felt like I was part of it—I was right in that car along with him. If you could talk to him, I think he'd say, 'Tell my dad to continue going to the race track.'"

16

It Was a Good Run

Standing behind North Wilkesboro Speedway's pit wall on a sunny Sunday afternoon in 1973, Travis Tiller was preparing to climb into his own Winston Cup stock car and share the track with the sport's legendary drivers. He'd worked and saved enough money to buy a refurbished Dodge Charger from Buddy Arrington and was about to make his maiden voyage, right after he put on his driver's uniform.

"Buddy qualified the car and did most of the practice to get it set up. I might have drove it six or eight laps," Tiller said. "Buddy started the race and then came in after the first lap. I didn't even have my suit on and my helmet on. I didn't expect him that soon. So he went back out for a couple of laps, came back in and I got in. That was the first time I'd really driven the car and my first time in traffic. You talk about raw, that was raw."

Tiller finished twenty-sixth in that thirty-car field, completing 335 of 400 laps before engine problems set in. The thirty-six-year-old marine corps veteran, business owner and NASCAR neophyte admitted nothing he'd ever done prepared him for rubbing fenders with racing's elite.

"I had no idea what I was getting into," Tiller said. "We went to Charlotte after that, and it was so fast. It was all bigger than life, and I was just trying to figure it out. I didn't know what I was getting into."

Tiller's first brush with NASCAR racing occurred a decade earlier, listening to radio broadcasters describe the scenes of Fireball Roberts, Rex White and Richard Petty battling wheel to wheel.

"I was in the marine corps stationed at Quantico, Virginia," Tiller recalled. "In that area, it was hard to find a station that carried the races, so on Sundays, I would drive toward Fredericksburg or Richmond to listen to the NASCAR races on the radio."

He grew up attending stock car races in Florida with his uncle, drag-raced a 1957 Ford and drove another Ford at a northern Virginia oval track, but he dreamed of competing with his Sunday afternoon heroes.

"Those broadcasts just inflamed it more. I knew I wanted to do it. Going about it and getting there was the biggest challenge for me. Just taking the step, but I did it strictly on my own, right out of the clear blue with no sponsors and nobody to encourage me," he said.

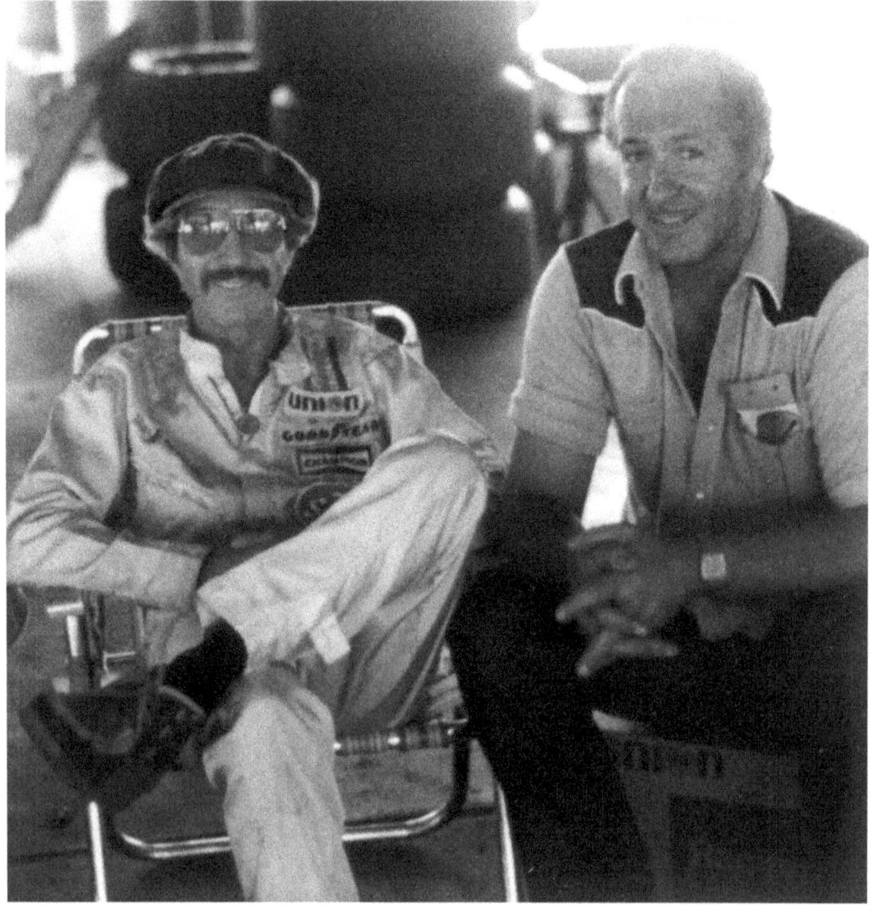

Travis Tiller (right) is seen with fellow racer and country music singer Marty Robbins. *Courtesy Travis Tiller.*

After eight years in the corps, Tiller built and operated drag strips in Tennessee and Virginia, ran a trucking operation and became a partner in a paving business in suburban Washington, D.C. After three years, he sold his interest in the paving company, drove straight to Buddy Arrington's Virginia race shop and picked up a Dodge Charger built and raced by Bobby Allison and, later, Marty Robbins.

After a couple starts in 1973, Tiller qualified for fourteen of thirty races in his rookie season but dropped out of twelve with some type of mechanical problem. Tiller's career-best Cup finish was a twelfth that year at the old Richmond, Virginia fairgrounds, but his bid for rookie of the year fell short for failing to make the minimum twenty races.

In a decade behind the wheel, Tiller never went to victory lane, never led a lap, never posted a top-ten finish nor finished on the lead lap in his more than fifty Grand National starts. Through the 1970s and early 1980s, Tiller was there helping make the sport's foundation as solid as the streets he once paved.

"If my car was ready to go and I had the money, I went. There was a lot of races where I didn't make the race. A lot of it was I didn't have a new set of tires to qualify on. I didn't miss going to very many, but I didn't always make the field," he said. "I struggled along. At that time, it was racing on a shoestring, and it was mighty thin. I came back to Southwest Virginia in 1975 and got into the coal business. I stayed on a shoestring. It was a rough go, but I enjoyed it more than anything I've ever enjoyed in my life."

There was scarcely any sponsorship and never a plane ride home.

"I'd always load up and come back as soon as the race was over with. I had to be back to go to work on Monday morning. Then you'd work on the race car half the night after work," Tiller said. "I was in business for myself, so it took more than a day's work to keep you going. It was a lot of hours. It was a struggle all those years."

The independents of his era did it strictly out of love.

"Ninety-nine percent were true strugglers like I was, but they were dedicated to the sport. They'd spent their life and their money to run the races. It was a lifestyle. All of them probably had a little job to help on the side, and some did work for other people at their shops to support their racing," he said.

Tiller was credited with ten starts in 1975, nine in 1976 and three in 1977. He sat out the 1978 season before making a handful of starts during each of the following five years. At superspeedways, he often raced the same car in the companion ARCA races, posting a solid twelfth-place finish at Talladega in 1976.

"All the equipment I had was worn out," he said. "I had a lot of overheating problems, but I couldn't afford to buy a new radiator. So I'd have to have it cleaned out. I finally bought a good used radiator."

Tiller campaigned that lone original Dodge from 1973 through the 1979 season, thanks in part to some generosity, since NASCAR had an age limit on cars. One day, Tiller drove to Petty Enterprises in Level Cross, North Carolina, seeking some sheet metal to reskin his aging Charger with a new Dodge Magnum body mandated by NASCAR. His list was short: a hood, two door skins, quarter panels, a top, a trunk lid, two bumpers and two rocker panels.

"Richard took my list, and he told me it wasn't enough. [He told me] that I needed more than two fenders and two doors, in case something happened," Tiller recalled. "I told him I couldn't afford any more than that, but he told those boys to put more stuff on my truck. I told him I couldn't afford it, and they would have to take some of it back."

When they handed Petty the paper, he said, "I didn't know it [would] be this much," and wrote, "Paid in full." Three decades later, Tiller's eyes still moisten as he tells that story.

"Richard Petty has always been and always will be my hero. He was always nice to me, but I guess he was always nice to everybody," Tiller said.

The Dodge was eventually replaced with an Oldsmobile, and after NASCAR downsized the cars in 1981, he raced a Buick and a Chevrolet.

Tiller became good friends with Marty Robbins, the late Grand Ole Opry singer and part-time race driver. Tiller cherishes a photo of himself, Robbins and Blackie Wangerin taken at Daytona in 1980, the same year a heart attack claimed Robbins.

Doing "99 percent" of the race car maintenance himself with only a few volunteer crew members, Tiller persevered through 1983. For the underfunded independents, everything from meals to travel arrangements was a challenge.

"There were a couple guys who would go with me or show up on the weekend. We'd usually end up with one or two motel rooms, and we ate a lot of bologna sandwiches and hoped whoever was parked next to us in the garage had a big budget," he said.

If there was a track, Tiller raced on it, but he preferred the short tracks to the larger, faster superspeedways.

"Most of the time you ran where you felt comfortable, hoped to survive the whole race and make enough money to go to the next one," he said. "You made sure those boys had your cans full of gas, so you'd make a pit stop late, but not with ten or fifteen laps to go because they wouldn't fill your gas cans up. You wanted that to put in the truck to get home. If you didn't qualify, you had to siphon gas out of your race car to get home on."

Tiller was also a part of a racing milestone, introducing the sport to a family of Virginia car dealers who went on to form Morgan-McClure Motorsports.

"Morgan-McClure had the Chevrolet dealership there in Coeburn, Virginia. They gave me a little bit of sponsor money, and I went to a couple of races for them. In Darlington, they gave me $1,200, and I finished fifteenth," Tiller said. They became one of the sport's preeminent teams of the 1990s.

Like most independents, there was no farewell tour nor commemorative souvenirs marking Tiller's departure from the sport he loved. He just stopped showing up.

"Money was the biggest reason I quit. It just got to be too much, and the coal business had slacked down a little bit," Tiller said. "I always said if I'd had good equipment, I could have run with any of them. And I feel sure there's a lot of other guys who could have, but it was a good run."

17

Kingsport's Golden Era

Few of life's events were actually as wonderful as rosy hindsight often suggests, except possibly Kingsport Speedway's golden era, from the late 1960s through the early 1980s. Former drivers, fans and officials universally pine for the time when the track was the very epicenter of NASCAR's Late Model Sportsman universe.

Winning races or a track championship is always an accomplishment, but that era was something special. Locals and invaders alike used those victories against all-star fields as springboards to national titles. Most years, about half the drivers ranked in the top ten nationally were Kingsport regulars. Six-time national champion and NASCAR Hall of Fame inductee Jack Ingram won Kingsport points titles in 1980 and 1981.

"Kingsport was as tough as any place in the country, and I ran at them all," Ingram said. "You had all the guys who traveled, and the locals were all good."

The centrally located speedway regularly attracted touring heavyweights, including Ingram, Jimmy Hensley, Morgan Shepherd, Sam Ard, Harry Gant, Butch Lindley, Tommy Houston, Bob Pressley and young Dale Earnhardt. But they found no easy pickings, encountering Gene Glover, Paul Lewis, Hank Maxwell, L.D. Ottinger, Mike Potter, Connie Saylor, Paul Shull, Brad Teague, John A. Utsman and Larry Utsman, among others.

"Kingsport, when everybody ran over there, had to be the best racing that's ever been—anywhere. I'm just thankful I got to be a part of it," said John A. Utsman, the 1972 track champion. "I didn't win all the time, but I won my share."

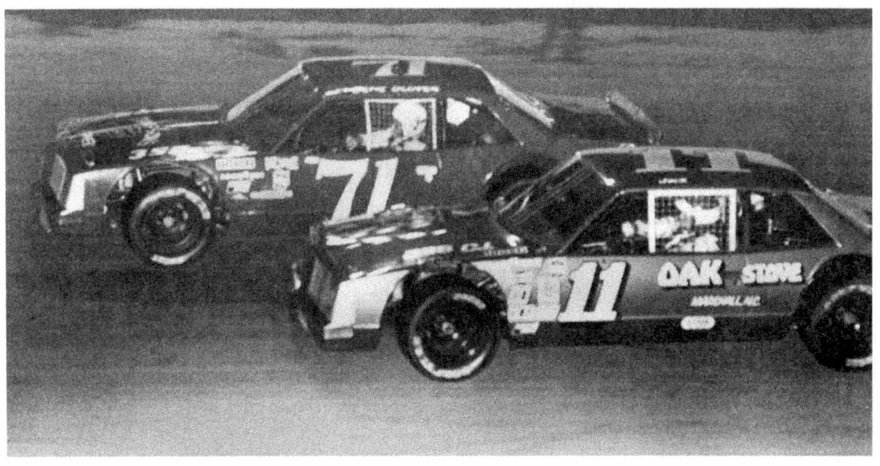

National champions Jack Ingram (11) and Gene Glover (71) battled often at Kingsport Speedway during the 1970s. *Mike O'Dell photo.*

Kingsport was tough in more ways than one. The track was short and narrow, so winning often meant using the bumper to move someone out of the way and postrace disagreements were sometimes settled with fists.

"You didn't know who was going to win, but you always knew that Jack Ingram and Harry Gant would be up front. I held my own, and when I drove Ed Whitaker's car, the last race I ran over there was a two-hundred-lapper. I wound up winning, Jack was second and Harry was third. If you could beat them, that was something to say, because they were tough," Utsman said.

Under NASCAR's unique program, drivers could accumulate points at weekly races and also at about thirty to forty national championship events. Kingsport typically hosted up to four of the national races each year in addition to its weekly shows. NASCAR points were also available an hour away at Lonesome Pine International Raceway in Coeburn, Virginia, enticing many to run both tracks each weekend.

Despite a four-hour drive from his home in Ridgeway, Virginia, Hensley raced at Kingsport nearly every week, winning three consecutive track titles from 1974 to 1976.

"There was a gang there every Friday night. I loved Kingsport. I won a lot of races there. It was a big deal because you had so many guys there capable of winning races," Hensley said, adding that he found the groove during his first-ever visit.

"We sat on the pole the first time I went there. We ran Manassas the night before. We hadn't been to bed [and] then drove all night to get to Kingsport for a Sunday afternoon race. Back then, you didn't do much to the car. We even ran the same tires we'd run the night before because we didn't have a lot of money. The old car handled pretty good, and I just adapted to it."

Kingsport's close quarters often produced bent fenders and hurt feelings. Large crowds came to see what would happen on the track and afterward in the pits. Utsman, for example, took offense to the actions of eventual national champion L.D. Ottinger.

"He put me out for no reason at all one night at Kingsport," Utsman said "I went over after the race and asked him if the track wasn't wide enough for both of us to race on. He said he thought he was farther ahead than he was, and it was his fault. I said, 'I know it was your fault. But you can afford to do that. You've got sponsors. I don't have, and I don't appreciate what you done.'

"The next week, he had his new car there, I still sat on the pole, which was six weeks in a row, and we got into a fender beatin'-bangin' duel. The first caution come out, and he was ahead. On the restart, he did one of those deals where you take off then hit his brakes. Well, Jimmy Hensley and Brad Teague both got around me. I passed Brad back, [and] then I ran Jimmy for seventy laps and got around him. I ran L.D. down, but I didn't have a chance of passing him."

After the race, Utsman lodged a protest against Ottinger's car, so Ottinger did likewise.

"We tore him down after the race, and he tore me down. But I was legal, and he was illegal. So I still wound up winning. That's when racing was really good fun," Utsman said.

Ottinger won Kingsport track titles in 1970 and 1973 and then back-to-back national championships in 1975–76. Hometown driver Glover won the 1978 track crown while finishing third in the national points. The following year, Glover took the national title. Another local racer and past track champion, Brad Teague, finished second in the national standings in 1981.

Among Kingsport's national race winners were Geoff Bodine, Tommy Ellis, Gant, Tommy Houston, Lindley, Pressley and locals Teague and Larry Utsman.

"I grew up on Late Model Sportsman racing going with my dad. I was a little kid, and you had all the top stars from the Carolinas come over and race at Kingsport all the time," sportswriter Jeff Birchfield said.

Kingsport's path to greatness began humbly in 1965, when it opened as a quarter-mile dirt track where local hot shots Glover, Bill Morton, Ken Hunley and Utsman raced Modifieds alongside a young Georgia driver named Buck Simmons. But track founder Ken Murray longed for something more, so in 1968, he expanded the track to three-eighths of a mile and added facing grandstands, much like Bristol's nearby NASCAR oval. Kingsport also gained NASCAR sanction and crowned Morton and Glover as its first NASCAR track champions, in Late Model and Modified, respectively.

NASCAR's new Grand Touring division for Chevrolet Camaros and Ford Mustangs was Kingsport's first series race on June 4, 1968. Slated for 267 laps around the reconfigured dirt oval, things didn't go smoothly.

Activities started four hours late as crews completed work on the track surface, and qualifying was rained out. So drivers drew for starting positions. The rough surface prompted Donnie Allison and Tiny Lund to withdraw. The green flag finally flew at 10:30 p.m., and the remainder of the field soldiered on until nearly midnight. Rather than risk breaking the track's curfew, officials stopped the race at lap 186 and declared Buck Baker the winner. He finished six laps ahead of second-place Roy Tyner and ten laps ahead of third-place Jim Vandiver—all driving Camaros—while Jack Ryan finished fourth in a Porsche.

The track was paved in 1969, and the GT series christened the new asphalt in April with a 500-lap torture test. While T.C. Hunt gets credit for the victory, he actually became ill before the halfway point, and crew member Russell Nelson wheeled the team's Camaro the final 325 laps. The caution flag flew twelve times for a total of 73 laps, often for multiple accidents on the same lap. Billy Yuma finished second, and fast qualifier Tiny Lund ran third in a Mercury Cougar prepared by Bud Moore.

That set the stage for the June 19, 1969 arrival of NASCAR's Grand National division for the Kingsport 250. The race was on a Thursday night, run between a 500-miler at Michigan International Speedway and a two-hundred-lap Saturday show at the half-mile dirt Greenville-Pickens Speedway in South Carolina.

A crowd of 8,500—nearly twice the announced GT race attendance—saw Richard Petty capitalize on Bobby Isaac's misfortune and claim the ninety-fifth win of his career. Isaac was the fast qualifier and led the first 187 laps, but he dropped out with engine failure in his K&K Insurance Dodge. Petty won by a lap over second-place John Sears and third-place David Pearson, all driving Fords.

NASCAR returned to Kingsport three times in 1970, with the GT cars rebranded as the Grand American series in May, followed by a Grand National encore in June and another Grand American show in September.

In the first race, Tiny Lund collected a Kingsport trophy driving his Camaro past the Cougar of Wayne Andrews. It was one of nineteen wins in thirty-five series starts for Lund that season. Fast qualifier Jim Paschal fell out early with mechanical problems in his Javelin.

A few weeks later, Petty dominated the 297-lap Grand National race, qualifying his Plymouth on the pole and leading 263 laps. Bobby Isaac was again a contender but blew a tire, hit the wall and settled for an eighth-place finish. James Hylton finished second, Dave Marcis was third and Bobby Allison and Neil Castles rounded out the top five. About 6,200 people attended the Friday night race, which had just two cautions for fourteen laps.

One relieved fan also got his front fender back unscathed. During practice, one driver scraped the wall, and NASCAR wouldn't allow him to race his Plymouth Roadrunner without the fender, which was too bent to repair. The announcer then asked if anyone drove a Roadrunner and would be willing to loan his fender, fan and photographer Chris Haverly recalled.

"So some guy out of the stands pulls his new Roadrunner down in the pits, they took the fender off and bolted it on the race car. It was the wildest thing I'd ever seen, but he got it back after the race," Haverly said.

The Grand American Series made its final Kingsport stop on Labor Day weekend 1970 as Jim Paschal exorcised past gremlins and drove his red, white and blue Javelin to victory over Wayne Andrews. Paschal led 249 of the race's 297 laps and scored his ninth win of the season. Buck Baker finished third after leading forty-seven circuits. Tiny Lund was the fastest qualifier but dropped out with a fuel pump failure.

NASCAR's top series underwent substantial changes in 1971, after sponsor R.J. Reynolds Tobacco and its Winston cigarette brand became the title sponsor. While it brought significant marketing and promotional dollars, the Winston Cup Series included only events of 250 miles or more. Drivers could still earn Grand National points at short-track events like Kingsport, but it and many tracks like it were about to be squeezed out as the sport ushered in its so-called modern era.

When the 1971 schedules were released, Kingsport originally had two Grand National dates—May 23 and October 3—but the second race never occurred, and NASCAR's Grand American Series also wasn't scheduled to return.

Much like Jim Paschal in 1970, Bobby Isaac finally collected his Kingsport debt that May. The defending Grand National champion captured the pole for the second time in three years and led 294 of the race's 300 laps. Richard Petty's Kingsport win streak evaporated in a cloud of smoke when the rear end of his Plymouth seized. Elmo Langley finished second, five laps behind the winner, as just 3,800 fans looked on.

The Late Model Sportsman series reached full bloom at Kingsport through the 1970s, but the track was also one of a handful of southern ovals to host the NASCAR Modified series. Seven-time national champion Richie Evans won there in 1979, while Geoff Bodine won the track's initial 250-lap Modified feature in November 1976. Ron Bouchard won Kingsport's other two Modified races, in 1977 and 1978.

Kingsport's golden era ended in 1982, when the Late Model Sportsman class evolved into the Busch Series. The track was sold to former NASCAR team owner J.D. Stacy, who converted it back to dirt.

18

Two-Time Champion

Three things stand out when L.D. Ottinger reflects on his NASCAR Late Model Sportsman career: the two national championships he won and the one he didn't.

Ottinger dominated the 1975 and 1976 seasons, winning a combined twenty-seven times in 140 races. Driving Chevrolets sponsored by coal magnate Kenny Childers and Black Diamond Coal of Bluefield, Virginia, Ottinger's consecutive titles represent the zenith of a forty-year career.

"I raced for the coal miner for three years and won the championships in 1975 and '76, and I wish I had stayed in '77 because I had the lead for six or eight weeks and didn't run a race," Ottinger said. "That would have been three straight times with the championship. Not too many have done that."

In truth, it might have been four consecutive championships because Childers and crew chief Ken Hunley teamed with Butch Lindley in 1977, and he steered the coal car to titles that season and the following year. A combination of frustration and health issues prompted Ottinger's early exit.

"I regretted it later because I just got fed up with it, and I was getting sick with ulcers," Ottinger said. "The guys were good. We should have won half those speedway races, but our strategy just wasn't good. They'd run me out of gas or wouldn't come into the pits at the right time."

Chasing a championship in that series required racing both close to home and traveling, so many teams competed three or four times each week. Ottinger ranked in the national top ten for seven straight seasons, which often meant racing Thursdays in Huntsville, Alabama; Fridays at Kingsport;

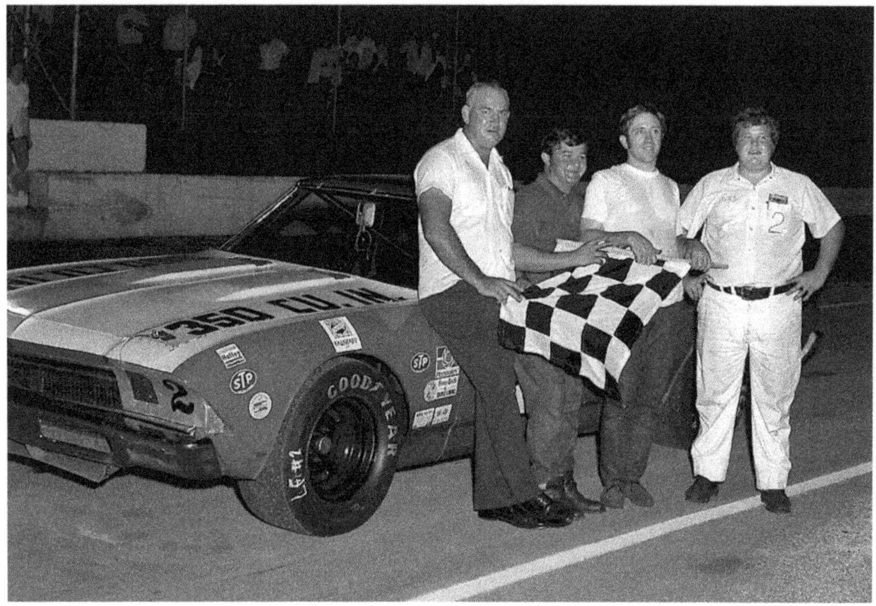

L.D. Ottinger of Newport laid the groundwork for consecutive NASCAR championships with regular wins at East Tennessee tracks like Smoky Mountain and Kingsport. *Ray Taylor photo.*

and Saturdays at Lonesome Pine Raceway in Virginia or Smoky Mountain Raceway—unless there was a national race somewhere. And those national races weren't just in Virginia or the Carolinas, sometimes requiring trips to Florida, New England and California.

"The traveling got so hard because we did 75 or 80 percent of the traveling in the truck," Ottinger said. "I flew when I had to. We had two rigs and sometimes would send one on to Barre, Vermont, or Oxford, Maine. One time, I raced in Virginia and then flew to Milwaukee. All the races paid like fifty points to win a weekly show, so the more you ran, the more points you could get."

Ottinger had already made a mark in the sport driving his own cars and those fielded by Russell Large, who had established the Lonesome Pine track. Ottinger picked off three Tennessee state championships and six combined track titles at Smoky Mountain and Kingsport. But teaming with Childers gave him the equipment and budget to go out and win a championship.

"He was looking to sponsor somebody, and he got involved with Gene Glover to start with. Then he came and talked to me, so I checked into see what he was into. I knew he'd bought a car for Gene and some high-dollar motors, but he wanted me to drive for him. So I started racing for him," Ottinger said. "We bought one or two of the cars from Large, and then we started getting our own cars from Mike Laughlin and Banjo Matthews."

Their 1977 split was ironic since Ottinger previously rejected an offer to drive in the Grand National series to remain with Childers. Ottinger's employer Stokely-Van Camp had long aided his racing efforts, and its Gatorade brand sponsored the DiGard Racing No. 88 entry at that time.

"They called me, wanted me to come drive that car. The plant manager was a friend, and he wanted me to go to Indianapolis and meet with Bill Gardner and Bill Stokely," Ottinger said. "That's when I was driving for the coal miner, and we had a gentleman's agreement—so I wouldn't take it. I thought about it and thought about, even talked to him about it. He gave me all the money we won, so I was making almost as much money as they were. And he paid all the bills."

Switching also would have required Ottinger to quit his job, a move he was unwilling to make.

"My job helped me a lot. I could get off about any time I wanted, [it] paid good and I had good retirement and benefits, because I had two kids," Ottinger said. "They furnished a lot of stuff for my cars. I never could have raced without them."

While travel was taxing, some connections provided real-life Ricky Bobby–style moments. Ottinger and Tiny Lund, for example, competed in an afternoon race at Kingsport and were scheduled to fly together to race in Canada. So Ottinger drove them to Tri-Cities airport in his new pickup.

"I parked in front of the main entrance, and we took our clothes in. There was a flight leaving to go to New York, but the guy said it was ready to go. Well, Tiny threw his suitcase on the counter and took off running down those steps, so I took off after him," Ottinger recalled. "They were pushing the plane back. And he stopped that plane, and they let us on. It was a 737, and there was one seat left. So Tiny got it, and I had to sit on the stewardess seat."

As the trip wore on, Lund began laughing and soon asked, "Where's your truck?"

"I had left it sitting, with the keys in it, right in front of the main entrance. I called Bear Hunley when we landed and told him to go get my truck, and they had towed it someplace. Oh, he was mad at me," Ottinger said.

Title contenders would sometimes try to trick the competition about where they might be racing. Ottinger had at least one such instance with Lund when a race in Hampton, Virginia, was rained out. There was another race four hundred miles away later that night in Asheville, North Carolina, but both men agreed not to go.

"We slipped off and left, and it was almost impossible to get back. We couldn't get flight connections, so we took off. We didn't get there until eight, but another guy qualified my car, and they waited on us," Ottinger said. "Tiny found out we were gone, and he was hot. He flew to the Asheville airport and made the highway patrol run him down the interstate at one hundred miles per hour. The race was about to start, and here he came. I blamed it on Bear. Neither one of us won that night, but he was mad at us for a while."

Ottinger returned to the Sportsman series after his health improved but didn't compete for another title. He went on to race seven full seasons in the NASCAR Busch Series, earning three victories, four poles and top-ten finishes in nearly half of his 206 series starts between 1982 and 1991. Victories came at Hampton, Virginia, in 1986; Martinsville, Virginia, in 1989; and Bristol in 1990—all tracks he knew well from his Late Model Sportsman days.

The Bristol win was overshadowed by events earlier in the race as Michael Waltrip walked away from a horrendous crash into the turn two gate.

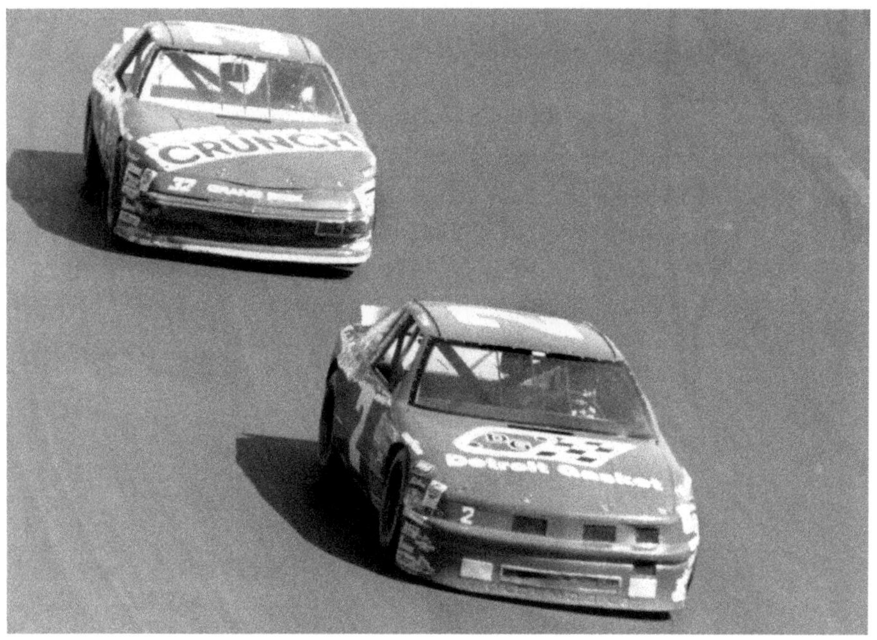

L.D. Ottinger (2) leads Dale Jarrett (32) en route to winning the 1990 Busch Series race at Bristol, his third series victory. *Author photo.*

Although a Busch Series title eluded him, Ottinger finished in the top ten for seven consecutive seasons.

Competing in NASCAR was a far cry from his career's humble, yet victorious beginning aboard a flathead-powered 1939 Ford at the old Oak Ridge Speedway in 1958.

"A friend gave us the old car, and the guys I ran around with decided to build a race car. This other guy drove it, but every time we'd go to Oak Ridge, we'd stop at the bars. He'd drink a few to build up his nerve, I guess. And he'd do pretty good, but he'd spin out," Ottinger recalled. "One night, he was plumb tight, and he spun out two or three times in practice. 'Let me drive that thing,' I said. So I got in it, and I was scared to death. I started about middle of the pack and went to the front and won."

He soon began racing Saturdays at the Tennessee-Carolina Speedway in Newport, and more wins quickly followed. Asphalt or dirt, Ottinger excelled at Smoky Mountain, 411, Newport and Atomic speedways. In eighteen races at 411 one year, Ottinger won sixteen times. He also racked up at Newport and won some big races at Atomic.

"The last race I won there was on [a] Sunday evening. The track got real hard and black on Saturday. I had a big old set of Firestone asphalt tires, so we came home and mounted those. We gambled and put those things on," Ottinger recalled. "Everybody told us it wouldn't work. But it took ten laps, and you talk about the class of the field."

Ottinger's reputation was a hard-nosed racer unafraid to use the bumper, and he admits he was more serious than others.

"It was a different world back then. There were a lot of good racers back in the day, but a lot of them didn't get the chance," Ottinger said. "I was lucky, but I gave up a lot. I didn't go to my kids' graduations because I was running for the championship, and you couldn't miss a race because it was so close. I regretted that later, in a way, but it was hard to do."

19
Like Father, Like Son

To anyone who watched Tony Glover grow up, it was no surprise cars he prepared won three Daytona 500s and a dozen other races in NASCAR's premier series. After all, he'd been spinning wrenches on race cars campaigned by his father, Gene, since he was scarcely tall enough to lean across the fenders.

Quiet and unassuming, Gene Glover won about three hundred short-track races, ten track championships, two NASCAR Tennessee state titles and the 1979 NASCAR Late Model Sportsman national championship. When he went Late Model Sportsman racing in 1970, Tony was a constant companion even though children weren't usually allowed in the pits.

The elder Glover became a terror around East Tennessee short tracks in the late 1950s and early 1960s, working out of Ken "Bear" Hunley's modest Church Hill garage with fellow racer Bill Morton.

"They would go to Cleveland Speedway on Friday, Chattanooga on Saturday and, if the cars weren't torn up, race at the Peach Bowl in Atlanta on Sunday and then drive all night to get back home to go to work. That was a routine," Morton's son Tony recalled.

Sometimes the friends would have a little fun with each other. Glover once won several weeks straight at a track in Richlands, Virginia, so the promoter put up a fifty-dollar bounty for anyone who could beat him. Hunley told Morton about the bounty, and he promptly drove up there and collected. Afterward, Hunley called Glover.

"Before hanging up, Hunley tells Gene he's going to go eat dinner with Daddy because he had an extra fifty dollars," Tony Morton said. "It got really quiet, and then Glover started cussing Hunley because he knew that's who told Daddy he was winning over there."

At Sportsman Speedway in the 1960s, Glover was racing hard with a driver from Newport and wound up getting wrecked. He responded by throwing rocks at the other driver's car every time it passed by, Morton said.

"After the race, Gene and the guy were arguing in the middle of the pit area, and this woman walks up with a pocketbook with a shoulder strap. She swung that pocketbook, hit Gene on the cheekbone and mirrors and lipstick flew everywhere," Morton recalled. "Glover turned around and looked, and she was about seven months pregnant. He didn't know what to say, so he and the driver got into a fight. But he said getting hit by the pocketbook hurt worse than the fight did, so he figured she had a pistol in there."

Glover also won at Chattanooga and, later, Smoky Mountain Raceway. When Kingsport Speedway opened in 1965, Glover and Bill Morton split its first five track championships.

By the late 1960s, Modified racing was becoming extinct while NASCAR's Late Model Sportsman class was emerging, so Glover prepared a Chevelle.

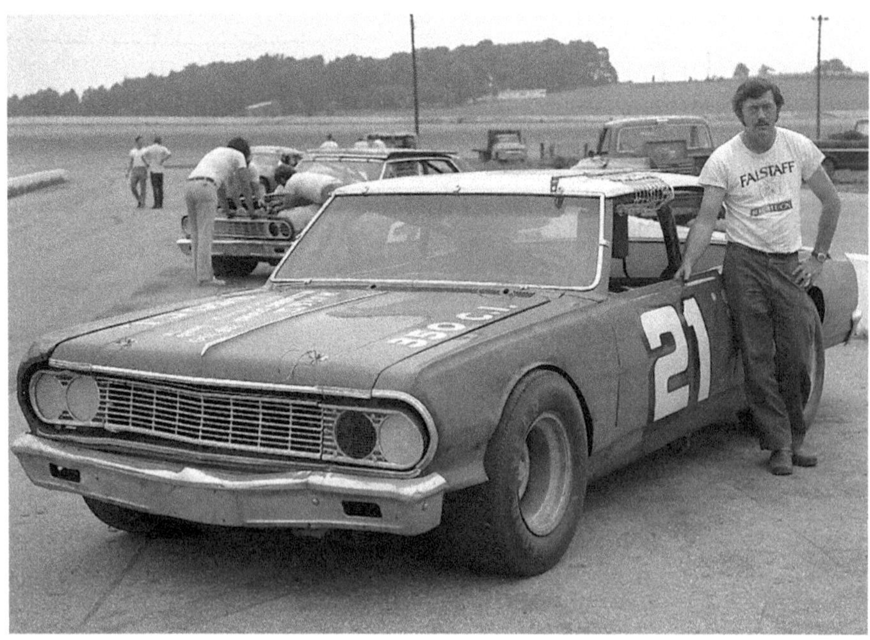

Gene Glover of Kingsport won extensively in Modifieds but found his greatest success in NASCAR Late Model Sportsman. *Ray Taylor photo.*

East Tennessee—already home to many talented drivers—became one of the nation's most competitive battlegrounds. The Glovers held their own as the 1970s wore on, progressing from top-ten finishes to top fives and victories. Gene placed in the top ten nationally five times in eight seasons, winning the 1979 national crown by more than 1,700 points over defending champion Butch Lindley.

"About the middle of 1978, we started going to race tracks that we'd never raced at in preparation for this year," Glover said just after winning the title. "I wanted to become familiar with as many tracks as I could before I started running for the national championship."

That strategy yielded a third-place points finish in 1978, competing at three tracks each in North Carolina and Virginia, plus Nashville and Kingsport in Tennessee. He scored four wins and thirty-five top-ten finishes in fifty-five races to take the 1979 title. No win was sweeter than that of October 21, when he won during "Gene Glover Day" at Kingsport.

"I sat on the pole and won the race that day, and it was the first race my son Tony had ever run in. I told him at the first of the year that he could run in the last race at Kingsport," Glover said after that season.

Glover placed third in the national points the following year, despite seeing his primary car destroyed in a vicious crash at Charlotte Motor Speedway.

He had slowed to avoid a spinning car, and Dale Jarrett plowed into the rear of his Pontiac, sending it into a series of violent flips. Glover was treated for minor injuries at a local hospital, while Jarrett suffered a broken ankle. A photograph of Glover's airborne red No. 71 appeared in newspapers nationwide as the car's trunk lid—adorned with sponsorship from Kingsport Speedway—was shown ripped loose by the impact.

"That was about the worst crash I ever saw," friend and rival Brad Teague recalled. "Gene was going slow, and Dale Jarrett came up behind him full speed and hit that car. And it just kept bouncing. I thought it probably killed him."

Glover finished ninth in the 1981 standings, but his equipment was all but worn out, just as the Late Model Sportsman series was evolving into what is now the Nationwide tour. He made one disappointing start at Bristol in the reconfigured series in 1982 but soon retired.

NASCAR champion Richard Petty, who also grew up in a racing family, recognized Tony's skills and offered him a job after Gene retired. Tony moved to Level Cross, North Carolina, and went to work for stock car racing's king, but he missed the hills of Tennessee. One day in 1983, his telephone rang.

Car dealers Larry and Ted McClure and their friend Tim Morgan pooled their money and purchased the assets of G.C. Spencer's former race team.

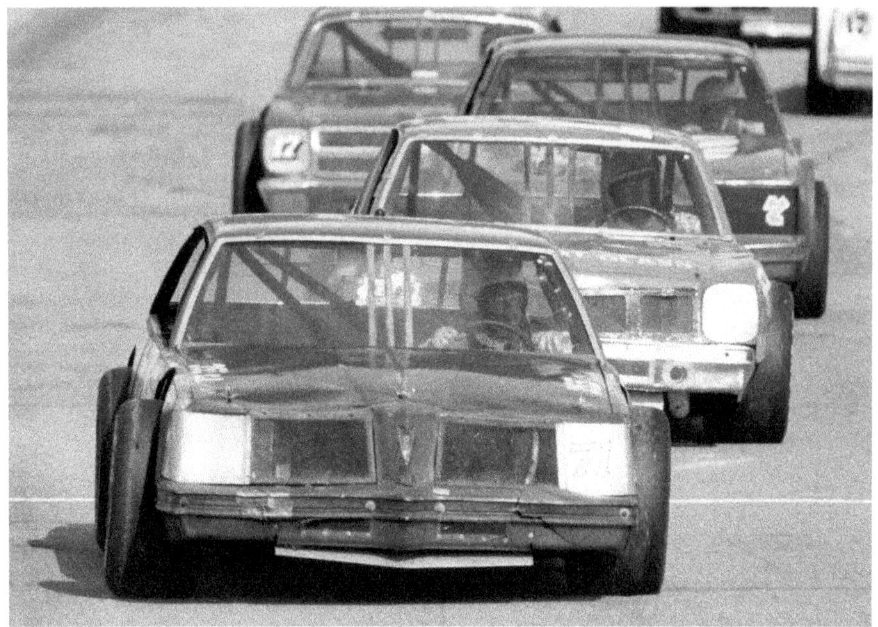

Gene Glover captured the 1979 NASCAR Late Model Sportsman national championship. *Bristol Motor Speedway collection.*

There were no sponsors, only a couple race cars and a small shop near Abingdon, Virginia—a half hour from Glover's boyhood home. The twenty-six-year-old jumped at the chance to become crew chief.

Through three ever-expanding race shops, a half dozen drivers and a case full of trophies, Tony and the Morgan-McClure team carved their names into the NASCAR record books. Their first pole came at Bristol in 1988 with Rick Wilson at the wheel. Young Ernie Irvan earned the team's first Winston Cup victory at Bristol, staving off reigning NASCAR champion Rusty Wallace in the 1990 August night race.

Over the next eight years, they claimed thirteen more wins, contended for a championship and established themselves as the team to beat when the series ran at its two biggest superspeedways. Nine of the team's wins came at Daytona and Talladega between 1991 and 1996. Irvan and successor Sterling Marlin regularly led those multicar packs and, more often than not, wound up putting the team's familiar yellow No. 4 Kodak-backed Chevrolets in victory lane.

Tony Glover was honored as the sport's top crew chief three times in the early 1990s. Competing as a single-car team against more heavily funded, multicar efforts, however, the team's edge eventually eroded, and so, too, did the chemistry.

Tony left during the 1996 campaign, relocating to North Carolina to become crew chief and manager for team owner Felix Sabates. Working with drivers Robby Gordon, Joe Nemechek, Kenny Irwin Jr. and once reunited with his old friend Marlin, Glover stayed there through 2011. That period included a merger with Chip Ganassi and working in a variety of administrative roles. Besides fourteen victories, his tenure atop a NASCAR pit box produced sixteen pole positions and 123 top-tens in more than four hundred races. The merged Ganassi-Sabates team also collected four wins while Glover was team manager.

Gene Glover died unexpectedly from kidney failure in 2008. In 2013, Tony began working for NASCAR at its research and development center in Mooresville, North Carolina.

20

Crazy about Racing

East Tennessee narrowly missed claiming another NASCAR Late Model Sportsman championship during the division's final season. Much like L.D. Ottinger and Gene Glover before, Johnson City's Brad Teague led the standings for about three months but ultimately finished second.

After enjoying more than a decade of success on dirt and pavement—highlighted by a string of solid runs in the Late Model Sportsman division—Teague began the 1980 season driving for Charlie Henderson, who owned a chain of grocery stores.

Competing primarily at Kingsport Speedway, Teague finished third in the track and Tennessee standings behind Hall of Fame driver Jack Ingram and longtime rival John A. Utsman. It didn't hurt his cause that Kingsport hosted four of thirty-six national championship races or that on October 19, Teague steered Henderson's Pontiac to victory in the Winston 300. Teague took the race lead after early leaders Butch Lindley and Ingram dropped out with engine failures and held off late charges from Glover and Utsman to collect the $5,350 top prize. Bob Pressley and Morgan Shepherd rounded out the top five.

Coming off a top-twenty finish in the 1980 national points, the team expected to improve in 1981. And it did. Teague raced to a solid eleventh-place finish in the season opener at Daytona, as David Pearson battled Rusty Wallace and Neil Bonnett for the win.

A week later, Teague roared to victory over Gene Glover in a 150-lap race at the Richmond, Virginia fairgrounds. He appeared headed for a second straight win the following week when disaster struck.

"We were leading at Rockingham [North Carolina]. I took the white flag and blew a right front tire, and it totaled the car," Teague said. Their ninth-place finish was no consolation for losing their best race car since they didn't have sufficient resources to replace it.

"We only had two cars, so we wound up running forty-seven races with one car," Teague said. "We led the points for three months, finished a lot of races and [ran] good, but we just wore our stuff out. If we'd had another car, I think we could have won it."

Tommy Ellis eventually claimed the title with six wins in the season's twenty-five national championship races. He bested Teague by 392 points, the second-closest margin in the final fourteen years of the series. Geoff Bodine, Jack Ingram and Sam Ard finished behind Brad.

As one of the race team's two full-time employees, Teague often drove the transporter on lengthy trips to compete at multiple races each week. "I would drive with a cooler beside me, with a rag in it. And I would get that rag out and wipe my face just to stay awake," Teague said. "I can remember a lot of nights stopping and getting out to walk around the truck just to stay awake."

For 1982, rather than take aim at NASCAR's new Budweiser Late Model Sportsman—later Busch—Series and its twenty-nine-race schedule, Teague and Henderson set their sights on Winston Cup.

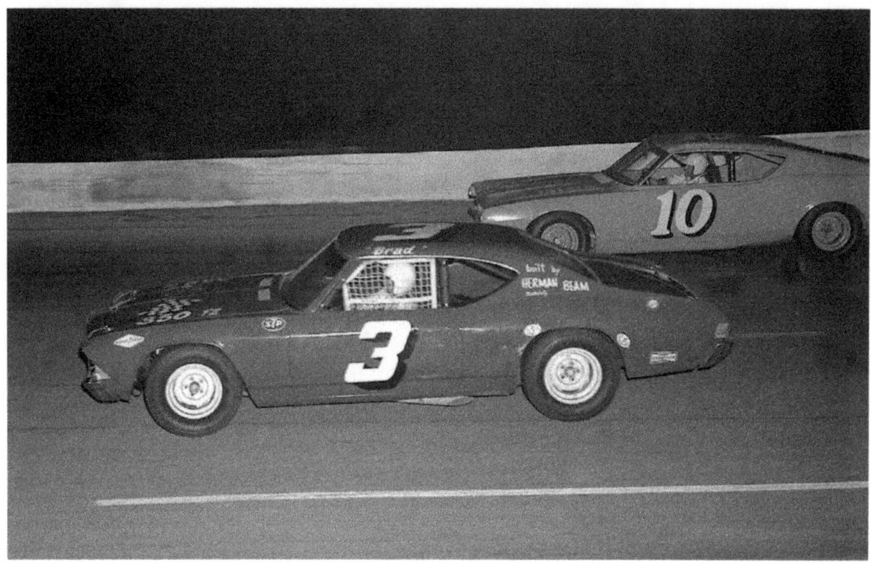

Brad Teague became a standout in the NASCAR Late Model Sportsman division and raced in all three of the sport's top-touring series. *Ray Taylor photo.*

"We were going to run for rookie of the year. Me, Mark Martin and Geoff Bodine, but we got wrecked at Daytona," Teague recalled of finishing twenty-sixth in the thirty-car qualifying race and missing the big show.

Regrouping in time for the spring Bristol race, Teague qualified twenty-third in the thirty-car field and posted a solid twelfth-place finish. His first Busch Series start came that same March weekend, as he qualified fourth and finished fifth. He qualified for eight more Cup races that year, finishing thirteenth at Atlanta and eleventh at Martinsville, but Henderson parked the operation following a fifteenth-place showing at Bristol's August night race.

"We just ran out of money. It was just too expensive," Teague said. "Even back then, NASCAR was getting too big, and they didn't really want the small person around."

Teague ran only one Busch Series race in 1983, as Henderson regrouped for a limited run the following year. They got back on track in 1984, posting four top-five and eight top-ten Busch Series finishes, including a pair of second-place efforts at Hickory, North Carolina.

The following year featured a serious run for the Busch title, competing in twenty-four of twenty-seven races. Teague earned poles at both Hickory stops; second- and third-place finishes at Darlington, South Carolina; and eight top-tens. Engine problems knocked them out of seven races, but they still managed to finish thirteenth nationally.

Problems surfaced again at the 1986 season opener in Daytona. Teague took the lead and was pulling away in the Goody's 300 when the new, smaller V-6 engine under his hood expired. Circumstances conspired to keep the team from more than one apparent win.

Fuel issues robbed him of chances at victory at both stops in Dover, Delaware. In one race, his Pontiac sputtered going down the backstretch after the team rolled the dice on fuel mileage. At the other, a late caution dashed his hopes for victory.

"I had a straightaway lead at Dover with five laps to go, when the caution came out," Teague ruefully recalled. "The turns and the straightaways are banked so steep, the fuel ran away from my fuel pickup. I had plenty of gas as long as it was under green, but because of the caution, I had to come in and get gas."

Not that the year was a complete throwaway, as the team scored one top-five finish and ten top-tens in twenty starts. All of which set the stage for a bid for the 1987 series title, punctuated by an early season victory at Martinsville and one of the most famous trophies in racing: a hardwood grandfather clock, handcrafted by the Ridgeway Clock Co.

"I always wanted to win at Martinsville and get me one of them clocks," Teague said. "I knew I had the winning car if I didn't have problems because that car was so good."

Teague qualified tenth at a place where track position is as highly prized as the concession stand's hotdogs, but the team had posted better efforts before only to see hope end in heartbreak. So, in addition to speed, crew chief Chris Carrier packed a bit of extra strategy for that weekend's two hundred laps.

"We planned on not pitting for tires or fuel," Teague said. "Some of them pitted early, and I was just cooling it. I knew, as soon as they pitted, we had it—as long as nothing happened. When I took the lead, there was no passing me back."

A string of near misses, mechanical failures and bum luck were suddenly distant memories. After the white flag flew, some of the sport's best drivers chased Teague to the checkers. Future Cup series champion Dale Jarrett finished second, followed by Rick Mast, former series champ Jack Ingram and Mike Alexander. Chevrolet later recognized the winning entry as the first downsized Celebrity body style to snatch a NASCAR victory.

Heading back home, the team was second in points, brimming with confidence and primed to run the full schedule. Teague led the standings briefly and posted nine top-ten finishes, but another win eluded him. A late season engine failure at Richmond, Virginia, and transmission woes at the second Martinsville race knocked the team from title contention. Teague ultimately settled for seventh place in the 1987 standings, sandwiched between Dale Jarrett and Mark Martin.

Self-described as "crazy" over racing and race cars since age five, Teague grew up in Buladean, North Carolina, a rural sawmill and farming town. Determined to break into racing, he later moved to Tennessee and the center of a racing hotbed that included a new NASCAR track at Bristol, where his youthful exuberance got him barred.

"Once a year, they would have an open-house day where people could drive their street cars on the race track," Teague said with a gleam in his eye. "Lettin' me in there was the wrong thing to do."

Teague quickly shifted from drag racing to the dirt ovals across East Tennessee and Southwest Virginia. Wheeling a homebuilt six-cylinder 1957 Chevrolet, he won the 1967 points championship at Johnson City's old Sportsman Speedway and soon progressed to the faster Late Models. Teamed with John Hodges and Jess Potter, he built a 1965 Chevelle that carried them to qualifying honors, track records and race wins from Rogersville, Tennessee, to Pulaski, Virginia.

"I told Jess Potter he needed to hire that boy that drives that '57 Chevrolet," former Grand National regular Brownie King said of Teague. "Jess asked why, and I told him anybody who could fight a steering wheel the way he does, if he had a good car, I guarantee he'd make you a good driver."

Potter had fielded cars in NASCAR's Grand National division during the 1950s and 1960s, so his vast mechanical knowledge proved invaluable.

After enjoying success on dirt, Teague finally fulfilled his dream of racing at Bristol in 1971, entering that same Chevelle in a NASCAR Late Model Sportsman race. He qualified with the third-fastest time and raced with the leaders throughout the three-hundred-lap grind—the longest race of his young career. Sharing the track with Bobby Allison, L.D. Ottinger and Cale Yarborough, Teague held on for a fourth-place finish.

"I could adapt to any race track pretty quick, but it was really hard to try not to run sideways," Teague recalled of his quick transition from dirt to asphalt. "I always felt I had the talent."

Running fender to fender with the nation's best, Teague established himself as one of the premier drivers in the Late Model Sportsman division. He won the 1975 Lonesome Pine International Raceway track championship—beating out Jimmy Hensley and Jack Ingram—and just missed winning the Kingsport title by two points. His seventeenth-place national finish was one spot ahead of a youngster named Dale Earnhardt.

The following year, Teague improved to eleventh in the national standings but watched as fellow East Tennessean Ottinger won his second straight championship. Virginia native Hensley swept the track championships at both Kingsport and Lonesome Pine that season, while Teague finished second at Kingsport and fourth at LPIR.

In the decades since his milestone Martinsville win, Teague bounced around NASCAR's Busch, Cup and Truck series. But the economic realities of modern racing often kept him from landing in competitive rides. There have been some memorable moments, like the unrealized potential of a 1988 Winston Cup run for car owner Bob Clark that Teague calls his "best opportunity" and a 1995 Bristol Busch Series race that he nearly won with an outdated car and volunteer pit crew.

"We qualified sixth, and that car was fast enough to win that race. I came in the pits first, and Rick Wilson blocked me in. I'd been running third and came out fifteenth. I got back up to sixth and that was as far as I could get," Teague said. It also represented the final time a V-6 engine would race in the Busch Series.

Much like his juvenile jaunt around the Bristol track, Brad Teague was never content to just ride around.

"There's nobody, nowhere that's loved racing as much as me."

21

A Snowball's Chance

Randy Bethea didn't set out to be a pioneer; he just wanted to race. But along the way, the man his competitors nicknamed "Snowball" helped desegregate a lily-white southern sport in the turbulent 1960s and '70s.

Articulate but soft spoken, Bethea was the first and possibly the only African American to compete in the old NASCAR Late Model Sportsman division that preceded the Busch- and Nationwide-sponsored series. Based in Newport, Bethea regularly competed alongside titans Jack Ingram, Harry Gant, Darrell Waltrip and Jimmy Hensley at tracks from Daytona and Charlotte to Bristol, Nashville and Martinsville.

He grew up hanging around the race shops of Banjo Mathews and Roy Tyner in Asheville, North Carolina, fascinated with the cars and the people who drove them. So when he slid behind the wheel of a 1955 Ford for the first time at Newport's Tennessee-Carolina Speedway, he was immediately hooked.

Bethea was disappointed the following year when the popular track didn't reopen. And Bethea's only outing of 1968 produced one of the few examples of overt racism he can recall.

"I went to race at Rogersville on July 4. I got to the track and asked somebody where to draw for positions," Bethea said. "The guy wanted to know who was driving the car, and I told him I was. He said, 'We've already drawn for you.' So I asked him where I started, and he said, 'Last.'

"Things like that went on, but as far as anyone saying anything about me being black, I do not recall that. All the people you raced with got

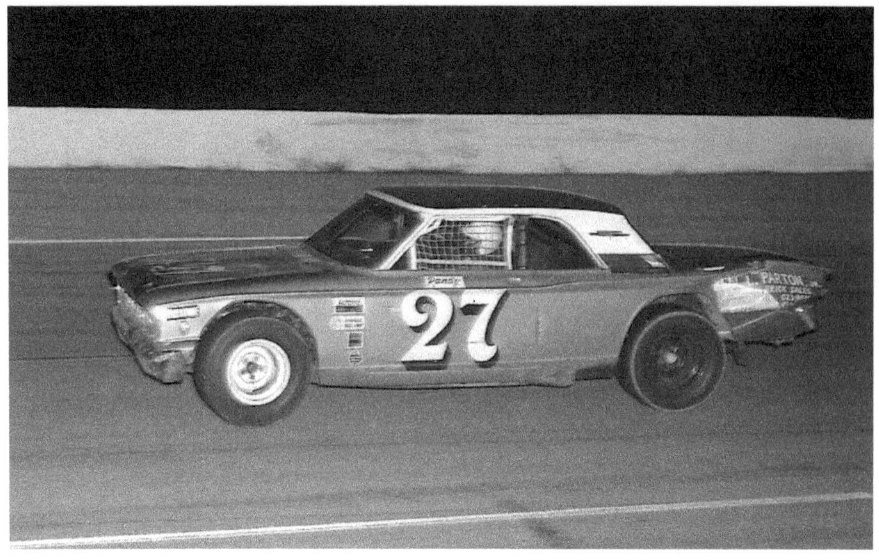

After Newport's Randy Bethea won the 1970 Tennessee NASCAR Hobby title, he raced for years in the Late Model Sportsman class. *Ray Taylor photo.*

along," Bethea said. "I do not know of any other black person that was racing, but I spent a lot of my racing career in situations like that. There were no horror stories."

In 1969, Bethea began competing in the Hobby division at Smoky Mountain Raceway, but he suffered a broken ankle in a hard crash that sidelined him for the rest of that season.

He built a new car for the 1970 season and, after prevailing over the protests of some fellow competitors, went on to notch one of his career highlights. Like many others in the class, Bethea mounted a 1963 Ford Falcon body on the longer 1955 Ford frame rails, except he shortened the wheelbase to fit the smaller car.

"A lot was being said about my car, so Pete Keller, who was over the NASCAR Late Model division, came to the race track and said my car was legal to race," Bethea said. "I had called him when I was building the car and told him I shortened the car. He said just to use the original [engine] mounts, which suited me because I had the engine way back in the car. Everybody else stuck that body on that '55 frame and had the radiator sticking out in front of the car."

Bethea isn't sure if the color of his skin motivated the protests or if other drivers were just upset about being outsmarted and outrun.

"Was race involved in that? I don't know. I don't know," he said. Either way, Bethea won more than his share that season and earned both the Smoky Mountain track title and NASCAR's Tennessee state championship. He finished ahead of Harold Moats and J.T. Kerr, who tied for second place.

"At the time, it was not a big deal to me, but actually it was," Bethea said.

He ran the same car the following year and continued winning races before some late season engine problems relegated him to tenth in the track points.

Bethea next set his sites on the highly competitive Late Model Sportsman division. Concentrating on Smoky Mountain, Kingsport and the new Lonesome Pine International Raceway in Virginia, Bethea logged a solid season. Racing regularly against L.D. Ottinger, Gene Glover, Paul Lewis, Tootle Estes and John A. Utsman, Bethea tied Ottinger for eighth place in the Lonesome Pine track standings, was twelfth at Smoky Mountain and thirteenth at Kingsport.

Bethea replaced his Fairlane with a gleaming gold, white and black Torino and began running many of NASCAR's national championship points events. Likely his brightest moment in the spotlight occurred in October 1973, when he outran seventy-one others to claim his only career pole for the Permatex Southern 400 at Nashville Fairgrounds Speedway.

"I usually did not have a lot of money to put into the race car," Bethea said. "At Nashville, I did have money to buy tires and could qualify on the same tires as everybody else qualified on, and I was able to race." That event featured a who's who of the era, including eventual winner and series champion Jack Ingram, Donnie Allison, Sam Ard, Neil Bonnett, Red Farmer, Harry Gant, Jimmy Hensley, L.D. Ottinger, Jody Ridley, Morgan Shepherd and Brad Teague.

The most surprised driver on the property was Darrell Waltrip, who appeared to have the pole locked up. However, Bethea's twenty-one-second lap denied the hometown hero the top spot and earned Bethea some national acclaim.

Waltrip had claimed ten wins and the Nashville track championship that year and skipped a Grand National show at Martinsville to compete. He finished eighth due to overheating problems, as Ingram won. The day also proved disappointing for Bethea, as the Torino's engine developed an oil leak that eventually put him out of the running.

As the 1974 season dawned, Bethea joined the rest of the Late Model Sportsman regulars for the season-opening Permatex 300 at Daytona Beach, Florida. But this trip offered a bold, new direction that would eventually sideline a once-promising career.

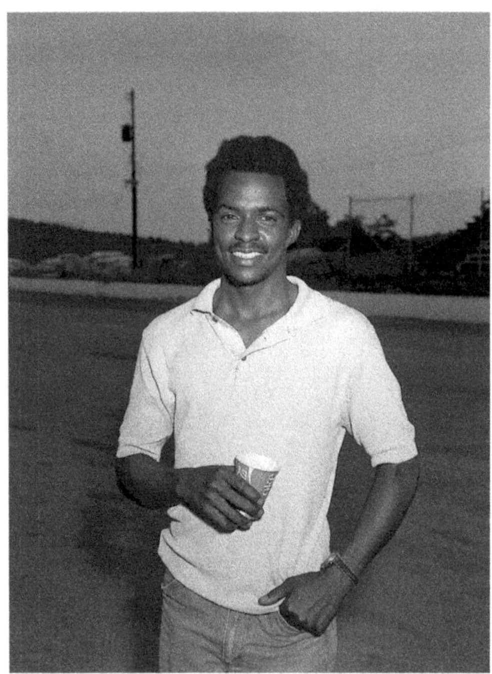

Randy Bethea was likely the only African American to race in NASCAR's Late Model Sportsman class during the 1970s. *Ray Taylor photo.*

"I was approached at Daytona to drive a Super Vee car for the Black American Racers Organization, sponsored by Brown & Williamson Tobacco Company and Viceroy. This was the beginning of the end of my racing," Bethea said. "It was a bad move on my part. Hindsight is twenty-twenty. I was beginning to do well in the Late Model Sportsman division when that opportunity came about. I left what I knew to go road racing, with no experience. And for two years did that and ended up crashing in that deal and broke my leg."

While he never found victory lane on the road courses, Bethea did manage a second-place finish in the 2.85-mile Bridgehampton, New York course before eventually returning to NASCAR.

"When I came back to NASCAR, everything I had—my crew and my sponsors—was gone," he said. "I had to start over again, and it was a struggle from that point on. I never really got it back to the point that it needed to be."

His lone Winston Cup Series start came in the 1975 World 600 at Charlotte, North Carolina. Driving a Chevrolet owned by D.K. Ulrich, Bethea qualified thirty-ninth in the forty-car field, but a blown engine left him thirty-third.

Bethea disappeared from the racing landscape during the next few years, working at Ford dealerships in the Virgin Islands, Puerto Rico and St. Croix, but he still itched to race.

"It was a hassle flying my wife and kids back and forth. I decided to come back home in 1987. Then my wife got sick with lung cancer and died in 1990. I took care of her until she died," he said.

Bethea drove an All-Pro Series Late Model racer on tracks in the Carolinas and Georgia in the early 1990s and then raced an open-wheel Modified car for a number of years around his former haunts of Newport, Kingsport, Coeburn and Hickory, plus some exhibition races in the Carolinas. His career came full circle when he again began racing a Late Model car on the asphalt track in Newport.

More than thirty years after the fact, he remains one of a handful of African Americans to start a race in NASCAR's top division. Bethea was once featured in a NASCAR television commercial about diversity.

"I was surprised. I had no idea. I got a phone call from a friend that said I was on TV. I watched for it, and it made me feel proud," he said. "I absolutely was not a pioneer. Racing was the only thing on my mind."

22

Heck of a Racer

From the mountains of North Carolina to northern Georgia and Tennessee, many of racing's early stars mastered car control negotiating treacherous mountain roads in hopped-up cars loaded with moonshine. At high speeds, a single slip could prove catastrophic, and more than one whiskey trip was made with state or federal agents hot on their trails, requiring a steady hand and intense concentration to deliver the goods.

In 1958, actor Robert Mitchum released *Thunder Road*, a popular film about southern boys running moonshine around Knoxville. Herbert "Tootle" Estes should have been given a starring role.

"Back in the early days growing up, he did about anything he could to make a dollar," his son, Rocky Estes, said.

Yes, Tootle was known to haul a little moonshine, but what he mostly hauled was ass.

Born during the Great Depression, Estes built a reputation as one of the Southeast's most prolific winners. He mostly made a living by racing, and some accounts claim he had 1,500 victories.

One season, Estes reportedly won 85 of 104 feature races while competing four to seven nights a week across the Southeast. He won in everything he drove, from Midgets and jalopies to balls-out open-wheel Modifieds nicknamed "Skeeters," dirt Late Models and NASCAR Late Model Sportsman cars.

You can't count the trophies because he never kept them, saying they didn't pay bills and he had a family to feed. One season, he won the same trophy

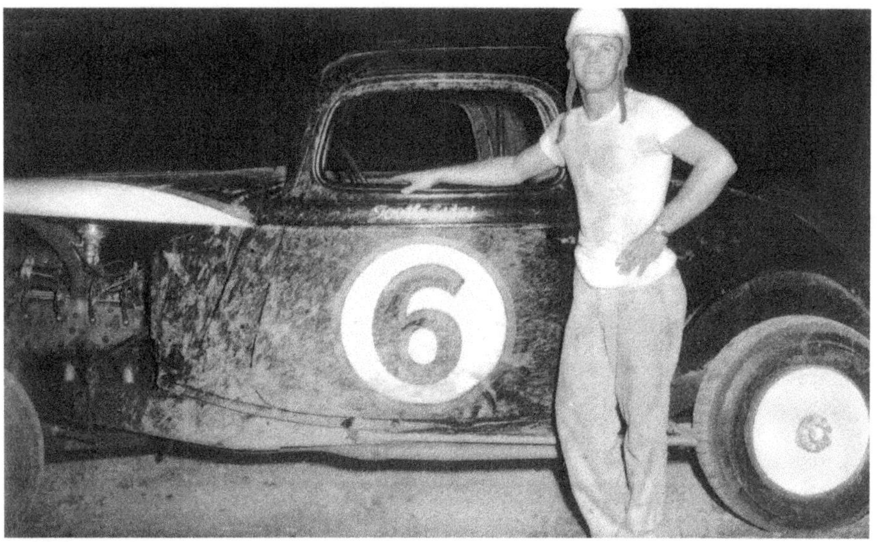

An early photo of Herb "Tootle" Estes, one of the nation's most prolific short-track winners. *Melvin Corum collection.*

seventeen straight weeks at Greenwood Speedway in South Carolina and then sold it back to the promoter after each race. Rocky Estes has just one trophy from Tootle's three decades of barnstorming: a silver cup representing a NASCAR Late Model Sportsman championship at Smoky Mountain Raceway. One of the men he beat for the 1970 title was L.D. Ottinger.

"He was a heck of a racer," Ottinger said. "He was a character. He worked for Ed Harvey, and he'd tell you he delivered moonshine. Tootle always dressed nice, always wore a white t-shirt and white lace-up shoes."

When he turned twenty-one, Estes began driving at the old Broadway Speedway in 1951. It wasn't long before fans started talking about the young man with the novel nickname, affixed at birth by an aunt who declared he was "too little to be a Herbert." Building on early successes at Broadway, Estes began conquering Tennessee-Carolina Speedway in Newport, Ashway Speedway in Strawberry Plains and other area tracks.

"They started traveling in the late 1950s, racing four and five nights a week in Georgia and the Carolinas," Rocky Estes said. "They raced more often and paid a little better down there. They could go over there and race Thursday through Sunday night, and [on] Memorial Day, July 4 and Labor Day, they would race seven straight nights."

During that time, Estes wheeled a flathead Ford-powered 1934 Ford sedan. He once won sixteen consecutive races at tracks in South Carolina,

Georgia and at Boyd's Speedway on the Tennessee-Georgia border, while competing against Buck Simmons, Charlie Mincey and the Fryar brothers. The streak ended when he suffered breakage, but he resumed winning after repairs were made.

Weekends often started on Thursdays in Greenwood, South Carolina; shifted to Anderson, South Carolina, on Fridays; and then went to Taccoa, Georgia, on Saturdays with some Sundays spent at Dallas, Cumming or Atlanta, Georgia—often racing twice on Sundays. He won at the Peach Bowl Speedway in Atlanta, a quarter-mile oval once promoted by NASCAR founder Bill France.

"About once a month, he'd come over here and run 411 Speedway and Ashway Speedway on Tuesday and Wednesday nights. Or he might go to Cleveland and Boyd's. In the winter, they'd go to Jacksonville, Florida, and Savannah, Georgia," Rocky Estes said.

NASCAR's Grand National and Convertible divisions beckoned briefly in 1958, but its rules fit like a tight pair of shoes. His first Grand National start came at Asheville-Weaverville's half-mile oval in North Carolina, where he qualified thirteenth and finished eleventh. He later appeared to have

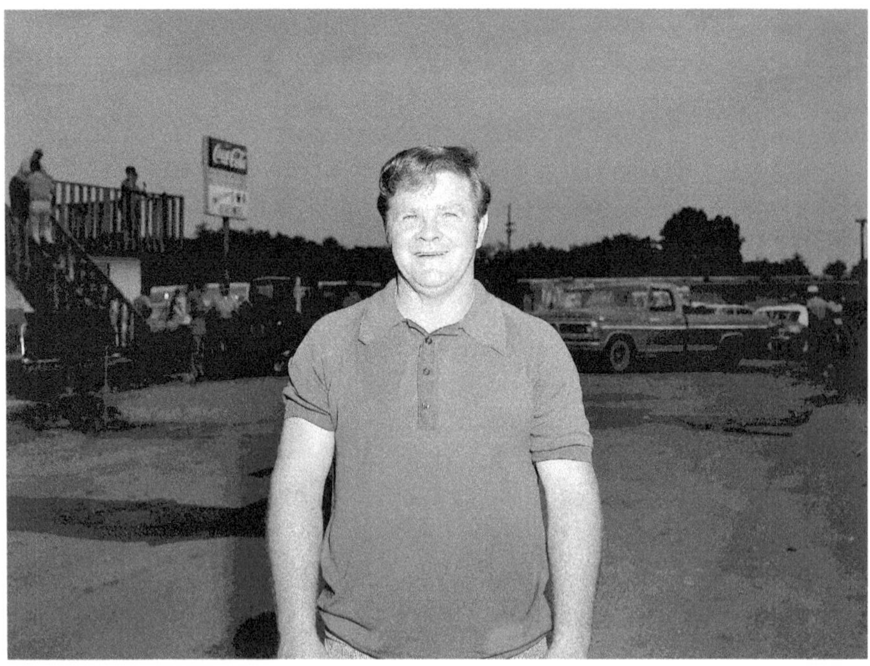

Tootle Estes competed at every level in just about every imaginable kind of race car and has a reputed 1,500 victories. *Ray Taylor photo.*

a Convertible division race won over in Wilson, North Carolina, but the official decision went to defending series champion Bob Welborn.

"It was mandatory that you make a pit stop, so he made his pit stop and got back up to second, and the leader hadn't made his pit stop," Rocky Estes said, repeating a story his father retold many times. "He was waiting on him, and the caution come out. Well the pace car came back to the guy leading the race, and it was a green-white-checker finish, and that guy never made a pit stop. Daddy said he almost beat him anyway."

Estes posted four top-ten finishes in twelve Grand National races and had three top tens in four Convertible series starts.

"We went to Trenton, New Jersey, when I was five years old, and he blew nine right front tires and finished eleventh," Rocky Estes recalled, proudly adding he also finished tenth in the Southern 500. "He only ran Cup a half a year. He didn't like their rules. He wasn't a real rule follower. He wasn't the type [of] person to do everything they wanted him to do, the way they wanted him to do it."

Around East Tennessee, people still recount his battles with Paul "the Ghost" Gose. The two friendly rivals ultimately agreed to visit different southern tracks so they wouldn't have to race each other, and both regularly captured the checkered flag. Estes piled up victories driving Ace Lawson's Ford, which was later banned from competing in Georgia, and a copper-colored, fuel-injected Ford coupe with a wing on its roof owned and prepared by James "Jabo" Bradberry of Athens, Georgia.

Life at the Estes household was often a study in contrasts.

"He was a regular dad. We weren't hardly allowed to talk about racing from Monday until Thursday, but from Thursday through Sunday, that's all there was—one racetrack to another," Rocky Estes said.

When the popularity of NASCAR's Late Model Sportsman cars grew, Estes began competing weekly at Smoky Mountain Raceway, where he won two track championships, besting Jim Hunter by ten points in 1967 and L.D. Ottinger by fifty-four points in 1970. That series also traveled, so Estes hit the road again to compete against many of the sport's biggest names.

He focused more on dirt after Atomic and Volunteer speedways opened in the 1970s. He captured about three hundred dirt Late Model wins, including the last race of his life. Estes held off longtime rival Ottinger to claim the checkered flag at Volunteer on August 20, 1982. After the race, Estes tried to sell Ottinger a 1960 Ford Thunderbird.

"Tootle was complaining about his arms hurting, but we didn't think much about it," Ottinger reflected. "We loaded up and got on the interstate,

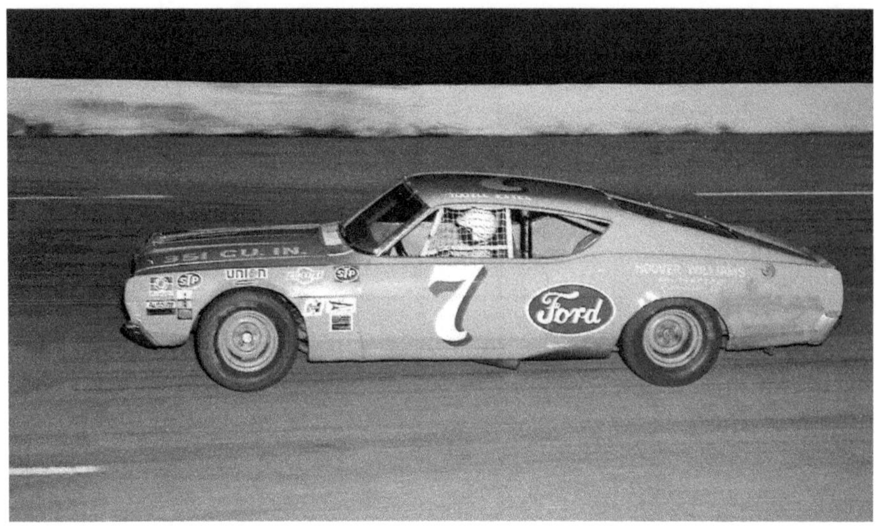

Tootle Estes captured two NASCAR Late Model Sportsman titles at Smoky Mountain Raceway, including one with this Ford in 1970. *Ray Taylor photo.*

and in a few minutes, that Thunderbird came by us doing one hundred miles per hour. Buddy Rogers was driving, and Tootle's wife was in the back with Tootle. They missed the exit for the Morristown hospital and stopped beside the road. We got Tootle out of the car and up on the bank to do CPR, but he was dead with a massive heart attack."

Estes was just fifty-two years old.

The following year, he was posthumously inducted into the East Tennessee racing hall of fame at Atomic, a track he once dominated. He was inducted into the Georgia Auto Racing Hall of Fame and the National Dirt Late Model Hall of Fame in Florence, Kentucky, in 2009.

Cars driven by Estes were displayed in the International Motorsports Hall of Fame in Talladega, Alabama, and the Memory Lane Museum in Mooresville, North Carolina.

23

Everybody Loved to Race Here

U.S. Highway 11 between Johnson City and Jonesborough was just two lanes back in 1958, and the old Skyline drive-in theater stood where a shopping center now operates. Across the road, a decomposing bowling alley stands in front of the dirt bank that once supported the grandstands and scoring tower of the old Sportsman Speedway.

Stand on that bank and look to the right. That's where turns one and two—really more like one continuous corner—were located. The backstretch began roughly parallel to what is now Industrial Drive but would have passed through the current Free Service Tire warehouse. Turn three was a wide, sweeping corner near an auto repair business, while turn four is now filled with another business. All that remains of the oddly shaped little clay third-mile track are memories.

Folks around here claim more drivers who made it to NASCAR's upper echelon raced at Sportsman than any other track. That might be tough to prove, but the list is impressive: Herman Beam, Gene Glover, George Green, Ken Hunley, Mark Hurley, Brownie King, Paul Lewis, L.D. Ottinger, Bill Morton, Connie Saylor, Brad Teague and members of the Utsman clan, including John A., Junior, Larry, Layman and Sherman. And those were just the locals. Tiny Lund spent much of one summer racing at Sportsman, as did Wendell Scott. Veteran G.C. Spencer stopped by, and so did a kid named Earnhardt.

Standing on that bank, looking right toward Leisure Lane, it isn't hard to imagine Lund and King roaring off into the corner side by side like they did more than five decades before. Ernie Collins doesn't have to imagine.

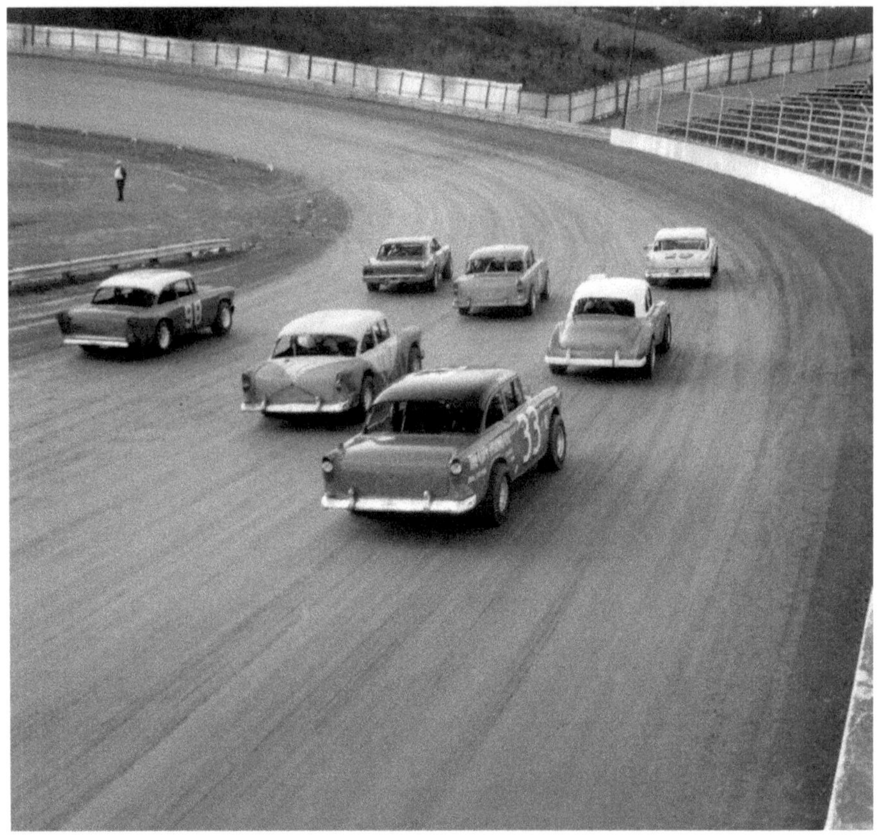

Cars race three wide into the narrow turns of Sportsman Speedway in Johnson City. *Ernie Collins collection.*

Collins grew up just two streets away and was there from the track's first race in the spring of 1958 through 1974, when track owner Paul Wiley made good on a promise to shut it down if drivers and owners wouldn't quit squabbling. Collins was sixteen when he helped park spectator cars and later learned how to score thirty speeding racers under the watchful eye of legendary promoter and announcer Hal Hamrick. Collins later served as the track's manager.

"Everybody loved to race here. If we could have gotten more land, with the shape of the track and the way it raced, it would be an icon today," Collins said. "This was a neat racetrack in spite of its shape. The Midget and Sprint drivers loved it. Merle Bettenhausen and those guys loved this track when they ran here in the late '60s and early '70s. Tiny Lund liked to race here."

Lund was a burly Iowan who relocated to South Carolina to pursue a career in big-league stock car racing. Years before he won the 1963 Daytona 500, Lund spent most of the 1960 season honing his skills at Sportsman.

"We ran twenty-one races that year. I won fourteen, and Tiny beat me five times," Brownie King said. "We battled every week. One time we ran a two-hundred-lapper and ran nearly every lap side by side. Years afterward, people would come up to me and tell me how they remembered me and Tiny."

King called his rival a "nice guy" who once visited his home for dinner.

"I'd be leading and Tiny would be trying to get around me, and he'd have that left arm outside the car holding onto the roof and just driving with that right hand," King said. "I never could understand how he had the strength to drive with that one hand because I was fighting that steering wheel for everything in the world trying to keep the car on the race track."

King was Sportsman's 1960 track champion but experienced his worst moment in a race car the next year.

"I was driving somebody else's Modified car and was passing Bill Morton for third place, and he motioned me to go around him on the outside. His right front wheel hit a rut and bounced into my left rear, sent me head-on into the fence," King recalled.

Hospitalized for two days, it was two weeks before King could remember why he was in that particular car.

John A. Utsman also suffered his worst crash at Sportsman a few years later.

"Every race car I ever had, I put 'In God we trust' because that's who I put my trust in," Utsman said. "I'm sure he was with me with that 1966 Fairlane because Brad Teague put me over the fence at Johnson City one night. I was passing him, and he was leading the race. I think he did it intentionally—but we're good friends, so there's no hard feelings. But it sure tore up a good race car. After that, I switched from dirt to asphalt." Utsman's brother Sherman was seriously injured in a 1959 accident at Sportsman, but he returned to driving in 1961.

Perched up on that hill, Sportsman was known for more than just stock car racing. There were big-name drivers from Indianapolis piloting Midget and Sprint cars, auto thrill shows, motorcycle stuntmen, fireworks on the Fourth of July and country music concerts—much like the array of events Larry Carrier staged at the nearby NASCAR-sanctioned Bristol speedway.

"I would watch him and get ideas. He started out with the bowling alleys and his vision—he could see way out in the future," Collins said. "He bought ads in my programs and I in his. I went up there a few times. He was temperamental. His secretary told me once not to piss him off, but I already knew that."

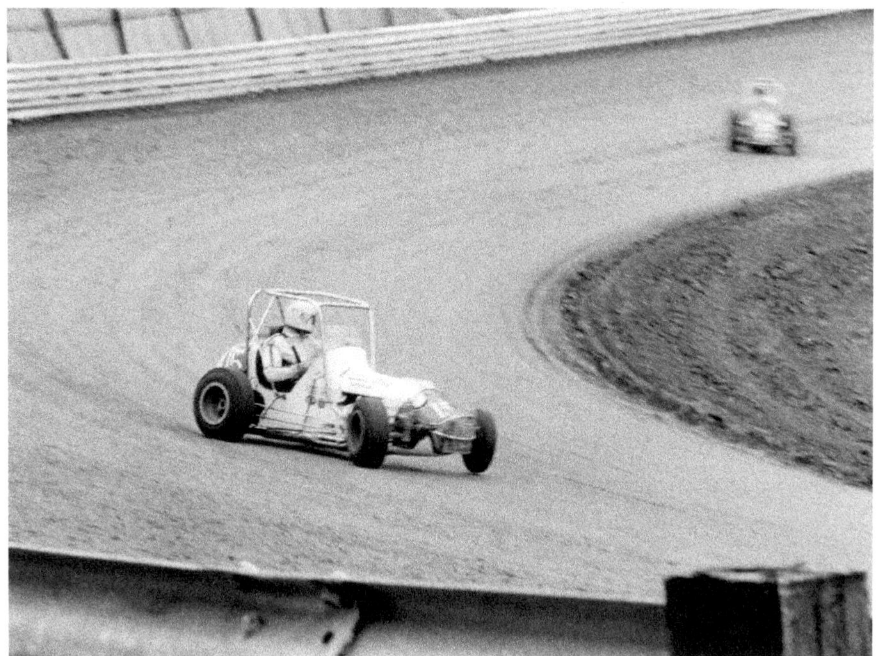

USAC Midget cars raced at both Sportsman and Appalachian speedways in the 1970s. *Ernie Collins collection.*

Sportsman's odd shape was out of necessity. Turns one and two fit within the property line and avoided two large sinkholes. The backstretch flared out wide toward turn three because the track's builders encountered rock and opted to bypass instead of dig, Collins said. The property included a junkyard, and many scrapped cars were later used to fill in the sinkholes.

A dramatic change occurred in the late 1960s when Sportsman track president Paul Dykes convinced two other businessmen to invest in constructing a modern half-mile dirt oval in nearby Kingsport. Built at a reported cost of $380,000, Appalachian Speedway was heralded as one of the South's finest facilities with wide, sweeping corners and modern amenities.

The partners hired former NASCAR driver Curtis "Crawfish" Crider to oversee construction. The South Carolina native moved into a trailer on the track property and later served as a race official. While Appalachian had much going for it, there were two problems: the more established Kingsport Speedway and its popular NASCAR-sanctioned Late Model Sportsman program operated about two miles away, and both tracks usually ran on Friday nights.

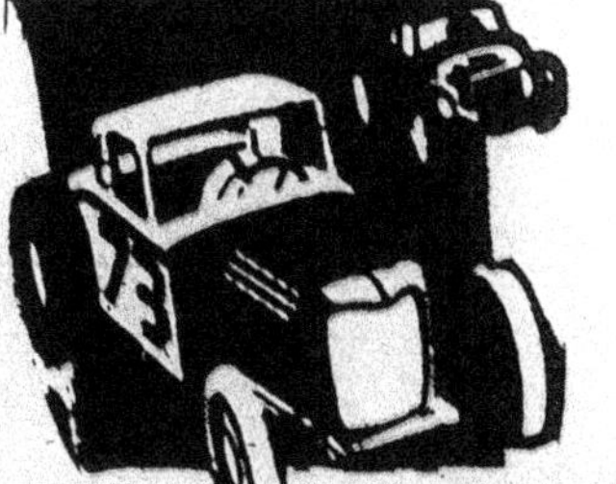

Sportsman Speedway in Johnson City offered a diverse racing program and other attractions. *Author's collection.*

"You could hear them running," Collins said of the other track. "We were in competition with Ken Murray, but we were just splitting the fans up. We did that for two or three years. Everybody was doing everything we could to survive."

The two dirt tracks ran a joint points system, but Appalachian put a strain on both tracks. Collins pursued a NASCAR sanction for both Sportsman and Appalachian around 1970, but that organization was rapidly evolving away from its dirt-track roots. The days of both tracks were numbered. Appalachian operated for four seasons, closed and then reopened for two years before shutting permanently in 1975. Sportsman faced a different kind of problem, Collins said, as relationships between racers and management grew strained.

"We had a lot of fighting. The crowd loved it, but we didn't. We had a fight up here in the pits one time, and it was ready to get out of hand. They had chains and tire tools," Collins said. "I had a guy who worked for me go down there and shut the lights off, and I mean it was dark. When he turned them back on, people were under cars. They didn't know if they were going to get hit upside the head or not, so they were crawling around on their hands and knees trying to hide."

Former driver turned track official Tom Eorgan told Collins, "Drivers and owners are temperamental. They're 99 percent temper and 1 percent mental." But the track's owner grew weary of the drama.

"He got so teed off at the drivers and owners for fighting all the time. He told them more than once he'd shut it down and build a bowling alley, and sure enough, he did," Collins said.

He wishes things could have turned out differently.

"I think if we could have salvaged Sportsman and never built Appalachian," his voice trails off, pondering what might have been. "Appalachian was a better race track, but it wasn't the Sportsman. It was kind of like Darlington; everybody loved Darlington. But there was so much competition for fans. Appalachian probably didn't help, but Bulls Gap was open by then, [with] Kingsport and Lonesome Pine in Virginia. Too much of anything is too much."

24

Ghosts of Atomic Speedway

Thousands travel Interstate 40 west of Knoxville daily, but in their seventy-mile-per-hour haste, most fail to recognize the specter lingering near exit 364.

A few, call them the faithful, still wistfully reflect on what once was. Conversations begin with "Remember when," as their minds' eyes picture two generations of racing legends battling fender to fender in a devil's bowl of dust and gasoline for a glimpse of swirling black and white and a drink from sweet victory's cup. Some truly ache for days gone by, but even the faithful speed past, changing conversations like radio stations as countryside and miles roll by.

But back off West Buttermilk Road, buried beneath the vast expanse of the Crete Carrier truck terminal, lies the shallow grave of Atomic Speedway. Once mentioned in the same breath as elite dirt tracks Eldora or Williams Grove, Atomic now lies silent. Most passersby couldn't comprehend the action that unfolded for thirty-six marvelous years on its banked third-mile oval.

Of East Tennessee's more than thirty ghost tracks, none can match the legacy of Atomic Speedway. In its day, Atomic hosted every major touring dirt Late Model series and everyone professing to be someone from that racing genre. Mining the rich pool of driving talent in its own backyard meant an Atomic feature win was cherished while a string of them was a statement and a step toward immortality.

Businessman and race fan Bob Martin secured a lease on forty-eight acres near the Roane-Loudon county line in 1969, intent on constructing a top-

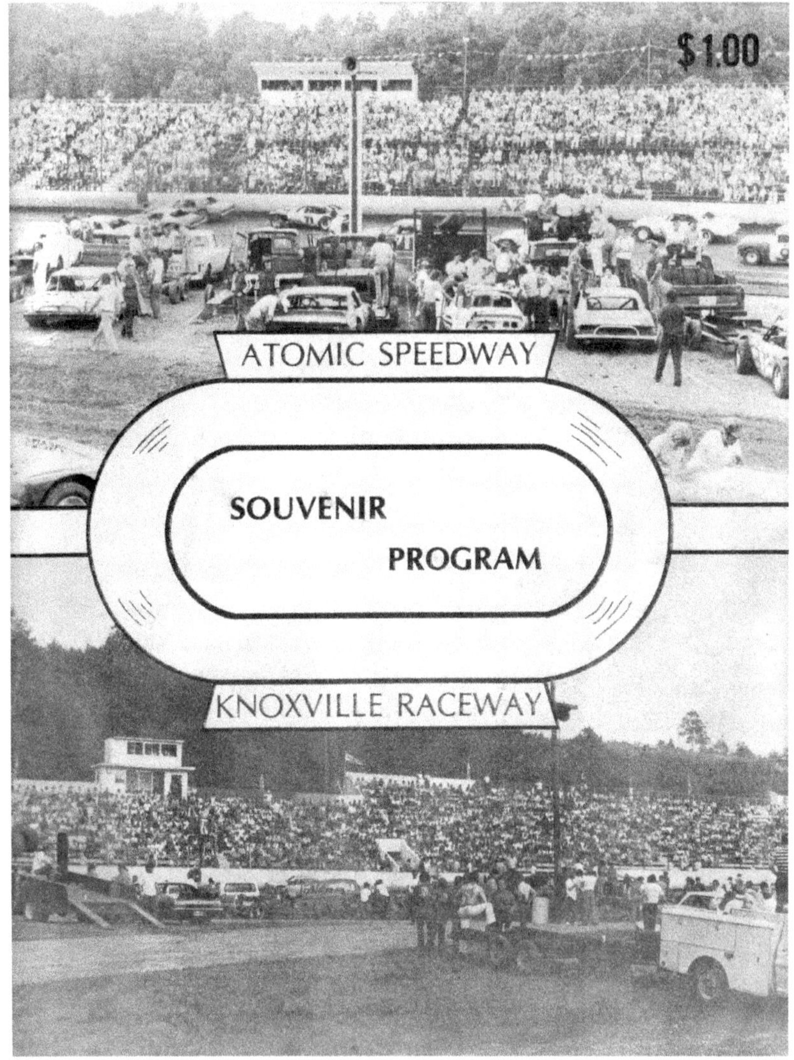

An early program from Atomic Speedway, which worked with Knoxville Raceway for a time in the 1970s. *Melvin Corum collection.*

shelf dirt track. He spent nearly a year creating a smallish oval with ample spectator seating.

The track opened in the spring of 1970 with 394 paying fans and a field of eleven drivers racing for a $700 total payout. Crowds and payouts grew right along with Atomic's reputation.

The Ogle family operated the track from the late 1970s through the 1990s when Atomic earned much of its acclaim. Carson Branum purchased Atomic in 1996, investing in a new racing surface and other upgrades to keep pace in an increasingly competitive arena.

Centrally positioned between rapidly sprawling Knoxville, Oak Ridge, Lenoir City and Kingston, its location was once a strength for attracting fans and competitors, but progress ultimately meant the site was worth more as something else.

Rumors of problems surfaced in 2002 amid diminishing attendance, and Branum eventually sold to Ed Adams, owner of a Knoxville concrete business, in January 2005. Despite a good product on the track, attendance didn't rebound, and Adams ultimately sold the land so the transportation company could consolidate operations from Knoxville and Johnson City into one $5 million facility.

Billy Ogle Jr. fittingly won the track's final feature race on November 4, 2006. Ogle captured five Atomic track championships at a facility once operated by his family. Atomic's gates closed forever, and the deal was consummated after Roane County commissioners approved a zoning change for the property. It was dismantled in 2007.

Its grandstands burned and were hauled away, and even the unique race car marquee that once beckoned to interstate travelers is gone, replaced by something far less audacious. Missing, too, are red clay dust clouds sent drifting across the landscape by frenetic feature races.

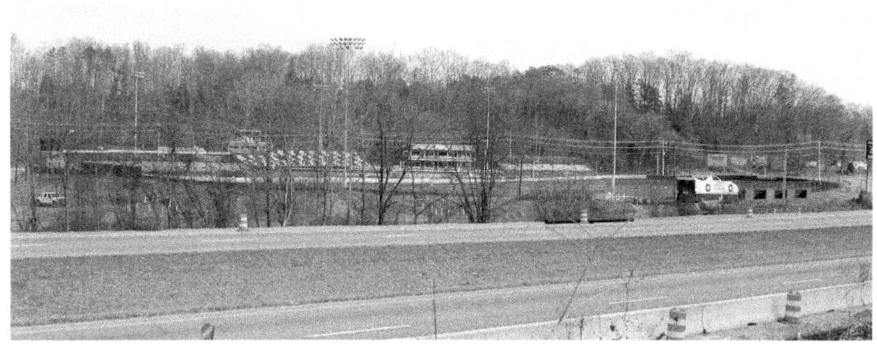

Atomic Speedway operated right next to bustling Interstate 40 from 1970 to 2006 but was dismantled soon after this photo was taken. *Michael Moats photo.*

The site now resembles a grave's vault, covered by a smooth layer of concrete and asphalt, as rows of diesel trucks seem to drone by endlessly. Lights rarely dim inside the massive building covering much of the former track and the infield where legends trod.

Thankfully, Atomic does have a tombstone. Just a few hundred yards down West Buttermilk Road, on a vacant green field resembling a cemetery, rests the track's former control tower building. Its red paint is flaking, and a section of the giant Pepsi sign decorating its roofline is missing, but the black-and-white checkered motif still harkens to past glories.

25

Greatest Show on Dirt

Sporting a showy black-and-white checkered vest and tie and flanked by beautiful, scantily clad women, an animated Robert Smawley flashed his trademark smile from behind mirrored sunglasses and reminded a grandstand full of paying customers they were about to watch the "greatest show on dirt."

Motorcycle racer turned ringmaster, Smawley single-handedly revolutionized dirt Late Model racing; turning a disjointed, grass-roots sport into a nationally recognized form of entertainment and its blue-collar drivers into celebrities. More than a forerunner to today's organizations, his Kingsport-based National Dirt Racing Association created the mold.

"I feel like if we quit tomorrow, we've already done more for dirt-track racing than anybody has done yet in its history," Smawley modestly told *Stock Car Racing* magazine in 1978, midway through its first season. And he meant it.

From his failure at promoting weekly shows at Kingsport's former Appalachian Speedway emerged a greater vision. Tracks like Ohio's Eldora Speedway were attracting the nation's top drivers to single events offering thousands of dollars to win. Why, reasoned Smawley, couldn't he stage a whole series of such races at tracks willing to pay his price?

The bold experiment began at East Tennessee's Newport Raceway on June 9 and 10, 1978. Smawley leased the then dirt oval for the "biggest dirt race in the U.S." His Southeastern Classic featured a $10,000 winner's prize at a time when $1,000 was substantial money. The total payout was

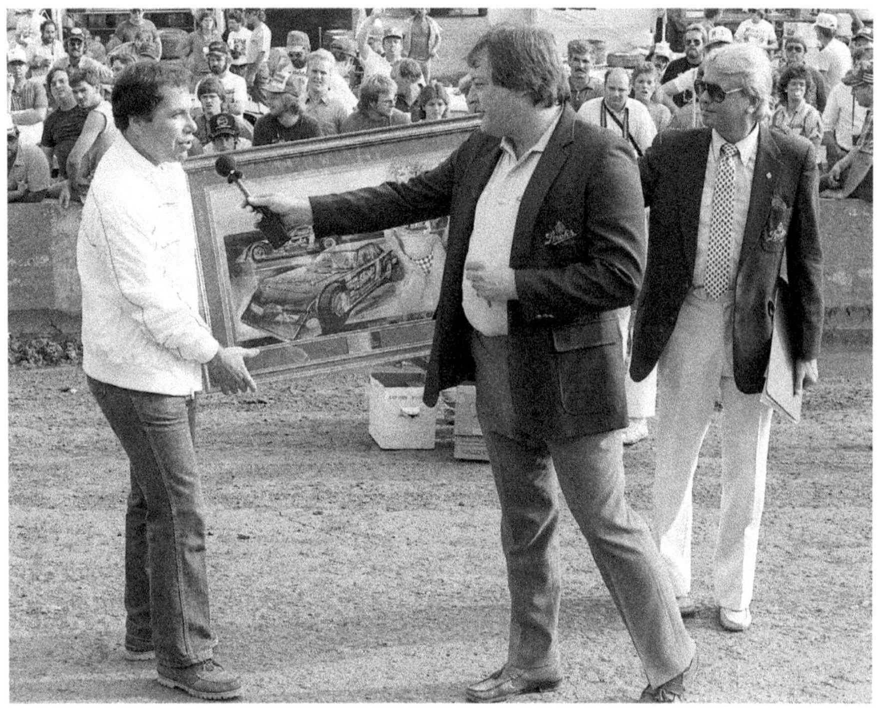

NDRA founder Robert Smawley (center) handles prerace festivities at the NDRA Stroh's Invitational at Kingsport in 1985. *Mike O'Dell photo.*

$22,000—the largest in the nation at that time—and the response was more than he dreamed. Grandstands were filled, and so was the pit area. When the dust settled, Georgia's Buck Simmons picked up the top prize.

"I thought it was [a] misprint," Simmons said of the $10,000. "I can remember many a night winning and getting $15."

A story in that first event's souvenir program offered a glimpse into the future: "Smawley is now working toward a sanctioning body for dirt track racing and is well under way in acquiring sponsorship for a $50,000 point fund for next season."

A few weeks later, the NDRA held its first official event in Phenix City, Alabama, and then claimed a crowd of thirteen thousand saw its second race in Gaffney, South Carolina. Another sellout followed at historic Myrtle Beach Speedway in South Carolina, where NASCAR great David Pearson finished second behind Leon Archer. The tour rolled into lightning-fast Atomic Speedway near Knoxville that October, where Ohio traveler Larry Moore collected the first of his nineteen series victories.

"NDRA is possibly now one of the biggest drawing cards that has ever hit racing in its entire history. We have run in three months on a parallel probably to the other organizations that have been in business for years. I believe it's because we've come in and put some class into the show," Smawley said in an early interview.

The formula included more than great racing. Smawley demanded a tight show that started on time. He brought a core group of officials in matching uniforms to conduct events, including a public address announcer and flagman to keep the program moving. Word of sellout crowds and high car counts prompted beleaguered promoters from the Gulf Coast to New York to sign up.

"Our rules for the cars are set up to cause a minimum of conflict and save arguments," Smawley said. "We looked at the majority of the cars participating in this sport throughout the major part of the country and have adopted our rules to fit what is actually happening."

In its 1979 advertising, NDRA claimed "dirt racing goes Wall Street," boasting a $500,000 series, a schedule with sponsors for all fourteen races and predetermined rain dates—all virtually unheard of at that time. Archer became the first series champion, despite having his a car stolen before a race at Atomic Speedway.

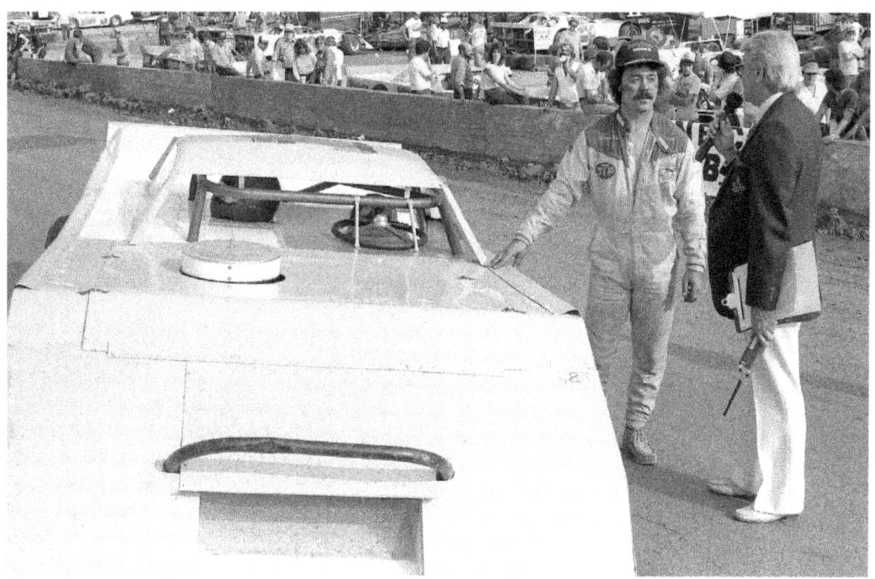

Future NASCAR star Ernie Irvan (left) talks about winning the Six-Cylinder championship at Kingsport. *Mike O'Dell photo.*

By 1981, the series expanded to twenty-eight races in sixteen states while attracting national sponsors and greater media attention. Winning its "Million Dollar Super Series" became a career-building springboard for drivers like Tennessean Jeff Purvis and Ohio's Rodney Combs, who leapt from dirt superstardom to NASCAR.

It wasn't perfect. NDRA was blamed for driving up the cost of dirt racing and the controversial evolution of wedge-shaped race car bodies. Wedge cars appeared to be going one hundred miles per hour sitting still but were either loved or despised since they bore scant resemblance to production cars.

NDRA's stakes and schedule also rendered homebuilt cars uncompetitive, forcing racers to purchase lighter, faster, professionally constructed machines able to withstand the rigors of competing night after night. As suspension and chassis components became more refined, drivers also needed more powerful, reliable engines. It was no coincidence that many of NDRA's sponsors produced those specialized components.

After star driver Jim Dunn perished in a fiery crash in 1983, Smawley successfully lobbied car builders, racers and promoters to improve safety standards.

In an effort to make the cars more like stock cars, Smawley published a series of more restrictive body rules for 1984. He also had an agreement with Hoosier to become the sole tire supplier to try to hold down costs.

Away from the track, life on the road for some in the NDRA circus included an endless string of parties as the serious approach to racing gave way to raucous abandon of booze, drugs and sex with the revelry often lasting until dawn.

After years of continued growth, Smawley's 1985 season appeared to offer unlimited potential with an impressive lineup of national sponsors, a robust schedule and a fleet of top-name drivers. Week after week, the series barreled along, staging events from Alabama and North Carolina to Missouri, Kansas and Arkansas and then on to Ohio and Michigan. Defending champ Purvis continued winning but shared the checkered flags with Billy Moyer, Charlie Swartz and Freddy Smith.

"Robert Smawley has done a good job getting dirt-track racing together," Moyer said that season.

"Everybody said dirt racing could not be organized," Smawley said. "It was hard to organize because no racetrack had the same rules. That made it hard on the drivers and resulted in nothing but mass confusion. We changed that."

In October 1985, NDRA offered the richest payout in dirt racing history, a $250,000 invitational weekend back home at East Tennessee's

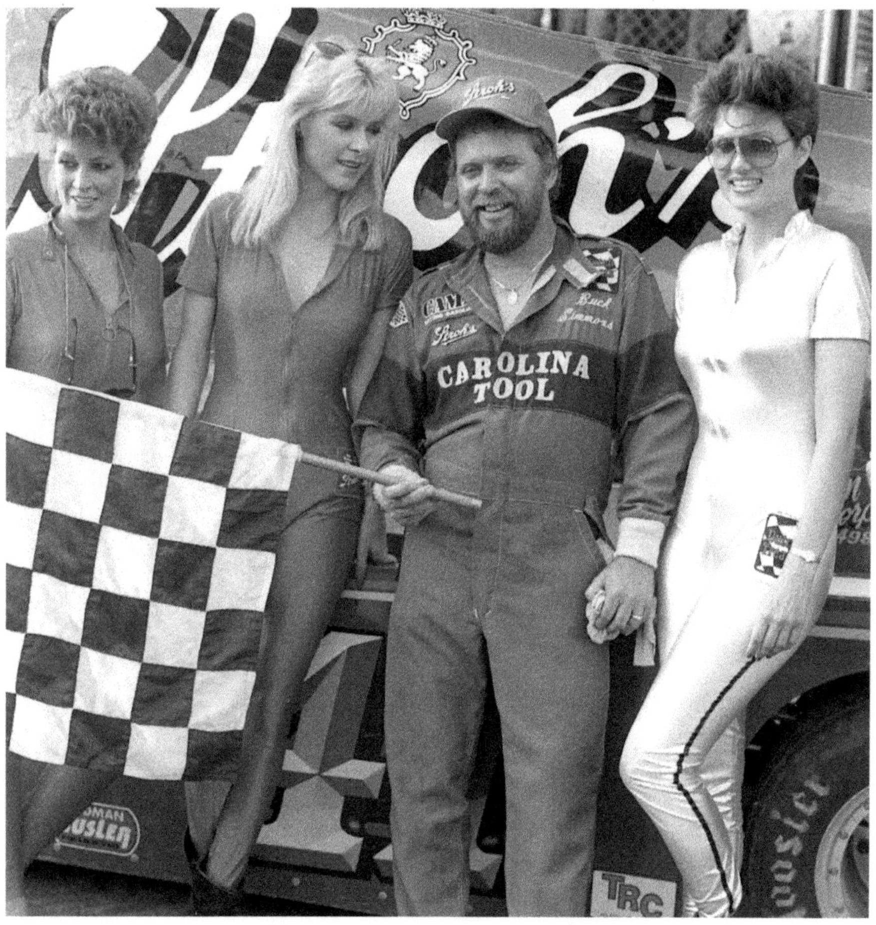

Kingsport Invitational winner Buck Simmons celebrates with a bevy of beauty queens. *Mike O'Dell photo.*

Kingsport Speedway. While the pits were filled with cars, attendance wasn't overwhelming. On the track, future NASCAR driver Ernie Irvan won a six-cylinder preliminary race and Georgian Buck Simmons led all one hundred laps to capture the main event and a $30,000 payday.

Behind the scenes, things came unraveled, and the aftermath remains a bit fuzzy. Series sponsor Stroh's abruptly withdrew its support while simultaneously dropping its program with the Bristol-based International Hot Rod Association drag racing series. NDRA champion Purvis didn't collect the $30,000 due him for winning the 1985 points title, and other NDRA bills went unpaid.

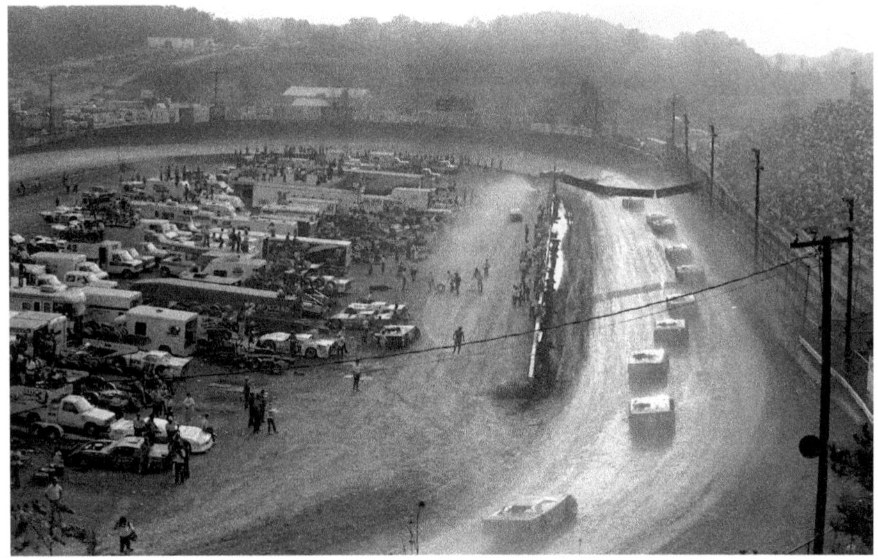

A dusty haze hangs over Kingsport Speedway as NDRA Late Model cars race around the track. *Mike O'Dell photo.*

One version of the story suggests the Kingsport race's mediocre attendance forced Smawley to use points fund money to pay the purse, while others blame the demise on a general downturn in the economy. Competing organizations were certainly gaining market share by using Smawley's own business model against him. For whatever reason, Smawley's reign over dirt racing ended just that quickly, and attempts to resuscitate the organization failed. Today, its former Clay Street office is home to a child development center.

"There is no telling how far Robert Smawley could have gone," former employee and racing publicist Robert Walden said. "He was so far ahead of his time, but he had his vices."

How significant was an organization that lasted just eight seasons? In 2001, Smawley and four series champions—Purvis, Simmons, Mike Duvall and Larry Moore—were part of the initial class inducted into the National Dirt Late Model Hall of Fame. Leon Archer, NDRA's first series champion, was inducted two years later, and the organization's twelve most successful drivers are now enshrined.

More importantly, dirt Late Model races with generous payouts continue to play out in every corner of the United States. The cars are safer, and grandstands are typically filled when the touring show comes to town—all of which would certainly bring a smile to Robert Smawley's face.

26

The People's Choice

The white-and-blue race car sits respectfully silent, parked alongside motorsports royalty in the International Motorsports Hall of Fame and Museum in Talladega, Alabama. Positioned among Bill Elliott's Winston Million–winning Ford, a Dodge donated by Richard Petty, an array of former Indianapolis 500 winners and a rocket-powered machine that reached 739 miles per hour on land sits a short-track Late Model stock car.

At first, it seems out of place, somehow unworthy to be in such company since thousands like it race all across America. But this one—a Ford from the fertile dirt tracks of East Tennessee—is a permanent part of one of the sport's most significant collections.

In 1993, John A. Utsman drove that car to simultaneous track championship titles at Volunteer Speedway in Bulls Gap and Kingsport Speedway. Utsman, a former NASCAR Late Model Sportsman series regular and part-time Winston Cup driver, won eighteen races and finished second six other times in the twenty-eight races entered. That was exceptional, especially in a region where legendary drivers seemed to grow on trees.

"The museum called here and asked if I had a driving suit, a helmet and a pair of shoes they could put on a mannequin. I thought it was a joke," Utsman recalled. "But I got a suit, helmet, shoes and took it down there. This woman also asked me to bring a bunch of pictures."

If he was unprepared for the first request, he was floored by the second.

"She asked if I was going to donate a car, but I told her I couldn't afford to do that," Utsman said. He politely presented the items, and while museum staffers copied his photos, Utsman and his brothers visited the museum adjacent to the Talladega Superspeedway. Even Utsman was taken aback by what happened next.

"We walked around that museum, and there were cars of Davey Allison and Bobby Allison, Dale Earnhardt, the Pettys and even Stan Barrett. I told [brothers] Layman and Sherman, I'm going to give them this race car if I don't ever race again. This is too much of an honor not to do it. It's an honor for me, but it's because you all did it before I ever came along."

The car represents thousands of weekend warriors who often perform in relative obscurity. So the brothers delivered that race-winning car.

"I feel really honored to be asked to do that. It was the first dirt-track car like that down there. There may be some more deserving; I don't know if there are or not. But for what we've done for racing in this area—not me, but my dad and my brothers—it's something just to be part of it."

Racing was always a family affair for the Utsmans.

"My dad had a race car, and he raced before I came along. Then my uncle Dub got out of service in 1946 or '47, and he drove dad's car," said the man known to one and all as John A. "There was an Island Park track there in Bluff City, and they used to race right there. I was six or seven years old. Then they went to the Tri-City airport, and Uncle Dub and Sherman [were]

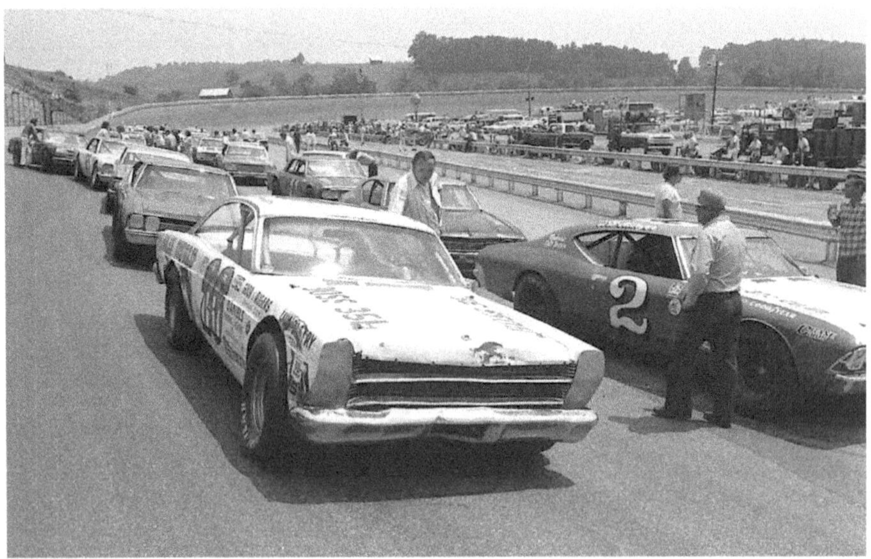

In June 1973, John A. Utsman qualified his Ford on the front row for a Bristol Late Model Sportsman race. He finished second behind polesitter L.D. Ottinger's Chevrolet. *John Beach photo.*

racing then in 1950–51. Then Layman started racing at Tri-City Speedway in open-wheel Modifieds in 1955. I started racing in 1960."

John A.'s career began on the dirt at the old Sportsman Speedway in Johnson City. The family might have continued to focus their energies on those short, dirt-covered race tracks until one day another track rose up out of a former dairy farm just a few miles away. In January 1961, Bristol businessmen Larry Carrier, Carl Moore and R.G. Pope announced plans to build Bristol International Speedway and host regular races for NASCAR's Grand National Series. The big time was coming to East Tennessee.

When the gleaming new track opened that July, three Utsmans—Layman, Dub and Sherman—qualified for the inaugural Volunteer 500. Layman finished last, dropping out after thirty-five laps with handling problems. Dub finished twenty-ninth after engine problems, but Sherman recorded a solid ninth-place finish in his first race since a serious crash in 1959.

The family continued competing in NASCAR and enjoying good success on the local level. John A. assembled a record worthy of a Hall of Fame. Known as "the people's choice" at tracks across East Tennessee and Southwest Virginia, Utsman won regularly on dirt and asphalt.

"I didn't win as many as some, but I really didn't have money to race on," he said. "We built our own cars and built our own engines. But I had a brother, Cecil, that made up the difference in money. He was more than just a brother. I raced for forty years, and he was right by my side."

Some of his greatest successes came in the NASCAR Late Model Sportsman class. Racing against L.D. Ottinger, Gene Glover, Jimmy Hensley and so many more, Utsman captured Kingsport's 1972 track championship. The following year, he nearly won the Permatex 300 at Bristol and made three starts in Winston Cup driving a Dodge owned and prepared by G.C. Spencer. Engine woes ended promising runs in the Daytona 500 and in Rockingham, North Carolina, but the team clicked when the tour came to Bristol in March. Utsman avoided trouble and posted his first top-ten finish on the day Cale Yarborough led all five hundred laps.

Series regular Benny Parsons finished fourth that afternoon and noticed Utsman's performance. When the tour returned in July, Parsons asked him to try out his Chevrolet in practice and stand by as a relief driver, since the grueling high-banked track often took its toll on drivers. Utsman was more than happy to oblige.

Parsons was leading the Volunteer 500 when he gave way to Utsman at the midway point. Utsman wheeled the car for 170 laps, taking the lead for good on lap 332 before switching again so Parsons could drive the final 80 circuits.

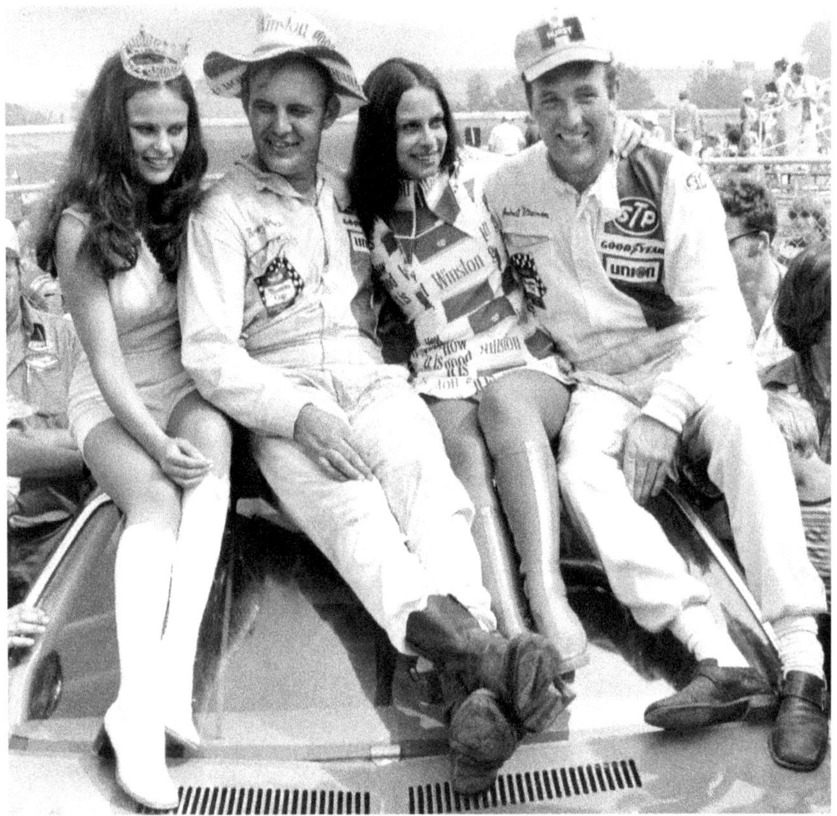

John A. Utsman (right) joined Benny Parsons's victory celebration after helping wheel Parsons's Chevrolet to the 1973 Volunteer 500 win. *John A. Utsman collection.*

"The biggest thrill I ever got was when Benny asked me to relief drive for him, and we won that race," Utsman said. "What really made it a thrill was, you know, how Cale Yarborough won that first race and led all five hundred laps. Well, the first thing I saw when I straightened that mirror up in Benny's car, was Cale Yarborough right behind me. He stuck his nose up beside me a time or two in traffic, but I could just drive off from him. That done me more good than anything to win that race."

The victory was Parsons's lone win en route to the 1973 championship. Among the most prized mementos from Utsman's driving career is a handwritten letter thanking him for his role in the win and the championship.

"If I'd wrecked, he wouldn't have won the championship. So I was part of the championship, even though I don't get credit for it, which is fine with me," Utsman said.

Official records include no mention of Utsman's participation, let alone his role. History shows Utsman's best Cup finish was that tenth-place finish in March 1973, but Utsman actually became a designated Bristol fill-in for Parsons and others.

"I relieved Benny four other times at Bristol and finished second, third and fourth. Then we crashed one other time," Utsman said. "Then I relieved Bobby Allison in 1976 after he injured some ribs in a crash at Rockingham, and we finished fifth. I got in Janet Guthrie's car thirteen laps down, and we finished sixth."

Parsons never forgot.

After he retired from driving, the taxi driver turned racing champion won an Emmy Award by bringing his cockpit-savvy analysis and folksy style to the TV broadcast booth. Two years before cancer cut short his life, Parsons reserved the back room of Ridgewood Restaurant—a world-renowned, down-home barbecue joint just a straightaway from Utsman's home—and invited his longtime friend and Utsman's wife, Ann, to join him. Parsons could have afforded any fancy restaurant with linen tablecloths and a gourmet chef, but Ridgewood's quaint surroundings, sweet iced tea, pulled pork and baked beans were just right for that celebration.

"I had a good time and made a lot of friends," Utsman said. "If I had my life to live over, I'd still race."

27

Dirt's Dale Earnhardt

A youthful Scott Bloomquist surveyed the Eldora Speedway pit area—stacked end to end with dirt racing's greatest drivers assembled for the annual World 100—and contemplated retreat. It was the long-haired Iowa native's first visit to rural, western Ohio and the hallowed ground of dirt Late Model racing's premier event.

Despite a résumé already filled with victories in California and across East Tennessee, the twenty-three-year-old was uncertain about suddenly plunging into the pool's deepest end.

"I went to the World 100 and almost left. There were 250 cars there. I'd never been there, never raced there, and there was a race at Atomic Speedway that paid $5,000 to win," Bloomquist said. "I never thought to look at what the payback was at that race. It was $21,000 to win and $5,000 for second. I thought, what in the hell makes you think you can even get second against 250 guys who have been coming here for years? I just about headed to Atomic because I figured I could get that $5,000."

Bloomquist relayed his uncertainty to a friend who worked for Hoosier Tire, who convinced him to stay.

"So we wound up sticking around and won that race. I was the first to ever win it as a rookie—someone who'd never raced there before," he said. "And that's when I started focusing on traveling and going to bigger shows and not underestimating yourself."

That 1988 pivot point in a remarkable career may have been the only time in three decades anyone ever underestimated Scott Bloomquist.

"We came back the next year and set [a] fast time. You could have multiple cars there to qualify, so we had first-, second- and third-fast[est] time[s], so people didn't think it was a fluke," he said. "We came back in 1990 and won the race again. That's when people took me serious."

Serious is an apt adjective for the enigmatic Bloomquist, an intensely focused man whose insatiable appetite for success makes him the most polarizing figure in dirt Late Model racing. He seems equally loved and reviled in the grandstands, a side effect from too much winning. But his souvenirs continually outsell all others just as he continues dominating the nation's racetracks. After thirty years of winning, he remains the face of his sport: dirt racing's Dale Earnhardt.

A Zen master of reading track surfaces and among the sport's most technically astute, Bloomquist has few peers and few remaining mountains to climb. He has accrued more than five hundred victories in dirt Late Model racing's most prestigious events against two generations of its finest drivers.

Hall of Fame? He was inducted more than one hundred victories ago in 2002.

"What has always motivated me is you cannot conquer this sport. It's more difficult every year," Bloomquist said. "Two or three years ago, I won twenty-some shows, and we don't run small shows. All the shows we win are big series events. It's going to be nearly impossible, if not impossible, for somebody to win every event. Because you can't conquer it, it continues to fascinate and compel me to continue the chase."

Winning every event in a season remains his goal, and he nearly accomplished it during his first season in East Tennessee. Now eligible for AARP membership, Bloomquist began his racing journey on a California dirt track at age sixteen when his father, a commercial airline pilot, bought a race car.

"The first night out he decided it just wasn't something he wanted to do. The lighting and the mud flying wasn't for him. He had always been around drag racing, everything really clean and bright lights and all that. We were at a track in Corona, California. It wasn't bright, and there was a lot of dust in the air. It wasn't something he saw pursuing," Bloomquist said. "He gave me a chance to drive the next week, and I did well enough to keep him interested. He was going to sell everything. We raced together for a couple years, and I did quite well, especially the second and third year."

At age eighteen, young Bloomquist dominated the largest Late Model race then held in California, setting fast times, lapping the field twice and pocketing $4,000. Flush with success and determined to make his mark,

Bloomquist knew that would require moving across the country, back to an area where he lived for one year while in third grade.

"I'd always kept up with what went on back here. I was a fan of Larry Phillips, and he came to California and just whipped everybody. But he had a harder time winning back here. So I was fascinated with why he couldn't dominate back here in Tennessee and all over the East," Bloomquist said. "When Robert Smawley got NDRA rolling, they were paying $10,000 to win at all these racetracks around here, and that's really what got my attention.

"I decided I really wanted to pursue this as a career, so that meant I needed to be near the hub, which, at that time, was Robert Smawley," he said. "My father was looking for a place to land when he retired from the airlines, and he found a nice place here. I lived here and just worked for him. He was either going to sell the stuff, or I could purchase it from him by working on the property. From that point, that's what we did. I worked here, lived here and raced when I could afford to."

"Here" was a farm in rural Mooresburg, located in East Tennessee's lakeway region midway between Kingsport and Knoxville. Bloomquist soon found a place to perfect his chosen craft.

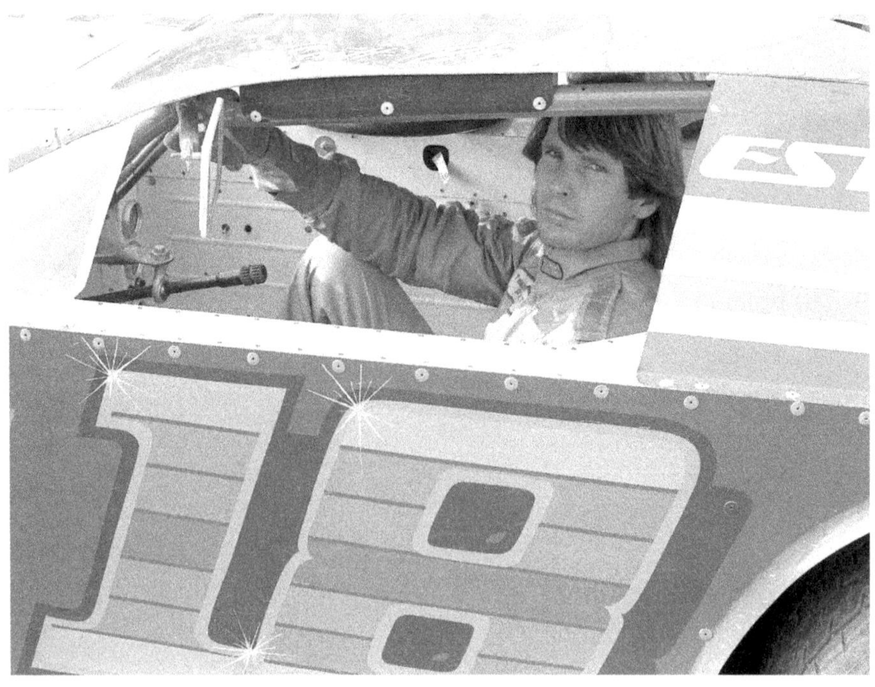

A young Scott Bloomquist captured the Kingsport Speedway Late Model championship in 1984, his first year living in East Tennessee. *Mike O'Dell photo.*

Former NASCAR race team owner J.D. Stacy bought the Kingsport Speedway, converted it back to dirt and began offering $2,500 to win each week in 1984. Armed with a new Barry Wright race car, Kingsport became Bloomquist's sole focus. His car wasn't ready for the season's first race, and he got quite a surprise the second week.

"We rolled in, and [Hall of Fame driver] Larry Moore was in the pits. I'll never forget, my dad looked at me and said, 'Well, there goes that $2,500.' I said, 'It ain't over yet,'" Bloomquist recalled.

Moore, one of dirt racing's all-time most successful drivers, set fast time while Bloomquist qualified second.

"Ten laps into the feature, he was in the way and I was pretty hungry, so I put the bumper to him and won the race. The next week, he was back. Well, we were fast time, he was second fast time, he got beat on the start and I never looked back and won that one. That was $2,500 and then another $2,500, so things were looking up," he said.

Moore didn't return for the next race, but Rodney Combs did. "Don't make me look too bad," the NDRA star and future NASCAR series driver told Bloomquist. "That's entirely up to you," Scott replied.

"I just never really was intimidated. Let's just call it [ignorance], but I never lacked confidence," Bloomquist said. "No matter how much money you have, you can only race one car at a time, one engine at a time and one set of tires at a time. I've always kept that attitude. We set fast time and beat him by a considerable margin, and he didn't come back the next week. We won every single race at Kingsport that year."

The only exception was an NDRA race in which Bloomquist qualified poorly, due to making a change to his car, but rallied to finish second to Mike Duvall.

His NDRA dream evaporated when that series folded after the 1985 season, and Bloomquist spent the next couple seasons racing and winning on the diverse array of East Tennessee tracks: Atomic, Kingsport, Newport, Smoky Mountain, Tazewell and Volunteer.

"That was a challenge," he said. "We won thirty-five of forty-five races in '86 at six different race tracks. It was a great season, and we won a lot [of] races. I never left East Tennessee until I felt I was ready. I couldn't afford to, but I wanted to be ready. Then I went to Isom, Kentucky, and that was where I won my first $10,000 show. Three weeks later, we went to the World 100."

Building on his Eldora success, Bloomquist hit the road, racing and winning from Florida to Wisconsin, from the Atlantic Coast to the Midwest. Name a prominent U.S. dirt track—Eldora, Knoxville, Charlotte, Florence,

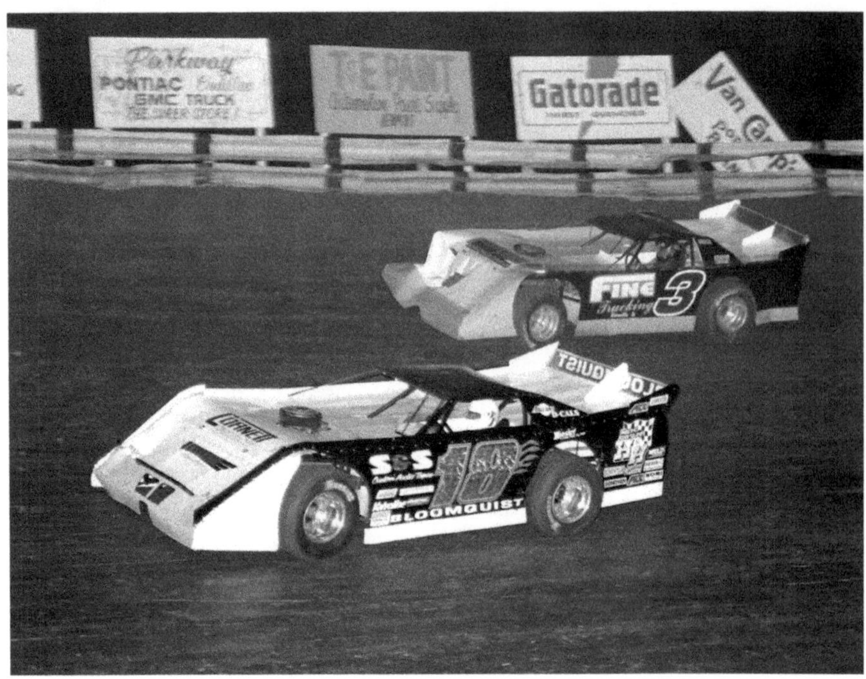

Scott Bloomquist (18) races with Steve Smith (3) during a 1990s Late Model action at Volunteer Speedway in Bulls Gap. *Joey Millard photo.*

Brownstown, Dixie, Volusia County, Pennsboro—and Bloomquist made multiple visits to victory lane. Name a rich, major event—World 100, Late Model Dream, Dirt Track World Championship, Show-Me 100, Outlaw 100, North-South 100—and Bloomquist has the trophy. Name a series—Hav-A-Tampa, Lucas Oil, UMP, Southern All-Star, STARS, UDTRA, World of Outlaws—and Bloomquist conquered it.

"There's not any race we haven't won, any championship we pursued that we haven't won with a whole lot of stuff to overcome," Bloomquist said. "If there is anything I would probably do different, I'd probably stay under the radar a little bit more. Winning puts a target on your back, and if you're a little outspoken…I've always given the other drivers credit because this is not an easy thing to win at. You might have a great year, but there is a tremendous effort being put forward by all the other competitors. And even if they've never worked together in the past, they'll all work together and share information if you dominate too much. They can make it hard on you."

During the early years, his cars carried number 18, but that switched to 0 in the 1990s. His cars still carry the tiny version of the 18 on each side—a tribute to his early success.

"I had intended on changing every year—19, 20, 21. At 18, we won the track championship and won some races. I also just liked how the number looked on each side of the car and the angle. I stuck with number 18 for fifteen years. I feel like I was on the cutting edge on decals and the look of the car, and everyone just kept looking closer and closer to pretty much what my look was," Bloomquist said.

The number change also signified a change in philosophy.

"It got to a point where I was ready to bring everything back home and start from ground zero. The first 0 car didn't have a sponsor's name on it. At the time, I felt like I was starting over, so zero was perfect," Bloomquist said. "I also liked the look of the number. There were so many possibilities with the zero. I really was just looking for a look, and it was a new beginning for me. We went through a bunch of things with the series [that] I felt were unjust. I felt they took the championship away from us so it was time to look at something different. I took some time off and assessed if I even wanted to do this anymore. Once I came back, I decided, yeah, I do have enough passion for it, enough love for it. I just had to have a different approach."

Bloomquist began building his own cars from the ground up and sharing once-secretive setups.

"I was just going to work with a few drivers to get some feedback. Some chassis builders sell cars to three hundred or four hundred people, and they get all this feedback. Everyone's got a little something to throw your way. You just need to hear those things, and that's what made me decide to do any cars for anyone else," he said.

A pursuit of technological perfection has also motivated his decision to remain in dirt racing.

"This sport is not going to be dominated by a computer anytime soon, and that's what makes me love it," he said. "I get bored easily, and I don't believe I'll ever get bored with this. The ability to think outside the box and apply it to your race car and not have NASCAR or someone step in and just strip you of something that might dominate. It's closer all the time, but we have such a bigger window than anyone in NASCAR to be able to free-think, build and experiment. I get as much joy out of that as racing."

Barring any health issues or accidents, Bloomquist expects to be behind the wheel for some time.

"I'm not feeling old, but I'm fifty. And I love this sport so much that I always want to be involved in it whether I'm driving or not. I feel like I have another fifteen years left, but if it gets to where I'm not competitive to the level I think I should be or if there is any physical handicap—ears, sight, whatever—that will keep me from racing at my full potential, then I might think about putting another driver, a younger driver, in the car. I don't think it's coming anytime soon," he said.

"It's been a nice ride, and it's not over yet."

28
Short-Track Legends

There must be something truly special in the East Tennessee soil. How else could one region generate so many legendary short-track drivers? Here are snapshots of some of the very best.

Walter Ball

With more than four hundred feature race victories, Walter Ball did more than just win—he dominated. In a career that spanned from the 1950s to 1978, Ball captured track championships at six facilities in two states. He saved his greatest season for Volunteer Speedway in 1977.

The Johnson City driver captured nineteen feature wins in twenty-one starts against the likes of Bill Corum, Tootle Estes, Herman Goddard, Bill Morton and H.E. Vineyard. It was Vineyard who regularly chased Ball to the checkered flag that season, finishing second fifteen times.

Ball won the prestigious Tri-Cities 200 twice, taking checkered flags in the 1968 and 1971 events. Besides Volunteer, Ball won track titles at Appalachian Speedway in Kingsport, Davy Crockett Speedway in Rogersville, Newport Raceway in Newport, Sportsman Speedway in Johnson City and Cedar Hills Speedway in Richlands, Virginia. He also ran in some NASCAR Late Model Sportsman races.

After hanging up his helmet, Ball served as crew chief for son Dale's racing efforts. He was rewarded with a number of wins, and they became the first father-son tandem to claim Volunteer track championships. Ball died after suffering a heart attack at the speedway on his seventieth birthday.

Bob Burcham

After first experiencing racing as a fan at Ashway Speedway when his family lived in Knoxville, Bob Burcham later relocated to the Chattanooga area and was soon competing at Boyd's and Cleveland Speedways. A quick study, Burcham won regularly at Boyd's and began running in Modified races across Georgia, Alabama and Tennessee.

In 1963, he ranked second nationally behind Bobby Allison in the Modified-Special class, winning the track title at Montgomery, Alabama, and placing in the top four at three other tracks. Burcham ranked sixth nationally in 1964 and was in the top ten at five different tracks.

He raced in the NASCAR Grand Touring division in the late 1960s, claiming a pole and second-place finish in Nashville in 1969.

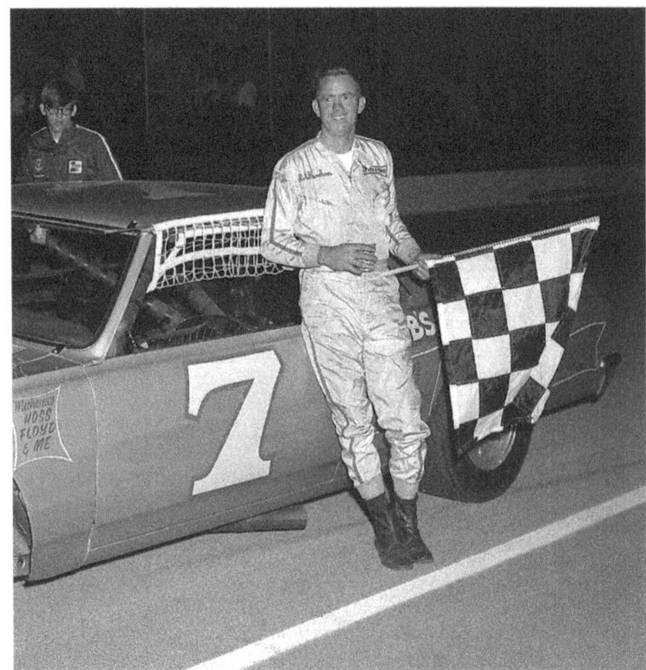

Bob Burcham of the Chattanooga area won a major NASCAR Late Model Sportsman race at Smoky Mountain in 1970, as well as the 1971 track championship. *Ray Taylor photo.*

He raced in the NASCAR Late Model Sportsman division at Smoky Mountain, Nashville and tracks in Georgia and Alabama, winning a three-hundred-lap race at Smoky Mountain in 1970 and the 1971 track championship. From 1968 to 1979, he made thirty-six NASCAR Grand National starts, including a dozen for Jack White, a successful machine shop operator from the Knoxville area.

Big Bill, Little Bill and Melvin Corum

Rural Maynardville is the home of the Corum family, which includes two brothers and a cousin who combined to win enough races and track championships to earn the dubious collective nickname "those damn Corums."

Melvin Corum was Big Bill's younger brother and grew up watching races at Broadway Speedway. At age nineteen, he was the first to begin driving,

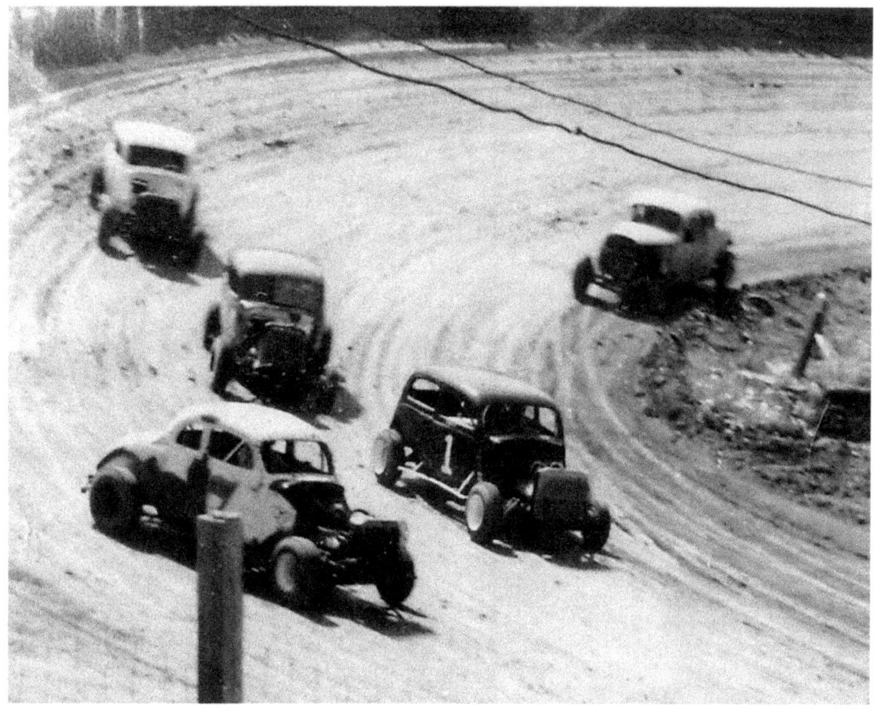

Big Bill Corum (7) races younger brother Melvin Corum (1) for the victory at Ashway Speedway. *Melvin Corum collection.*

getting his first win in the amateur class at Ashway Speedway in 1959. Soon, his older brother got interested and began competing. When their cousin began racing, the nicknames helped separate them.

Melvin captured more than three hundred short-track wins across East Tennessee and Kentucky. He won a points championship and a two-hundred-lap race at Ashway Speedway in 1962 and seven track titles at Tazewell Speedway in both the Modified and Late Model divisions between 1966 and 1977. He was Knoxville Raceway's 1975 champion and the 1984 titlist in the 9:1 Late Model class at Atomic. He was a 1991 inductee into the East Tennessee Racing Hall of Fame and has worked tirelessly to preserve the region's racing history.

Big Bill recorded a number of wins, but his career was cut short by a fatal heart attack in 1973.

Since the brothers won so often, Little Bill set out to carve his own niche and often ran at tracks where they didn't. He became a regular at Tazewell, 411, Volunteer and Atomic speedways, winning many of their biggest races and finishing his career with more than two hundred feature victories.

Freddy Fryar

From coupe-bodied Modifieds to Skeeters, Late Models and Grand National stockers, Chattanooga native Freddy Fryar wheeled them all, winning more than eight hundred times at many levels in his illustrious thirty-seven-year driving career.

He began racing at age fourteen at Warner Park and then later competed at Moccasin Bend and Boyd's Speedway around Chattanooga. He twice drove a Modified on Florida's old Daytona Beach & Road Course. He captured seven NASCAR Modified and Sportsman track championships during the 1960s in Nashville and tracks in Louisiana, Mississippi and Texas, as well as three state titles.

He finished second behind Bobby Allison for the 1964 NASCAR Modified national championship, third in the 1967 national points and sixth in the 1968 Late Model Sportsman championship. He won thirty-four times in forty-five starts in 1968 and was selected as the division's most popular driver. Fryar again finished third in the 1969 points, trailing Red Farmer and Harry Gant for the national championship.

Fryar made six Grand National starts for Charley Griffith, Herb Adcox and Buster Davis, but his true niche was in Late Model racing. He captured the 1983 All-Pro Series title and 1984 All-Pro Truck Series championship. He had at least ten All-Pro wins and two victories in the prestigious Snowball Derby. After retiring from driving in 1987, he served as crew chief for a number of NASCAR teams and, later, as a driving instructor for Richard Petty's driving school.

Older brother Harold was also an outstanding southeastern short-track racer but died as a result of injuries suffered in a race in Gadsden, Alabama, in 1971. Freddy Fryar was inducted into both the Alabama Auto Racing Hall of Fame and Ozark Racing Hall of Fame in 2013.

Herman Goddard

At an age when most slow down, Knoxville's Herman Goddard continued pushing the pedal. The last of his more than five hundred dirt Late Model victories came in 2008, at age seventy-two, at Volunteer Speedway. He retired from driving at seventy-four.

Goddard made his first start at Broadway Speedway in Knoxville at age nineteen. He soon raced and won regularly across the region at 411 and Newport when both were dirt, plus Volunteer and Atomic speedways. Perhaps his greatest success came at Atomic, the legendary, third-mile oval just west of Knoxville. Displaying a knack for the dizzying pace and unique car control it demanded, Goddard won the 1984 Tennessee dirt track championship one-hundred-lap race there and a bevy of track titles.

The youngest of three Goddard brothers, Herman made the fast-paced Volunteer oval look easy by winning the 1990 championship, and he later received a lifetime achievement award for a career marked by multiple victories and outstanding sportsmanship. Beyond racing, he has long been active in his church.

The family operates Goddard Performance Parts in Knoxville, which includes building Warrior brand dirt Late Model race cars. In 2008, Herman Goddard became the fifth Tennessee driver inducted into the National Dirt Late Model Hall of Fame.

Paul Gose

Despite nearly always arriving late at racetracks, Paul Gose nearly always finished first beneath the checkered flag. Driving a 1932 Ford coupe powered by a flathead Ford V-8 engine, Gose dominated the racing scene across East Tennessee and much of the South.

Competitors recalled Gose regularly showed up after practice and qualifying was complete, fell in at the rear of the field but left them eating his dust. The Morristown driver nicknamed "the Ghost" won more than 540 feature races and a bevy of championships during a career than began in 1949 at the old Tri-City Speedway near Blountville and continued through the early 1970s.

A World War II army veteran, Gose worked as an engine builder and racer and never held a regular job. He began racing motorcycles but soon switched to cars. Gose specialized in building the fastest flathead engines around and racked up track championships at nine Tennessee facilities: Appalachian Speedway, Davy Crockett Speedway, Kingsport Speedway, Knoxville Raceway, McMinnville Raceway, Oak Ridge Speedway, Sportsman Speedway, Tazewell Speedway, Tennessee-Carolina Speedway and 411 Raceway.

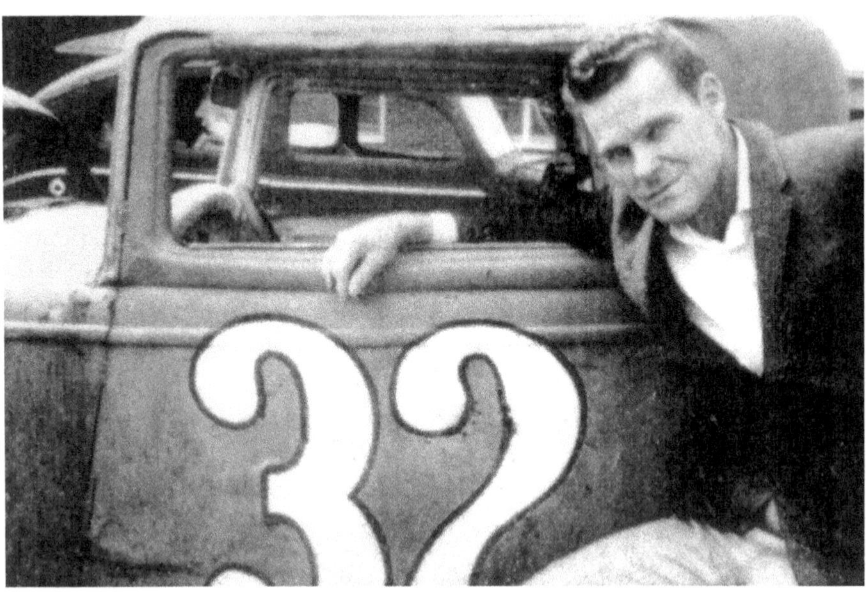

Paul Gose of Morristown was one of the region's most successful drivers, winning hundreds of races and championships at ten tracks. *Melvin Corum collection.*

But the Ghost's exploits weren't limited to Tennessee. He also regularly raced and won at Athens Speedway and Boyd's Speedway in Georgia, Corbin and Monticello speedways in Kentucky, Harris Speedway and Rutherford County Speedway in North Carolina, along with Anderson, Cherokee, Golden Strip and Mountainview speedways in South Carolina. Nowhere were his skills more evident than Cherokee Speedway, where he won all forty-seven races entered.

Ken "Bear" Hunley

From the cockpit to beneath the hood, Ken "Bear" Hunley made quite a mark on racing both in East Tennessee and across the nation. Others hailed him as an innovator and mechanical genius.

As a driver, Hunley won with regularity in the old dirt Modifieds, racing a six-cylinder-powered car from the Tri-Cities to Chattanooga. Winning usually meant beating Gene Glover and Bill Morton, who also raced out of Hunley's Church Hill shop.

Hunley retired from driving to work at Kingsport Speedway, but he racked up his greatest achievements as a crew chief by winning four consecutive NASCAR Late Model Sportsman championships. He helped guide L.D. Ottinger to the 1975–76 crowns and, after Ottinger left, won two more titles with Butch Lindley. He also assisted old friend Glover during his run to the 1979 championship.

When car owner Kenny Childers stepped up to Winston Cup, Hunley was crew chief for a succession of drivers including Lindley, Donnie Allison, Harry Gant, Jack Ingram, Lennie Pond and Buck Simmons.

Ronnie Johnson

Racing beneath the considerable shadow of a famous father, Joe Lee Johnson, Ronnie Johnson proved more than capable of upholding the family name. Beginning in the 1970s, Ronnie amassed more than four hundred dirt Late Model feature race wins, including some of the country's most prestigious events.

Johnson is a three-time Southern All-Stars series champion; a two-time winner of the Dirt Track World Championship in Pennsboro, West Virginia;

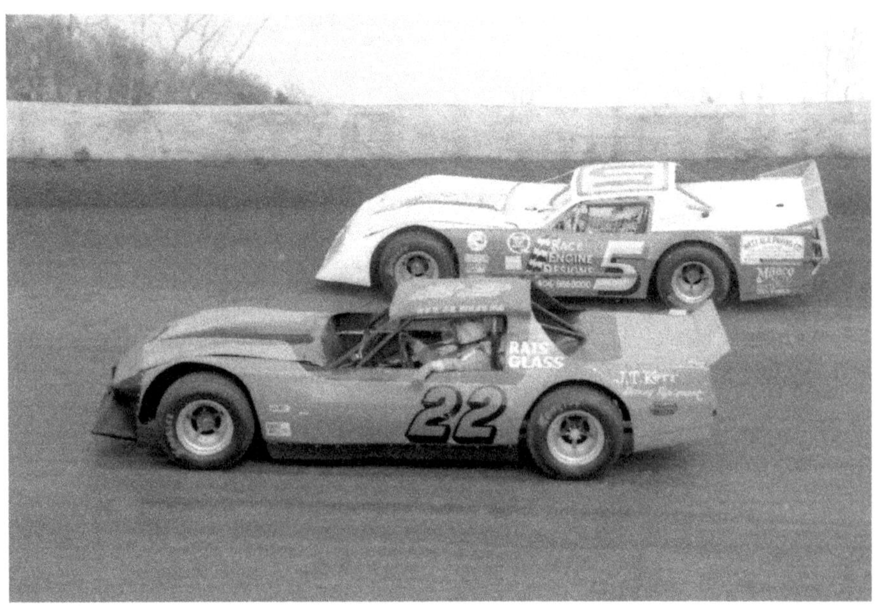

Herman Goddard (22) runs alongside Ronnie Johnson (5) during a major event at Atomic Speedway. *Mike O'Dell photo.*

and a three-time winner of the Hall of Fame 200 at Atomic Speedway. Johnson won races under at least five sanctioning groups, including the National Dirt Racing Association, Hav-A-Tampa Series, Short Track Auto Racing Series and NASCAR Southern All-Star Racing Series.

He captured checkered flags from Florida to Louisiana, the Carolinas, Georgia and Alabama, but some of his greatest success occurred closer to home. Johnson won a string of important races at Atomic, Newport, Volunteer, Smoky Mountain, Tazewell, Crossville and Cleveland—the track long promoted by his famous father.

In 2004, Johnson became the first East Tennessee native and third Volunteer State resident inducted into the National Dirt Late Model Hall of Fame.

J.T. Kerr

While he began racing later in life than most, J.T. Kerr immersed himself in both driving a Late Model stock car and supplying parts to his competitors.

He began driving at age thirty-eight but still accumulated more than two hundred feature victories. Kerr finished second in points in the Hobby class at Smoky Mountain Raceway in his rookie season. The following year, he became NASCAR's Tennessee state Hobby champion, winning the track title at Smoky Mountain and finishing in the top ten at Kingsport.

He advanced to Late Models, began clicking off wins with regularity and claimed the 1989 Volunteer Speedway championship at age fifty-nine. Four years later, Kerr captured fifteen wins and the Late Model championship at 411 Motor Speedway. Combined with top-ten finishes in all forty-four of his starts, Kerr finished runner-up to Larry Phillips for the 1993 NASCAR Racing Series Mid-American regional championship.

Every win was followed by a unique ritual: exit the car, wave to the crowd and perform twenty push-ups—a testament to early mornings spent in the gym. Kerr retired in 1994, at age sixty-four, right after winning at Smoky Mountain Raceway. He later fielded a car for his grandson Tommy.

A mechanic and machinist, Kerr opened an auto salvage business near Knoxville in 1964 and later changed it to J.T. Kerr Racing Equipment. Some forty years later, the business serves a national clientele and continues operating despite his death in 2011 at age eighty-one.

Scott Sexton

Scott Sexton proudly carried the nickname "Superman" for both his relationship with race fans and his nearly two hundred Late Model victories during a career cut tragically short by illness.

A standout high school athlete from Pigeon Forge, Sexton captured eight World Karting Association go-kart championships before jumping into a Late Model stock car in 1986. He raced and won regularly at Atomic and Volunteer Speedways and was a mainstay in the Southern All-Stars series, where he collected ten feature wins. Hall of Fame driver John A. Utsman called Sexton "as good as anybody" he ever raced against.

Sexton's largest payday came in 1992 when he won $12,500 over a stellar field at Volunteer. He also captured that track's 1991 and 1995 championships. After years out of the cockpit, Sexton made the most of a start in late 2009 when he won the national steel-head Late Model championship against a forty-car field at 411 Speedway in Seymour.

Outside the car, Sexton participated in charitable events, donated his trophies to children and was always ready to sign an autograph. He died in 2013 at the age of forty-six, following a seven-year battle with a rare blood-clotting disorder.

Larry Utsman

For someone who approached racing as a hobby, Larry Utsman accomplished much.

A cousin of East Tennessee's racing Utsman family, Larry raced for more than thirty years at the local and national levels. Competing against many of the nation's best NASCAR Late Model Sportsman drivers, Utsman won Kingsport Speedway track championships in 1977 with car owner Ed Whitaker and in 1979 for Charlie Henderson. He finished tenth in the national points standings in 1977 and twelfth in 1979, the same year he won a national Late Model race at Kingsport. He also posted a sixth-place finish in the first NASCAR Busch Series race run at Bristol in 1982.

Utsman regularly placed in the top ten in points at both Kingsport and Lonesome Pine Raceway in Virginia. His career began in 1971, and he won track championships at both Sportsman and Appalachian Speedways, claiming twenty-three wins in thirty-one starts.

"I just enjoyed being part of it," Utsman said.

H.E. Vineyard

Whether on dirt or asphalt, racing a coupe or a Late Model, H.E. Vineyard of Powell ranks among the nation's most prolific winners. His five hundred career feature victories across the southeastern United States earned him a spot in the 2007 class of the National Dirt Late Model Hall of Fame.

Beginning in the 1960s at Knoxville Raceway and continuing through the late 1990s, Vineyard captured major local races and touring events run by the National Dirt Racing Association and United Midwestern Promoters. From Florida to Kentucky, with a heavy concentration at high-speed Tennessee tracks like Atomic, Volunteer and Tazewell speedways, Vineyard assembled an impressive list of victories.

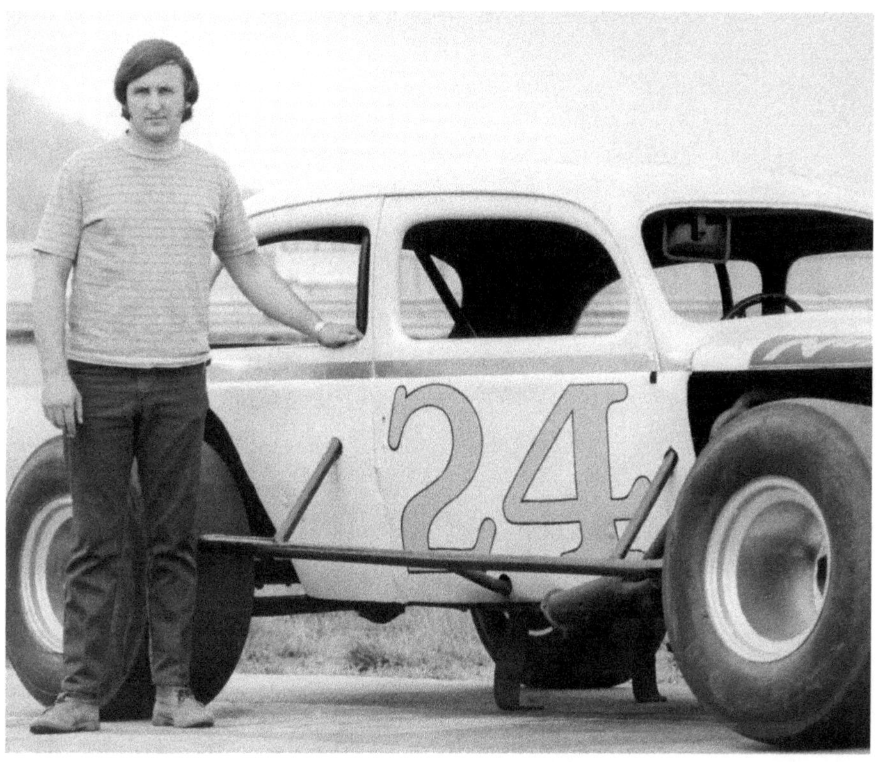

H.E. Vineyard was named to the National Dirt Late Model Hall of Fame for his success on short tracks all over the Southeast, but he also won in this asphalt Modified. *Melvin Corum collection.*

He captured the 1987 Tennessee Dirt Track Championship at Atomic Speedway; NDRA victories at Volunteer, Kingsport and Tazewell; a number of Kentucky Dirt Track Series races; and back-to-back wins in Atomic Speedway's Tootle Estes Memorial race, which honored his longtime friend.

He captured four Volunteer Speedway season championships in 1978, 1979, 1981 and 1984, and the final win of his career came at Bulls Gap in 1998.

Appendix A

NASCAR Statistics for Regional Drivers

(Minimum 10 starts)

Grant Adcox, Chattanooga

Grand National/Winston Cup

Years	Starts	Poles	Wins	Top 5	6-10	Miles Run	Money
1974–89	60	0	0	1	5	19,266	$132,505

Busch Series

Years	Starts	Poles	Wins	Top 5	6-10	Miles Run	Money
1989	1	0	0	0	0	198	$445

George Althiede, Morristown

Grand National/Winston Cup

YEARS	STARTS	POLES	WINS	TOP 5	6-10	MILES RUN	MONEY
1971–72	16	0	0	0	0	4,617	$15,025

Herman Beam, Johnson City

Grand National

YEARS	STARTS	POLES	WINS	TOP 5	6-10	MILES RUN	MONEY
1957–63	194	0	0	3	54	28,005	$38,965

Convertible

YEARS	STARTS	POLES	WINS	TOP 5	6-10	MILES RUN	MONEY
1959	2	0	0	0	0	335	$100

Jeff Berry, Kingsport

Busch Series

YEARS	STARTS	POLES	WINS	TOP 5	6-10	MILES RUN	MONEY
1982–90	14	0	0	0	4	1,059	$8,030

Bill Ervin, Tellico Plains

Grand National

YEARS	STARTS	POLES	WINS	TOP 5	6-10	MILES RUN	MONEY
1967–69	24	0	0	0	0	1,399	$2,805

Herbert "Tootle" Estes, Knoxville

Grand National

YEARS	STARTS	POLES	WINS	TOP 5	6-10	MILES RUN	MONEY
1956–58	12	0	0	0	4	1,747	$2,609

Convertible

YEARS	STARTS	POLES	WINS	TOP 5	6-10	MILES RUN	MONEY
1958	4	0	0	1	2	319	$1,010

George Green, Johnson City

Grand National

YEARS	STARTS	POLES	WINS	TOP 5	6-10	MILES RUN	MONEY
1956–63	116	0	0	3	26	12,088	$16,460

Convertible

Years	Starts	Poles	Wins	Top 5	6-10	Miles Run	Money
1959	12	0	0	1	0	1,017	$1,407

Charley Griffith, Chattanooga

Grand National

Years	Starts	Poles	Wins	Top 5	6-10	Miles Run	Money
1958–63	17	0	0	1	2	2,157	$7,155

Raymond "Friday" Hassler, Chattanooga

Grand National/Winston Cup

Years	Starts	Poles	Wins	Top 5	6-10	Miles Run	Money
1960–72	135	2	0	12	36	30,022	$114,320

Chuck Huckabee, Chattanooga

Grand National

Years	Starts	Poles	Wins	Top 5	6-10	Miles Run	Money
1963–64	12	0	0	0	1	391	$1,280

Harry Mark Hurley, Johnson City

Grand National

YEARS	STARTS	POLES	WINS	TOP 5	6-10	MILES RUN	MONEY
1961–64	16	0	0	1	1	1,011	$2,630

Joe Lee Johnson, Chattanooga

Grand National

YEARS	STARTS	POLES	WINS	TOP 5	6-10	MILES RUN	MONEY
1957–62	55	0	2	10	10	7,137	$45,666

Convertible

YEARS	STARTS	POLES	WINS	TOP 5	6-10	MILES RUN	MONEY
1958–59	16	0	2	7	3	1,540	$7,206

Herman "Brownie" King, Johnson City

Grand National

YEARS	STARTS	POLES	WINS	TOP 5	6-10	MILES RUN	MONEY
1956–61	97	0	0	2	25	9,710	$12,309

Convertible

YEARS	STARTS	POLES	WINS	TOP 5	6-10	MILES RUN	MONEY
1956–59	24	0	0	3	4	2,282	$4,064

William Paul Lewis, Johnson City

Grand National

YEARS	STARTS	POLES	WINS	TOP 5	6-10	MILES RUN	MONEY
1960–68	114	1	1	16	29	19,337	$52,869

Bill McMahan, Dandridge

Grand National

YEARS	STARTS	POLES	WINS	TOP 5	6-10	MILES RUN	MONEY
1964–65	21	0	0	1	3	2,897	$7,305

Doug Moore, Chattanooga

Grand National

YEARS	STARTS	POLES	WINS	TOP 5	6-10	MILES RUN	MONEY
1964–65	29	0	0	0	6	2,322	$6,335

Bill Morton, Church Hill

Grand National

Years	Starts	Poles	Wins	Top 5	6-10	Miles Run	Money
1955–65	35	0	0	0	9	4,842	$7,535

Convertible

Years	Starts	Poles	Wins	Top 5	6-10	Miles Run	Money
1958–59	11	0	0	2	2	1,329	$1,717

L.D. Ottinger, Newport

Grand National/Winston Cup

Years	Starts	Poles	Wins	Top 5	6-10	Miles Run	Money
1966–84	10	0	0	1	1	2,080	$20,087

Busch Series

Years	Starts	Poles	Wins	Top 5	6-10	Miles Run	Money
1982–91	206	4	3	45	39	25,758	$667,622

Mike Potter, Johnson City

Grand National/Winston Cup

YEARS	STARTS	POLES	WINS	TOP 5	6-10	MILES RUN	MONEY
1979–93	60	0	0	0	0	13,623	$181,795

Busch Series

YEARS	STARTS	POLES	WINS	TOP 5	6-10	MILES RUN	MONEY
1982–2004	15	15	0	0	0	259	$170,897

Connie Saylor, Johnson City

Grand National/Winston Cup

YEARS	STARTS	POLES	WINS	TOP 5	6-10	MILES RUN	MONEY
1978–88	58	0	0	0	1	17,018	$198,790

Busch Series

YEARS	STARTS	POLES	WINS	TOP 5	6-10	MILES RUN	MONEY
1982–84	4	0	0	0	0	490	$3,260

Grover Clinton [G.C.] Spencer, Bluff City/Jonesborough

Grand National/Winston Cup

YEARS	STARTS	POLES	WINS	TOP 5	6-10	MILES RUN	MONEY
1958–77	415	1	0	55	83	62,282	$253,158

Convertible

YEARS	STARTS	POLES	WINS	TOP 5	6-10	MILES RUN	MONEY
1959	8	0	0	1	4	887	$1,376

Don Tarr, Miami Beach, Florida/Mountain City

Grand National/Winston Cup

YEARS	STARTS	POLES	WINS	TOP 5	6-10	MILES RUN	MONEY
1967–71	48	0	0	0	9	10,229	$43,627

Brad Teague, Johnson City

Grand National/Winston Cup

YEARS	STARTS	POLES	WINS	TOP 5	6-10	MILES RUN	MONEY
1982–94	44	0	0	0	0	11,583	$185,045

Busch Series

YEARS	STARTS	POLES	WINS	TOP 5	6-10	MILES RUN	MONEY
1982–2013	240	2	1	11	32	24,935	$2,082,852

Truck Series

YEARS	STARTS	POLES	WINS	TOP 5	6-10	MILES RUN	MONEY
1997–2004	9	0	0	0	0	1,044	$57,085

Travis Tiller, Triangle, Virginia/Kingsport

Winston Cup

Years	Starts	Poles	Wins	Top 5	6-10	Miles Run	Money
1974–83	51	0	0	0	0	9,521	$47,865

John A. Utsman, Bluff City

Winston Cup

Years	Starts	Poles	Wins	Top 5	6-10	Miles Run	Money
1973–80	14	0	0	0	1	4,537	$26,155

Busch Series

Years	Starts	Poles	Wins	Top 5	6-10	Miles Run	Money
1982–83	7	0	0	0	1	738	$4,200

Sherman Utsman, Bluff City

Grand National

Years	Starts	Poles	Wins	Top 5	6-10	Miles Run	Money
1956–63	21	0	0	1	8	3,559	$5,060

Appendix B

East Tennessee Touring Series Results

NASCAR Grand National/Winston Cup

(Prior to NASCAR's "modern era")

July 11, 1971	Bristol	Charlie Glotzbach/Friday Hassler
May 23, 1971	Kingsport	Bobby Isaac
April 15, 1971	Maryville	Richard Petty
March 28, 1971	Bristol	David Pearson
July 24, 1970	Maryville	Richard Petty
July 19, 1970	Bristol	Bobby Allison
June 26, 1970	Kingsport	Richard Petty
May 28, 1970	Maryville	Bobby Isaac
April 5, 1970	Bristol	Donnie Allison
July 27, 1969	Maryville	Richard Petty
July 20, 1969	Bristol	David Pearson
June 19, 1969	Kingsport	Richard Petty
June 5, 1969	Maryville	Bobby Isaac
March 23, 1969	Bristol	Bobby Allison
July 25, 1968	Maryville	Richard Petty
July 21, 1968	Bristol	David Pearson
June 6, 1968	Maryville	Richard Petty
March 17, 1968	Bristol	David Pearson
July 27, 1967	Maryville	Dick Hutcherson
July 23, 1967	Bristol	Richard Petty
June 8, 1967	Maryville	Richard Petty
March 19, 1967	Bristol	David Pearson
July 28, 1966	Maryville	Paul Lewis
July 24, 1966	Bristol	Paul Goldsmith
June 9, 1966	Maryville	David Pearson
March 20, 1966	Bristol	Dick Hutcherson
August 13, 1965	Maryville	Dick Hutcherson
July 25, 1965	Bristol	Ned Jarrett

May 2, 1965	Bristol	Junior Johnson
July 26, 1964	Bristol	Fred Lorenzen
June 19, 1964	Chattanooga	David Pearson
March 22, 1964	Bristol	Fred Lorenzen
July 28, 1963	Bristol	Fred Lorenzen
March 31, 1963	Bristol	Fireball Roberts
August 3, 1962	Chattanooga	Joe Weatherly
July 29, 1962	Bristol	Jim Paschal
April 29, 1962	Bristol	Bobby Johns
October 22, 1961	Bristol	Joe Weatherly
July 30, 1961	Bristol	Jack Smith
June 15, 1957	Newport *	Fireball Roberts
October 7, 1956	Newport *	Fireball Roberts

*Fairgrounds

NASCAR Late Model Sportsman

(Partial listing)

August 8, 1981	Kingsport	Jack Ingram
June 21, 1981	Kingsport	Jack Ingram
March 28, 1981	Kingsport	Tommy Ellis
October 19, 1980	Kingsport	Brad Teague
August 9, 1980	Kingsport	John A. Utsman
June 29, 1980	Kingsport	Jack Ingram
June 1, 1980	Kingsport	Geoff Bodine
October 21, 1979	Kingsport	Gene Glover
August 11, 1979	Kingsport	Larry Utsman
July 1, 1979	Kingsport	Jack Ingram
April 28, 1979	Kingsport	Bob Pressley
August 18, 1978	Kingsport	Bob Pressley
July 30, 1978	Maryville	Butch Lindley
June 30, 1978	Kingsport	Bob Pressley
June 4, 1978	Bristol	Jack Ingram
April 28, 1978	Kingsport	Butch Lindley
April 9, 1978	Maryville	Jack Ingram
Aug. 12, 1977	Kingsport	Butch Lindley
July 15, 1977	Kingsport	Harry Gant
May 31, 1977	Bristol	Bob Pressley
May 27, 1977	Kingsport	Harry Gant
April 15, 1977	Kingsport	Tommy Houston
May 30, 1976	Bristol	Harry Gant
May 31 (June 10), 1973	Bristol	L.D. Ottinger
November 5, 1972	Bristol	David Pearson
October 16, 1971	Maryville	L.D. Ottinger
August 8, 1971	Bristol	James Hamm
November 1, 1970	Maryville	Bob Burcham

NASCAR Grand National East Series

May 14, 1972	Maryville	Neil Castles

NASCAR Grand American Series

September 5, 1970	Kingsport	Jim Paschal
June 20, 1970	Maryville	Tiny Lund
May 3, 1970	Kingsport	Tiny Lund

NASCAR Grand Touring Series

May 3, 1969	Maryville	Tiny Lund
April 13, 1969	Kingsport	T.C. Hunt
August 10, 1968	Maryville	Tiny Lund
July 20, 1968	Bristol	Donnie Allison
June 4, 1968	Kingsport	Buck Baker

NASCAR Modified

October 21, 1979	Kingsport	Richie Evans
October 28, 1978	Kingsport	Ron Bouchard
October 23, 1977	Kingsport	Ron Bouchard
November 14, 1976	Kingsport	Geoff Bodine
September 9, 1962	Bristol	Malcolm Brady; Joe Bill Adams
October 21, 1961	Bristol	Red Farmer

NASCAR/ARTGO

June 27, 1987	Bristol	Dick Trickle
August 2, 1986	Bristol	Dave Mader III

American Speed Association/All-Pro

July 2, 1983	Bristol	Butch Miller

ARCA [MARC] Series

September 3, 1973	Seymour	Wayne Watercutter
May 18, 1969	Bristol	Ramo Stott
November 17, 1968	Bristol	Bobby Watson
May 25, 1968	Knoxville	Les Snow

April 7, 1963	Newport *	Iggy Katona
October 28, 1962	Newport *	Iggy Katona
May 18, 1957	Broadway	Nelson Stacy
April 7, 1957	Broadway	Roz Howard
October 28, 1956	Broadway	Russ Hepler

* Fairgrounds

AAA/USAC Stock Cars

August 3, 1957	Broadway	Sherman Utsman
August 4, 1956	Broadway	Les Snow
June 16, 1956	Broadway	Marshall Teague
May 5, 1956	Broadway	Nelson Stacy
August 6, 1955	Broadway	Frank Mundy
July 2, 1955	Broadway	Frank Mundy
April 30, 1955	Broadway	Frank Mundy
August 7, 1954	Broadway	Marshall Teague
May 2, 1954	Broadway	Frank Mundy

National Dirt Racing Association

October 13, 1985	Kingsport	Buck Simmons
April 20, 1985	Atomic	Jeff Purvis
March 30, 1985	Kingsport	Freddy Smith
September 23, 1984	Maryville	Tom Helfrich
August 19, 1984	Kingsport	Mike Duvall
June 2, 1984	Atomic	Ronnie Johnson
August 27, 1983	Atomic	Mike Duvall
April 17, 1983	Atomic	Freddy Smith
September 18, 1982	Atomic	Mike Duvall
June 26, 1982	Bulls Gap	Rodney Combs
May 8, 1982	Maryville	Rodney Combs
November 8, 1981	Atomic	Bill Corum
July 25, 1981	Bulls Gap	Leon Archer
July 3, 1981	Bulls Gap	Buck Simmons
June 25, 1981	Tazewell	Buck Simmons
April 25, 1981	Maryville	Buck Simmons
October 26, 1980	Bulls Gap	Freddy Smith
July 26, 1980	Bulls Gap	Buck Simmons
October 7, 1979	Bulls Gap	Ronnie Johnson
June 9, 1979	Bulls Gap	H.E. Vineyard
October 29, 1978	Atomic	Larry Moore
June 10, 1978	Newport	Buck Simmons

Hav-a-Tampa Dirt Racing Series

September 1, 2003	Atomic	Dan Schlieper
June 28, 2003	Tazewell	Scott Bloomquist
September 1, 2002	Atomic	Skip Arp
July 19, 2002	Atomic	Rick Eckert
May 3, 2002	Oneida	Dale McDowell
October 2, 2001	Atomic	Wendell Wallace
September 2, 2001	Atomic	Scott Bloomquist
June 2, 2001	Bristol	Scott Bloomquist
June 1, 2001	Bristol	Jimmy Mars
May 31, 2001	Bristol	Scott Bloomquist
September 3, 2000	Atomic	Scott Bloomquist
September 2, 2000	Atomic	Dan Schlieper
July 29, 2000	Bulls Gap	Billy Moyer
July 14, 2000	Atomic	Ray Cook
June 3, 2000	Bristol	Dale McDowell
May 6, 2000	Tazewell	Scott Bloomquist
April 1, 2000	Atomic	Donnie Moran
March 31, 2000	Atomic	Wendell Wallace
September 18, 1999	Bulls Gap	Freddy Smith
September 5, 1999	Atomic	Marshall Green
June 4, 1999	Atomic	Marshall Green
May 22, 1999	Tazewell	Marshall Green
March 28, 1999	Atomic	Rick Eckert
September 6, 1998	Atomic	Scott Bloomquist
May 30, 1998	Tazewell	Billy Ogle Jr.
April 4, 1998	Bulls Gap	Scott Bloomquist
August 30, 1997	Atomic	Billy Moyer
July 26, 1997	Tazewell	Wendell Wallace
July 25, 1996	Atomic	Wendell Wallace
July 13, 1996	Cleveland	Scott Bloomquist
May 31, 1996	Atomic	Scott Bloomquist
May 5, 1996	Cleveland	Scott Bloomquist
May 4, 1996	Bulls Gap	Freddy Smith
August 13, 1995	Maryville	Rex Richey
August 12, 1995	Cleveland	Dale McDowell
July 8, 1995	Atomic	Skip Arp
June 24, 1995	Bulls Gap	Scott Bloomquist
April 22, 1995	Cleveland	Freddy Smith
March 25, 1995	Kingsport	Bill Frye
August 25, 1994	Kingsport	Scott Bloomquist
August 13, 1994	Cleveland	Scott Bloomquist
July 17, 1994	Maryville	Scott Bloomquist
April 30, 1994	Maryville	Scott Bloomquist
July 18, 1993	Maryville	Mike Head

June 5, 1993	Cleveland	Rex Richey
June 4, 1993	Maryville	Dale McDowell
May 1, 1993	Bulls Gap	Freddy Smith
March 28, 1993	Cleveland	Clint Smith
March 21, 1993	Atomic	Dale McDowell
July 11, 1992	Cleveland	Ronnie Johnson
May 17, 1992	Kingsport	Rex Richey
May 16, 1992	Bulls Gap	Gary Myers
April 25, 1992	Atomic	Ronnie Johnson
June 15, 1991	Cleveland	Dale McDowell
June 7, 1991	Bulls Gap	Skip Arp
March 24, 1991	Atomic	Jack Boggs
September 15, 1990	Atomic	Gary Hall
September 1, 1990	Cleveland	Dale McDowell

World of Outlaws Dirt Late Model Series

April 26, 2013	Maryville	Shane Clanton
April 28, 2012	Tazewell	Bub McCool
July 3, 2011	Tazewell	Chris Madden
July 3, 2010	Tazewell	Shane Clanton
July 2, 2010	Wartburg	Tim McCreadie
August 21, 2008	Bulls Gap	Shane Clanton
August 20, 2008	Bulls Gap	Jimmy Owens
October 13, 2007	Bulls Gap	Steve Francis
August 23, 2007	Bulls Gap	Chris Madden
September 4, 2004	Atomic	Scott Bloomquist
April 30, 2004	Maryville	Rick Eckert
March 27, 2004	Bulls Gap	Brian Birkhofer
March 14, 2004	Atomic	Dale McDowell
March 13, 2004	Atomic	Billy Moyer

AAA Midget Series

May 5, 1956	Broadway	Chuck Weyant
July 24, 1953	Broadway	George Tichenor
Sept. 26, 1952	Broadway	Bill Homeier
July 24, 1952	Broadway	Johnnie Tolan
July 22, 1952	Broadway	Jimmy Bryan
June 24, 1952	Broadway	Johnnie Tolan
November 11, 1951	Broadway	Dick Frazier
July 24, 1951	Broadway	Rex Easton

Bibliography

Allison, Bobby, and Tim Packman. *Bobby Allison: A Racer's Racer*. Champaign, IL: Sports Publishing LLC, 2003.

Bledsoe, Jerry. *World's Number One, Flat-Out, All-Time Great Stock Car Racing Book*. Asheboro, NC: Down Home Press, 1975.

Brown, Allan E. *The History of America's Speedways, Past & Present*. Comstock Park, MI: n.p., 2003.

Clifton, Jon H. *In Pursuit of Speed*. Johnson City, TN: Overmountain Press, 1998.

Fielden, Greg. *Charlotte Motor Speedway*: Osceola, WI: MBI Publishing Co., 2000.

———. *Forty Years of Stock Car Racing*. Vols. 1–4. Surfside Beach, SC: Galfield Press, 1990.

———. *Forty Years of Stock Car Racing Plus Four*: Surfside Beach, SC: Galfield Press, 1994.

Gabbard, Alex. *Return to Thunder Road: The Story Behind the Legend*. Lenoir City, TN: Gabbard Publications, 1992.

Golenbock, Peter, and Greg Fielden. *NASCAR Encyclopedia: The Complete Record of America's Most Popular Sport*: St. Paul, MN: Motorbooks International, 2003.

Granger, Gene. *American Racing Classics*. Concord, NC: Griggs Publishing Co. Inc., 1992.

Hunter, Jim. *Darlington Raceway: 50th Anniversary*. Charlotte, NC: UMI Publications, 1999.

Kirkland, Tom, and David Thompson. *Darlington International Raceway: 1950–1967*. Osceola, WI: Motor Books International, 1999.

McGee, David M., and Sonya Haskins. *Bristol Motor Speedway: Images of Sports*. Charleston, SC: Arcadia Publishing, 2006.

McGee, David M. *Tales of Bristol Motor Speedway*. Charleston, SC: The History Press, 2011.

Moore, J.S. *Gathering Leaves*. Denver, CO: Outskirts Press, 2008.

NASCAR. *NASCAR Sprint Cup Series Media Guide*. Daytona Beach, FL: NASCAR Media Group, 2012.

Phillips, Benny. *Bristol Motor Speedway: 40 Years of Thunder*. Charlotte, NC: UMI Publications, 2001.

Pierce, Daniel S. *Real NASCAR: White Lightning, Red Clay and Big Bill France*. Chapel Hill: University of North Carolina Press, 2010.
Radbruch, Don. *Roaring Roadsters*. Veyo, UT: Hot Rod Library Inc., 2000.
Yarborough, Cale, and William Neely. *Cale: The Hazardous Life and Times of the World's Greatest Stock Car Driver*. New York: Times Books, 1986.

Newspapers and Periodicals

Bristol (VA) Herald Courier
Chattanooga (TN) News Times-Free Press
Circle Track Magazine
(Maryville, TN) Daily Times
Kingsport (TN) Times News
Knoxville (TN) Journal
Knoxville (TN) News Sentinel
Johnson City (TN) Press
Mid-American Auto Racing News
NASCAR Scene (formerly *Grand National Scene* and *Winston Cup Scene*)
National Speed Sport News
Southern Motorsports Journal
Stock Car Racing
Speedway Illustrated

Internet Reference Sites

arcaracing.com
ashwayspeedway.net
boydsspeedway.net
bristolmotorspeedway.com
champcarstats.com
chattanoogan.com
clevelandspeedway.net
dirtondirt.com
georgiaracinghistory.com
i81motorsportspark.com
knoxnews.com
midwestracingarchives.com
mrmracinng.net/tribute
nashvillefairgrounds.blogspot.com
newkingsportspeedway.com
newportspeedway.weebly.com
racersreunion.com
racingphotoarchives.com
racing-reference.info
sasdirt.com
smokymountainspeedway.com
springcityraceway.net
studebakerracing.com
tazewellspeedway.net
tennesseeracer.com
thunderroadusa.com
timesfreepress.com
ultimateracinghistory.com
volunteerspeedway.com
wartburgspeedway.net
wheelsofspeed.com
winfield.50megs.com

Index

J

K

L

M

N

O

P

S

T

U

V

W

Y

About the Author

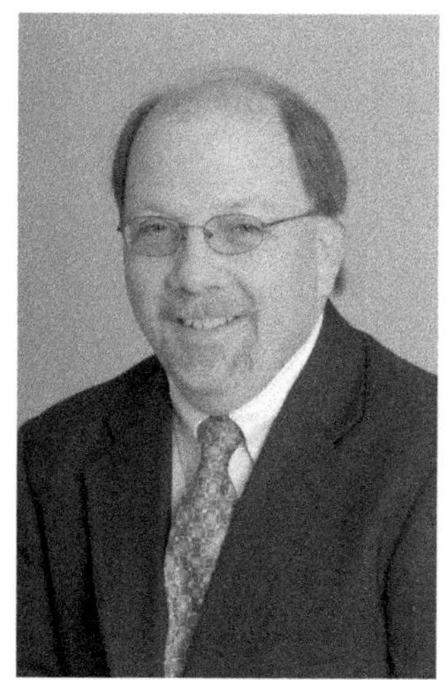

David M. McGee is the author of other books on racing history, including *Tales of Bristol Motor Speedway* and *Bristol Dragway: Images of Sports*, and is the coauthor of *NASCAR Bristol Motor Speedway*. He is the senior member of the Bristol Motor Speedway and Bristol Dragway public address announcing team and the track historian. He is also a member of the executive committee of the Kentucky Motorsports Hall of Fame. He lives in Bristol, Tennessee, and is employed as an award-winning journalist for the *Bristol Herald Courier* in Bristol, Virginia. A Kentucky native with a lifelong passion for motorsports, McGee is a graduate of Morehead State University with a degree in journalism.

Visit us at
www.historypress.net

....

This title is also available as an e-book